Nuno Ribeiro

Enhancing Digital Information Awareness

Nuno Ribeiro

Enhancing Digital Information Awareness

Humanising User Interfaces with Speech-based Assistants

VDM Verlag Dr. Müller

Impressum/Imprint (nur für Deutschland/ only for Germany)

Bibliografische Information der Deutschen Nationalbibliothek: Die Deutsche Nationalbibliothek verzeichnet diese Publikation in der Deutschen Nationalbibliografie; detaillierte bibliografische Daten sind im Internet über http://dnb.d-nb.de abrufbar.

Alle in diesem Buch genannten Marken und Produktnamen unterliegen warenzeichen-, marken- oder patentrechtlichem Schutz bzw. sind Warenzeichen oder eingetragene Warenzeichen der jeweiligen Inhaber. Die Wiedergabe von Marken, Produktnamen, Gebrauchsnamen, Handelsnamen, Warenbezeichnungen u.s.w. in diesem Werk berechtigt auch ohne besondere Kennzeichnung nicht zu der Annahme, dass solche Namen im Sinne der Warenzeichen- und Markenschutzgesetzgebung als frei zu betrachten wären und daher von jedermann benutzt werden dürften.

Coverbild: www.purestockx.com

Verlag: VDM Verlag Dr. Müller Aktiengesellschaft & Co. KG
Dudweiler Landstr. 99, 66123 Saarbrücken, Deutschland
Telefon +49 681 9100-698, Telefax +49 681 9100-988, Email: info@vdm-verlag.de
Zugl.: York, University of York, PhD Thesis, 2002

Herstellung in Deutschland:
Schaltungsdienst Lange o.H.G., Berlin
Books on Demand GmbH, Norderstedt
Reha GmbH, Saarbrücken
Amazon Distribution GmbH, Leipzig
ISBN: 978-3-639-15629-4

Imprint (only for USA, GB)

Bibliographic information published by the Deutsche Nationalbibliothek: The Deutsche Nationalbibliothek lists this publication in the Deutsche Nationalbibliografie; detailed bibliographic data are available in the Internet at http://dnb.d-nb.de.

Any brand names and product names mentioned in this book are subject to trademark, brand or patent protection and are trademarks or registered trademarks of their respective holders. The use of brand names, product names, common names, trade names, product descriptions etc. even without a particular marking in this works is in no way to be construed to mean that such names may be regarded as unrestricted in respect of trademark and brand protection legislation and could thus be used by anyone.

Cover image: www.purestockx.com

Publisher:
VDM Verlag Dr. Müller Aktiengesellschaft & Co. KG
Dudweiler Landstr. 99, 66123 Saarbrücken, Germany
Phone +49 681 9100-698, Fax +49 681 9100-988, Email: info@vdm-publishing.com
York, University of York, PhD Thesis, 2002

Printed in the U.S.A.
Printed in the U.K. by (see last page)
ISBN: 978-3-639-15629-4

To

Lurdes and Francisca

TABLE OF CONTENTS

LIST OF ILLUSTRATIONS

LIST OF TABLES

ACKNOWLEDGEMENTS

This book is the result of many years of effort in a PhD programme and would not have been possible without the contributions of my friends and my family.

First, I would like to thank my supervisor, Ian Benest, for making my PhD one of the most memorable and enjoyable experiences of my life. I would like to thank him for his unconditional support, his availability and enthusiasm to spend long hours discussing new ideas, his suggestions that enhanced the quality of this work, his help in guiding me through the demanding milestones of the PhD programme, his effort and patience in reviewing this book manuscript, and for all the encouragement he offered me since the very beginning of my project. I truly believe that his knowledge and experience have helped me to become a better researcher. I would especially like to thank Anna, Ian and Robert for excelling themselves in making me feel at home when I was staying in York. I hope our friendship may continue for many years.

I would like to thank Feliz Gouveia, my friend and co-supervisor at Universidade Fernando Pessoa, for all the encouragement he gave me in pursuing my PhD since I became a member of CEREM. I would like to thank him for his insightful suggestions, his continued interest in my work, his availability to discuss my progress, his useful advice, and for helping me with the financial requirements for frequent travel to York.

During my time in the Computer Science department, I have been privileged to exchange ideas with a number of remarkable people who have contributed to expand my knowledge in various areas related to this research. I would like to thank my former assessor Dr. Patrick Olivier, my assessor Dr. Alistair Edwards, and Dr. Chris Kimble for their interest in my work, their pertinent suggestions, and for participating actively in the realisation of my PhD project.

I am grateful to Fundação Fernando Pessoa, in particular to Prof. Doutor Salvato Trigo and to Dra. Manuela Trigo, for encouraging me to realise this project, for providing the financial support without which this PhD work would not have been possible, and for creating the necessary conditions that allowed me to concentrate exclusively on my PhD research work.

Special thanks go to my friend José Vasconcelos with whom I had the pleasure of sharing the best moments of my PhD experience in York. His support was invaluable at critical times, and his objective approach to the research process has helped me to stay focussed on many occasions. I hope our genuine friendship will continue to grow in the years ahead.

Very special thanks go also to my friend David Lamas who helped me to shape this research since the early days. His ideas and his vast knowledge have helped to broaden my own curiosity. I thank him for the time he spent discussing the details of the architecture and of the empirical study. I hope our enthusiastic co-operation and friendship will continue for many years.

Since the first moment I arrived in England (I mean in Yorkshire) I have been fortunate to meet an outstanding friend, Paul Hildreth, who immediately included me in his life. The friendship he offered me has been warm and sustaining. I would like to thank Maggie, Paul and Tom for the wonderful times we spent together – my fondest memories of York include them.

I would like to thank my mother, Maria Zulmira, my father, Jorge Manuel, and my sister, Maria Estela, for their love and enthusiasm, and for offering me the stability I needed to accomplish my project. My mother taught me in my formative years and gave me the most solid foundation on which I could develop my skills. I thank her for teaching me her moral principles, for all her loving and caring attention, and her enormous effort to make sure I would survive away from home. My father has been the best example to guide me through life; he taught me the importance of hard work, dedication, persistence and honesty. My parents were the first persons that believed I was able to pursue this project - I thank them for encouraging me to expand my horizons, and for making me a better person. I thank my sister for being my eternal friend and ally, for drowning me with her kindness, and for patiently helping me to focus on my work. I hope I can bring as much happiness to her life as she has brought to mine.

I would also like to thank my father-, mother- and brother-in-law, Emília Machado, Vitorino Teixeira, and Manuel António, for their continued support during these years. Their presence has been reassuring and they have created the conditions that allowed me to focus on my work.

The people who deserve the greatest acknowledgement are the ones to whom this book is dedicated: my loving and beautiful wife, Lurdes, and my stunning daughter, Francisca. Lurdes is an extraordinary person and her contribution to this work is apparent in every word, she pushed me forward at all times, she gave me constant support and stimulation, she fostered my best ideas, she listened patiently to my constant divagations, and she offered me more understanding than I could ever imagine. I love her dearly and I wish I could one day have the opportunity to help her realise her most ambitious dreams in the way she helped me to realise mine. During my PhD, I was extremely fortunate to experience one of the most rewarding and joyful moments of my life: the birth of my daughter Francisca. I only wish I can offer her the same wisdom that her grandparents gave to me. I would like to emphasise Lurdes's unlimited strength to act as both a mother and a father while I was away from home. I thank you with all my heart - this book would never have been possible without you by my side.

Chapter 1

INTRODUCTION

1.1 Motivation

1.1.1. Problems with current interfaces

The desire for all personal information acquired over time to be stored, organised and accessed using a computer (Bell, 2001) is strong (Bell, 1997), but current interface metaphors emphasise a graphical approach to such information management that is far from optimal. Furthermore, the exponential growth in almost everything related to personal computing is bound to produce a level of information and communication chaos (Olsen, 1999) that is well beyond the principles that supported the original design of current interfaces. In fact, current graphical interfaces for personal information management (PIM) are based on principles, mostly arising from the desktop metaphor, that limit the computer-human interface (Gentner and Nielsen, 1996) in many ways.

First, *finding hidden information*, such as information nested in a hierarchy or hidden behind opened windows, is distracting. In fact, because screen real estate is at a premium, it is often not possible to display every piece of information that might be needed to accomplish a certain task. Information that is hidden from view requires cognitive effort for it to be searched and found, and this can adversely attract attention from the user's main activity. While growing volumes of information overwhelm people, they still need to be *aware* of information that is important to them. For example, many people care when important e-mail arrives from their family, when their document is held up behind other large jobs in the printer queue, when they should not miss a critical meeting or forget important birthdays, and when there is a good opportunity to make profitable investments. Thus, these people wish to be able to appreciate the significance of desired sources of information. Therefore, this status information should be readily available and it should be delivered in an unobtrusive way.

A second interaction problem is directly related to the *lack of semantics in alerting cues* presented to users. When people need to be notified of new or updated information, current interface approaches rely on playing a sound or blinking an icon to obtain users' attention. However, these techniques do not provide sufficient information about the interruption and require users to investigate further. Where systems display a notification window, often with an incomprehensible message (which should be of no concern to users) it obscures any information already being displayed (Raskin, 2000) due to limitations in screen display space (Shneiderman, 1993). In both cases, these alerting techniques interrupt the user and may cause serious disruption to the user's current activity.

Moreover, existing approaches that alert users do not include an evaluation of its importance before interrupting. As a result users are often interrupted with needless notifications that distract attention, causing a loss in concentration and reducing productivity. Because designers seldom pay any attention to users' possible level of engagement with their activity, there is a clear *lack of awareness and co-ordination between high-priority and unimportant alerts* that are conveyed by the interface.

Finally, a *lack of integration for alerts* itself may also cause problems. Often applications that interrupt make use of their own icons or notification windows. This lack of a unified interrupting scheme poses a serious burden on the user who has to remember and recognise the source of the information being provided (Sawhney and Schmandt, 2000).

In effect, personal information should be made available to users in their workplace in an active and unobtrusive way, based on their degree of interruptability and commitment to a task. The interface should be responsible for sensing users, for detecting their context and acting accordingly. This is a crucial aspect as far as alerts, which can be notifications or reminders, are concerned. In this book, *notifications* are viewed as alerts to the imminence or occurrence of *new* events whereas *reminders* are viewed as alerts to *past* events of which users needs to be reminded. From this alerting perspective, open research issues (Silverman, 1997) which further motivate the research described in this book include the following:

- What effects do systems, which convey many simultaneous alerts or a series of sequential alerts, have on users?

- To date there is no acceptable theory about what kind of message content provides the most efficient alerts. What is then the most beneficial content for notification and reminding? Is it dependent on user types and activity types?

1.1.2.   The case for a humanised approach

One way to address those limitations is to humanise the computer (Maes, 1997a), to endow the machine with human characteristics in order to make it less unpleasant and more suitable for people. This would establish a relationship between users and the computers. After all, there is a natural and almost universal tendency to personify inanimate objects (for example ocean-going liners are referred to as "she"). Furthermore, the interfaces to computer-based applications exploit metaphors that are designed to communicate familiar behaviour (Laurel, 1997). The tendency to anthropomorphise - to project human characteristics onto non-human and inanimate objects - can be triggered by any action appearing in the least intelligent (Norman, 1994).

Current research suggests that anthropomorphism can be supported by and deployed through interface agents: characters enacted by the computer (Laurel, 1997) who act on behalf of the user in a computer-based environment (Erickson, 1997; Laurel, 1997; Maes, 1994). So why would it be appropriate to anthropomorphise interface agents? Laurel (1997) suggests both psychological and functional reasons: psychologically, humans are "quite adept at relating to and communicating with other people" (Laurel, 1997), and the way we use this ability in dealing with inanimate objects is through the process of anthropomorphism. It is clear that our social responses do not disappear while we are interacting with machines: we get annoyed when machines do not work properly, we become happy when a difficult task is completed smoothly, we even attribute human motives to their inanimate behaviours (Ball and Breese, 2000).

Indeed, extensive research carried out on the tendency of people to use their knowledge of people and social rules to make judgements about computers (Reeves and Nass, 1996) resulted in at least two surprising and interesting aspects. First, Reeves and Nass (1996) show that *very small cues* can trigger people's readiness to apply social rules to computers. For example, the simple fact that the computer uses a human voice is sufficient to cause a person to apply social rules to the computer (Nass and Steuer, 1993). This suggests that as soon as people's natural predisposition to anthropomorphise is triggered, they start to behave socially towards the inanimate object that provided the trigger cue. The second surprising result is the finding that people *do* apply social rules when making judgements about machines: for example people find the praise more meaningful when computer A praises computer B than when computer A praises itself (Nass et al., 1994).

Thus people respond psychologically to interactive computers as if they were human: it has been demonstrated that strong social responses are evoked even when the computer does not have an explicit anthropomorphic representation (Reeves and Nass, 1996). The suggestion is that humans have evolved to attribute special meaning to the movement and language produced by other people, and that people cannot avoid responding to current communication technology as if another person produced it.

The finding that people are, indeed, willing to apply their social heuristics to computers is in fact *surprising*, particularly since the cues that trigger the application of these social rules can be as small as the simple use of voice at the interface. Furthermore, people vociferously deny treating the computer as if a human. The interesting implication of these results for the research presented in this book is that, since interaction is a two-way channel, just as people respond socially to computers, so computers should also respond socially to people (Erickson, 1997). In fact, the natural tendency to respond socially to computers is likely to become much stronger when there is a spoken conversation with a computer (Ball and Breese, 2000). The reason may be because humans do not possess the resources to overcome their fundamental instincts concerning speech (Nass and Gong, 2000). Thus, people behave toward and make attributions about speech systems using the same heuristics they would normally apply to other people. Therefore, the *willingness* of people to apply social rules to computers, in particular speaking computers, which should be able to hold their side of an expected social interaction, raises important research problems as far as user interface design is concerned.

1.1.3.   Pitfalls of a humanised approach

It is true, however, that many anthropomorphic scenarios designed in the past have been rejected by consumers because they confused and distracted users, and made them lose the feeling that they were in control (Shneiderman, 1997). For example, previous usability studies showed that some users seek the "feelings of mastery, competence, and understanding that come from a predictable and controllable interface" (Shneiderman, 1997), in contrast with anthropomorphised interfaces that create the illusion of an intelligent machine with all the variations that humans deploy. In fact, the attribution of human-like traits to computers requires extensive user testing to find out what specific types of user really want or need. For example, the lack of this kind of user testing may explain the failure of the incorporation of speech I/O in talking cars and vending machines.

It is clear that current anthropomorphic systems create unrealistic user expectations that lead to errors and subsequent disappointment with the system. Previous research in human factors has even indicated that there can be negative reactions to user interfaces that are too cute or too talkative. However, since this data was collected with early screen-based systems and user inputs via keyboard, it is possible that, with the capabilities of current spoken language systems matching more closely the capabilities of humans, the negatives associated with anthropomorphic interfaces have been attenuated (Boyce, 1999). Clearly, only carefully designed user tests can provide any indication of whether this is a true assertion.

It is important to note that, beyond the unpredictability raised by anthropomorphism (Shneiderman, 1992), previous research also suggests that such user interfaces are potentially dangerous because attributing intelligence, independent activity and free-will to computers can mislead the user; it may suggest more flexibility than the anthropomorphic system is capable of delivering, and can ultimately lead to deception with the user feeling poorly treated (Shneiderman, 1993). Kay (1984) supports this argument by noting that "if the projected illusion is that of intelligence and the reality falls far short, users will be disappointed". Hence, while it is desirable to invoke anthropomorphism so as to improve the interaction, the level of intelligence must be truthfully conveyed - although some researchers believe that *artificial consciousness* is possible and will emerge in future computers (Buttazzo, 2001).

Ensuring that the level of intelligence is correctly conveyed is hampered by the addition of a face. "As soon as we put a human face into the model, perhaps with reasonably appropriate dynamic facial expressions, carefully tuned speech characteristics and human-like language interactions, we build on natural expectations for human-like intelligence, understanding and actions" (Norman, 1994). Instead of completely anthropomorphising the interface, the way to exploit the advantages of anthropomorphism, while trying to avoid its pitfalls, is to *humanise* some aspects of the interaction, while retaining the desirable qualities of predictability and controllability that are inherent in *direct manipulation*[1] user-interfaces (Shneiderman, 1997).

In the context of this book, *humanising* does not mean that relations with the computer are exactly the same as relating with other people; it is instead "the application of a metaphor with all its concomitant selectivity" (Laurel, 1997). This means that humanising the interface is *not* about

---

[1] Direct manipulation interfaces are often graphical interfaces that include icons based on a "real world" metaphor.

creating a completely artificial personality in all its subtle complexity, but instead, choosing by careful design, only those traits that are useful in a particular context. This is a crucial observation as far as the research work described herein is concerned. This book shows the importance of properly designing an interface exhibiting a set of human traits that help in addressing the alerting problems associated with current interfaces.

1.1.4.   Exploiting speech output to enhance information awareness

The problem then is how the information awareness problems identified at the beginning of this chapter can be addressed through the humanisation of the interface.

A possible way to tackle the limitations imposed by current interfaces might be to use speech induced anthropomorphism to enhance the awareness of information that is visually hidden. Speech output might complement, rather than replace, the graphical user-interface and provide what are the indispensable cues that support an enhanced awareness of personal information. These cues might be designed to convey the semantics of visually hidden information, while making the speech-based interface exhibit an anthropomorphic behaviour in terms of a selected number of appropriate human-like conversational traits. Indeed, research is required to determine the kinds of information processing environments for which spoken output is a benefit and is in fact preferred (Cohen and Oviatt, 1995). Information awareness is one such target process for which speech output might provide a number of benefits and constitute the preferred means for acquiring information.

Furthermore, instead of investigating only the beneficial aspects of speaking utterances[2] as compared with other means of presenting the same information, research should also evaluate users' preferences in terms of the content being communicated (Cohen and Oviatt, 1995).

In summary, speech output has the potential to offer a complementary solution to the issues of conveying visually hidden information, including sufficient semantics in alert cues, and promoting a sense of integration for what are otherwise disparate alerts.

---

[2] In this book the term "utterance" is used instead of "sentence" to refer to the units of spoken language.

1.2   Key contributions of this work

There is a growing belief in the research community that the use of software agent techniques in computer interfaces is both desirable and necessary due to the increasing volumes of information being accessed and processed. Recent research has been investigating the application of anthropomorphic interface agents to various application domains, in particular to personal information management. The system described in this book aims to provide a human-like assistant that automates the delivery of information a person wishes to be aware of through a style of interaction that is based on human conversation norms.

However, relatively little empirical evaluation has been performed, which addresses the effects on humans caused by having a computer show social behaviours, in particular when using speech at the interface. In this context, the specific objectives of the research described in this book are as follows.

The research investigated whether the exploitation of speech, used as part of a complementary alerting mechanism to a graphical user-interface, offers *benefits* over a purely graphical approach to information awareness. The research also investigated whether anthropomorphising the delivery of speech-based information reinforces the social acceptability of the computer and, thus, the perception of a humanised work companion.

The research investigated how to *design* and *implement* an *architecture*, based on software agent techniques, for an experimental environment that displays anthropomorphic characteristics, founded on typical human conversation norms, such as: knowing when and how to interrupt, adopting linguistic variation, and conveying polite behaviour through speech output.

Finally, this research evaluated the importance and the usefulness of humanised speech-based interfaces as an interaction style, with a particular emphasis on evaluating how effectively the perception of a humanised work companion for personal information awareness is implemented through the combined use of those human conversation norms.

1.2.1.   Benefits of speech in the user-interface

Speech is an ideal medium for intense interactive communication between people, but the state of the technology hinders its adoption for human-computer interaction. The technology cannot yet provide an almost error free recognition of human utterances, and continually repeating oneself is as irritating as if it were with another person who is hard-of-hearing. Furthermore, a computer that incessantly "chatters" is wearisome. Speech should complement and enhance a graphical user-interface rather than duplicate or replace it (Cohen, 1992). Here are at least some of the situations where speech may be employed to good effect.

First, using speech output for notifying and reminding the user should enable interruptions to be less disruptive since the user's attention can be obtained without interfering with the visual "locus of attention" (Raskin, 2000). Second, speech output potentially allows for the provision of more meaningful alerts: it can be used both to alert the user as to the occurrence of an event and to provide sufficient semantics about that event. Finally, usage of speech output should enable the creation of an integrated mechanism for conveying alerts since the same output channel can be used to deliver timely information from disparate source domains, such as e-mail, diary or printing.

However, the speech channel is strictly serial in nature so it is best exploited when succinct and precise information needs to be conveyed (Arons and Mynatt, 1994). Thus an overview of the event should be conveyed first (Walker et al., 1998), enabling users to be aware of potentially interesting information. In this way, users are able subsequently to make use of the graphical user-interface to select specific items of interest for viewing the full details at a time that is most convenient for them. From this perspective, a speech output system can be seen as complementing the graphical delivery of information.

On the other hand, as a complementary modality, speech input also enables users to access visually hidden information since it eliminates the need for the user to perform a visual search, for example for a specific folder or for a document icon, while trying to find the required information. Indeed, Cohen (1992) suggests that speech recognition and direct manipulation interfaces possess "complementary strengths and weaknesses", and that in multimodal user-interfaces, the strengths can be exploited to overcome the weaknesses. It has also been suggested that user interface performance and acceptance may increase by combining direct manipulation and speech and exploiting their best features (Cohen and Oviatt, 1995).

1.2.2.   Linguistic variation in a humanised system

Though people are aware that computers do not require the same social treatment that they would afford another human, they unconsciously treat people and computers in much the same way, but deny doing so (Reeves and Nass, 1996). Hence, if people respond socially to computers, then computers should also respond socially to people. This means that, to humanise the interaction, it is not sufficient to use a typical human communication medium such as speech. The reception of speech demands that the interface reflect human social norms. One of those norms is variation in utterances, particularly when asked to repeat.

For visual interfaces it is paramount to ensure that consistency is maintained so that users do not make any incorrect inferences that might result from the inclusion of variations. But for speech output the consistency issue is more complex. The same spoken message must be semantically consistent, but expressed with variation (Witten, 1982) so as to avoid irritating the user. Ideally, not only should the words in the sentence be varied and spoken with the appropriate intonation and prosody (Zue, 1997), but individual words should also be spoken with slight variations. If the computer regularly speaks a word in the same irritating manner (and it might only be irritating to that person) then it will distract users from their activity.

Of course it is important that the dialogue in a film remains constant, but, for example, an on-line lecture (Benest, 1997) - a narrated sequence of slides with illustrative and indicative animation - may require some level of variation. The act of requesting a repetition of a sequence might be an implied signal from the user that the narration was not properly understood and that a different explanation, whilst still maintaining the same semantic meaning, would be beneficial.

It is very common to think that a conversational interface relies on the quality and accuracy of the speech recognition engine. However, creating an effective conversational interface must also exploit other aspects of the human dialogue such as the naturalness of the speech output and this is mainly achieved by incorporating variation. In terms of the design, this linguistic variation may be achieved both at the sentence construction level - employing lexical and syntactical variation, and at the speech synthesis level - by varying the intonation and the prosody of utterances.

1.2.3.   Avoiding rudeness in a humanised system

To create a humanised interface that employs speech requires at least two further norms to be perceived sub-consciously. The first is for the system to know when and how to interrupt, and the second is for it to be polite. If either or both of these characteristics are ignored, rudeness ensues (e.g. a confirmation dialogue box that appears in front of the user's current window). Above all, alerts (either notifications or reminders) should be relevant and unobtrusive.

The ability to manage interruptions effectively has also been stressed by Ball et al. (1997): when it is necessary to initiate an interaction with the user, the system needs to recognise the possibility that the user is engaged in a very different activity, perhaps requiring a high-level of cognition. The system may be able to recognise that the user is typing or that the user is engaged in an on-line presentation, and should wait until an appropriate pause occurs, depending on its *precedence* the interruption may take in the chain of activities needing the user's attention. But even when the user is apparently idle, the person might be engaged in deep thought, and unimportant alerts should still be avoided.

A recent study on the nature of interruptions in the workplace (O'Conaill and Frohlich, 1995) suggests that preventing interruptions is *not* necessarily wise because it would also prevent beneficial interactions from occurring. Thus, the preferred way to deal with interruptions would be to have a filtering mechanism that would take into account a particular user's interests and work environment characteristics. In terms of design, this aspect may be taken into account through an interruption mechanism that obtains the *precedence* of an interruption based on the *urgency* (the immediate relevance of information to its user's current activities) and the *priority* (relevance of information in relation to its user's long-term interests) of the interruption.

Politeness is an important element in terms of further attenuating the irritating effect of interruptions. But including politeness as another aspect of the system design raises at least one important ethical problem: since the polite behaviour derives from higher levels of human cognition, and depends on human emotion, which is obviously not yet available in the computer, the fact that the computer says for example *"Excuse me!"* might be deceiving. Nevertheless, if the system does not raise false expectations regarding its non-existent intelligence, the polite behaviour may contribute to smooth the interaction, in particular in the case where a considerable number of interruptions are being generated. In addition, the presence of these spoken expressions of politeness also direct the user to attending the aural channel.

1.2.4.   Enhancing information awareness

While using speech might provide advantages for maintaining awareness of the contents of personal information sources, it is not sufficient just to investigate the way speech-based messages should be delivered. In order to enhance information awareness effectively, there must also be a proper design of the *contents* of speech-based notifications and reminders. The fundamental concepts that should drive the design of the alerting messages are those that relate to the psychological principles that underlie the processes people use in personal information management.

Personal information can be defined as all the information that is handled by individuals, be it organisational or private data. The data contained in a personal information system belongs to a user's information repository and each data item is part of a personal context. Personal information management systems (PIMS) include the methods and rules that a person uses for acquiring, organising, storing, maintaining and retrieving information (Barreau, 1995). The processes that must be supported by any system for personal information management include those of information awareness, information handling, and information storage and retrieval. Human memory plays a crucial role in all processes. Hence, the psychological findings related to human memory can and should be used to guide the design of any personal information management system.

Within these psychological principles, one is relevant to the design of notifications and reminders, which characterises the human memory for recognition and recall. Recognition refers to the awareness that something perceived has been perceived before. Recall denotes the process of summoning back to awareness of a subject or situation at hand; that is, the process of remembering, bringing back or restoring a piece of information. The psychological evidence states that *recognition is superior to recall* (Houston, 1986). The implication of this fact is that a system that attempts to enhance information awareness should support the weaker recall function, in order to bring information to awareness. This may be followed by a recognition-based scanning when users search their personal information repository. In terms of the design of alerts, and looking at a humanised system from the perspective of complementing the graphical presentation of notifications and reminders, this suggests exploiting speech for the provision of support for the initial recall-directed function (for example by presenting a suitable overview of new information), leaving the recognition function (the presentation of the full details) for the most suitable graphical presentation.

The other important evidence concerning human memory relates to the fact that humans have a *poor memory for details* (Houston, 1986). In fact, people interpret information in the context in which it appears, rather than storing that information in memory exactly as it has been acquired. This fact prompts the need to provide recallable and recognisable characteristics in order to improve information recall, and these are provided by contextual elements, or *cues*, that characterise the situation in which an event occurs (Barreau, 1995), including such elements as the subject matter, the addresses of the information or the intended use for the information. This evidence has a profound impact on the design of the contents (or semantics) of spoken notifications and reminders. The speech-based alerts must convey the right cues, which prompt the user to the occurrence of events, and these cues must be extracted from the personal information items that are relevant to the user.

1.2.5.   Designing an anthropomorphic speaking assistant

There is the need to evaluate both whether a humanised speech output system reinforces the social acceptability of the computer, and whether such an approach enhances information awareness. This requires the creation of a suitable experimental environment which exhibits speech-based anthropomorphic behaviours, and which gathers and delivers the necessary cues that assist human memory in maintaining awareness of information that is hidden from view.

The background technology for such an environment must enable the application of social science theory to computer-based systems, and must promote the perception of the computer as a personal assistant. In this regard, the techniques provided by research in software agents (Bradshaw, 1997) appear to provide an adequate support for the required properties of the humanised system. Software agents are a special kind of software entity that have the following distinctive properties: software agents are *autonomous* - they operate on behalf of their users with minimal supervision by them, *adaptive* - they take into account users' preferences, interests and habits as they change over time and customise their assistance according to these aspects, and *collaborative* - they communicate with other software agents.

Now there is the need to include a set of specialised and autonomous entities that capture the context of events related to personal information, extract the appropriate context elements that characterise those events, and communicate that information.

In addition, there is the need for an interface mechanism that generates the appropriate utterances to be delivered to the user and these should be based upon the context elements extracted by the other software agents. Furthermore, the choice of this mechanism must also take into account such anthropomorphic aspects as the proper management of interruptions, linguistic variation and politeness. Interface agents (Maes, 1994) appear to provide the key functionality for the development of software systems to which users can delegate certain computer-based tasks, including those that maintain people's awareness of their personal information. Maes stresses the fact that agents are not substitutes for a user interface, and that whenever there is an interface agent, there is also the need for a good application interface, because the user is mainly interacting with the application and the agent is only assisting (Shneiderman and Maes, 1997).

The generation of appropriate speech-based messages can be guided by techniques that stem from research in conversational interfaces (e.g. (Ball et al., 1997; Langley et al., 1999)), and from research in spoken language systems (e.g. (Cole et al., 1995; Gardner-Bonneau, 1999)) that attempt to model a natural dialogue between a user and a machine.

Conversational interfaces need to support large-vocabulary spontaneous spoken language exchanged as part of a "fluid" dialogue between the user and the computer, by providing support to the parallel natural language processing required for both input and output between a human and a computer (Oviatt and Adams, 2000). Conversational interfaces also need to support other elements of typical human conversation. These elements include a range of anthropomorphic social behaviours as diverse as expressing emotion and personality (Ball and Breese, 2000), or reproducing the human facial expressions and gestures in embodied conversational agents (Cassel, 2000). These anthropomorphic behaviours have been incorporated in the design of a variety of animated software characters (e.g. see (André et al., 2000) and (Badler et al., 2000)), which aim to facilitate human-computer conversational exchange (Oviatt and Adams, 2000).

In presenting the design of such an experimental environment, this book highlights an approach which addresses a number of issues related to the adoption of agent-based techniques that create an assistant-like system; one that humanises information awareness through the use of speech induced anthropomorphism to convey context cues as part of alerts. The design illustrates how to split the environment functionality into a number of specialised software agents together with an interface agent. It also illustrates how to develop a generic software architecture that includes those types of software agent, how to design the internal architecture of each software agent in a way that it senses and communicates contextual information, how to enable the agents to communicate between themselves in order to decentralise the control, how to transform collected information into appropriate spoken messages designed to alert the user, and how to deliver spoken information, adopting a number of anthropomorphic traits so as to reinforce the social acceptability of the speech-based system.

1.2.6.   Evaluating the humanised interaction style

The fact that people respond socially to computers should be understood by user-interface designers; they should try to adapt computer systems to the psychological needs of users (Ball and Breese, 2000). However, there is relatively little empirical evaluation devoted to the real needs of users concerning humanised interfaces, and on the effects caused by having a computer exhibit typical human social behaviours.

In fact, unlike other human-computer interaction areas, systems that attempt to establish a spoken dialogue with users have been difficult to evaluate, mainly because it is not possible to say what is the single most correct dialogue. Furthermore, it is even more complicated to separate and evaluate only the response generation part of the spoken language system. As a consequence, there has been very little work on finding out the right way to measure the success of a spoken language generation system, and even less on evaluating its anthropomorphic aspects and their impact on users.

Some authors argue that current speech output systems lack the required variability and flexibility necessary in high-quality synthetic speech and this leads to rejection by users (Larrey et al., 1998). Furthermore, they identify a set of requirements according to two main criteria: message quality and communication efficiency. The most interesting is the *message quality* requirement, since it aggregates a set of aspects against which an anthropomorphic approach to speech output could be evaluated. These aspects include (Larrey et al., 1998): the *intelligibility* - the ability given to users to understand the message and its contents, the *conviviality* - the degree of sociability, liveliness and warmth conveyed by the system, the *prosodic* adequacy - the use of the right melodic and rhythmic patterns and correct speaking style according the dialogue context, the *naturalness* - vaguely seen as the proximity to human speech, and the *continuity* - the absence of inappropriate pauses or gaps.

With these evaluation criteria in mind, there is a need to identify a suitable evaluation process that allows for the measurement of those criteria. Some possibilities for the process of evaluation of a language generation system were suggested by Sagisaka et al. (1996) who investigated how well a user can complete a task requiring interaction with a system that generates spoken responses. They asked users to indicate their satisfaction with system responses and performed a preference analysis between different types of text. They also degraded the response generation system and tested the resulting user satisfaction.

Another evaluation possibility consists of a framework, called PARADISE (Walker et al., 1997b), designed to evaluate spoken language dialogue agents. This method defines a single performance function as a weighted linear combination of both a task success measure and a dialogue cost measure. The weights were obtained by correlating users' satisfaction (a usability related objective) with performance. Although interesting, this approach did not seem well suited to the evaluation of the kinds of criteria of interest in this book. In fact, this evaluation method seemed to be more concerned with complete dialogues between speaking agents and users, and treated the process as a whole, making it very difficult to evaluate just the *message quality* output aspects identified above.

Yet another evaluation technique that was applied to conversational interfaces and natural language dialogue systems consisted of simulation studies known as Wizard of Oz studies (Dahlback et al., 1992; Oviatt and Adams, 2000). These studies involve collecting data for the purpose of system design, in advance of building a fully functional system, and involve test subjects who believe they are using a fully functional system, while a test assistant at a remote location provides *simulated* system responses (Oviatt and Adams, 2000).

The problem with simulations is that, while they allow for the evaluation of system responses and inform the design before any design decision is made, they do not allow for the evaluation of how well a certain architecture is suited to support a particular system feature. Simulations are indeed an invaluable tool for early stages of system design, and constitute a tool to be considered whenever there is the need to evaluate a set of alternative concepts that should be incorporated in a design.

Thus, as far as evaluation is concerned, the research problem lies in designing an adequate experiment that allows for the assessment of the incorporation of humanised aspects in the spoken output of information. Combining the ideas suggested by Larrey et al. (1998) and Sagisaka et al. (1996), and focussing the evaluation on the perceptions and effects caused by having a system exhibit anthropomorphic behaviour, an initial empirical study has been designed following a quasi-experimental model. This study was designed for the purpose of testing whether speech employed as part of a complementary mechanism for interruption, notification and reminding, and conveyed using typical human conversational behaviours, promotes the perception of a work companion. The emphasis was on users' perceptions, and the main goal was to uncover whether users want, or need, such behaviour as part of an interface that actively assists them in staying aware of their personal information.

The study described in this book uncovered such aspects as the adequacy of a number of humanised behaviours (for example getting a user's attention prior to interrupting, employing politeness and incorporating linguistic variation) as well as the impact that the combination of these behaviours has on the perception of the assistance the system provides. The study revealed some interesting tendencies in terms of a person's psychological preferences for acquiring information: people who tended to adopt a heuristic approach to information acquisition also tended to find the humanised characteristics more adequate than people who tended to adopt a more analytic approach.

The observations that resulted from the study deserve further research in order to validate them with less restricted and more heterogeneous groups of users. However, the results of the initial study show that, as far as the interruption for notification and reminding functions are concerned, users feel that more attention should be devoted to the incorporation of appropriate social norms when speech is employed in the interface, so as to avoid degrading their experience when unnatural or socially inappropriate behaviour is generated. In a similar way, users tended to find the employment of speech useful and appropriate for addressing current limitations of purely graphical-based approaches to information awareness.

1.3   How to design a work companion?

The goal of the thesis presented in this book is to determine whether the adoption of human-like characteristics, conveyed using speech as part of a complementary assistant to a graphical user-interface, reinforces the perception of a socially competent system, and leads users to establish an enhanced rapport with the system. To this end, it is hypothesised that:

A computer-based system, designed to enhance information awareness by incorporating speech, invokes social reactions; when these are reinforced by anthropomorphic behaviours, it is perceived to be a work companion.

The concept of a w*ork companion* is possibly a much better way to approach human-computer interaction than simply to regard the computer as a *tool*. Users and computers should be peers, and the dependence on computers should not imply that people feel inferior or superior. Ideally, people should feel that they are in the same team with the computer. Being in the same team encourages people to think that the computerised work environment is more enjoyable and efficient, which in turn should promote better performance (Nass et al., 1996). In fact, making the machine more human-like is a way to empower the user, who is obviously able to interact more naturally and productively with other humans than with machines (Massaro et al., 1999).

In this book, a *"work companion"* is characterised as a speaking assistant that is imbued with a set of chosen social norms that mimic typical human conversational behaviour: knowing when to interrupt, what to say so as to properly interrupt and get a user's attention, how to interrupt the audio channel, how to speak with a degree of appropriate linguistic variation, and how to avoid rudeness. The emphasis is on the correct design of this behaviour, and on the issues that must be addressed for designing and implementing a software architecture that includes these norms as part of a personal assistant for information awareness. *Information awareness* is the process that enables people to appreciate the significance of sets of desired information.

In summary, this research was guided by the hypothesis that a speaking assistant will facilitate the awareness of personal information, and encourage and support personal information management through the computer. The work described in this book is a step towards the understanding of how to achieve the goal of providing a more enjoyable (because it is more humanised) and a more productive (because it better assists users in maintaining awareness of personal information) work environment that stimulates and assists users in their daily personal information management activities, whilst respecting their determination for what is next to be achieved. In order to explore the hypothesis sketched above, the following research methodology was applied.

1.4   Research methodology

1.4.1.   Delineation of the problem space

First, an extensive literature review was performed, which identified the problems with current interfaces as far as information awareness is concerned, along with the relevant literature on the psychology of personal information management. Background literature on social interfaces, anthropomorphism, conversational interfaces, software agents and spoken dialogue systems were also covered with the objective of providing a framework of key concepts and technologies on which to base the design of an architecture that addressed the issue of information awareness. In this way the literature review indicated a niche demanding investigation.

1.4.2.   Spoken message design

The second step in the methodology consisted of the design of a typology of speech-based messages to be conveyed by the speaking assistant. To this end, a number of categories for speech-based information delivery were identified together with the corresponding types of message. This was followed by the identification of a number of key elements that characterised the context surrounding the occurrence of events in a user's personal information space. These pieces of contextual evidence provided the semantic elements that constitute the content that spoken messages convey.

1.4.3.   Designing and prototyping the experimental environment

A suitable agent-based architecture for the experimental environment was then devised that was founded on a number of specialised agents which monitored particular sources of personal information, detected the occurrence of events, extracted context elements, and composed messages that corresponded to those events. An inter-agent communication protocol was then designed which allowed the specialised agents to send asynchronous messages to an interface agent (the speaking agent).

The internal architecture of the speaking agent reflected the design requirements for a humanised delivery of speech, and included the mechanisms for the proper management of interruptions, the generation of English-language sentences incorporating linguistic variation and politeness, and the creation of the corresponding spoken messages with the correct intonation and prosody.

In order to demonstrate the applicability of the approach and provide a concrete environment for evaluation, a prototype was developed that implemented a number of specialised agents (which monitored events in the e-mail, diary and printing domains), and a fully functioning speaking agent, for the Windows NT desktop environment.

1.4.4.   Evaluating the concept

Following the implementation of a working prototype, an initial empirical study was devised with the main purpose of uncovering users' *subjective* perceptions about the importance of the humanised characteristics incorporated in the speaking assistant in reinforcing the social acceptability of the computer. Thus, the study aimed to test how effective was the resulting perception of a work companion, and to collect users' opinions and suggestions which allowed finding out whether the anthropomorphic speech-based approach enhanced their awareness of information that is hidden from view.

To this end, the empirical study included a restricted sample of fifteen participants selected from the Computer Science department population, and collected their subjective perceptions through carefully designed questionnaires. These were prepared in order to elicit users' opinions concerning the *adequacy* of the selected anthropomorphic behaviours, and the degree of *usefulness* and *humanisation* of the speaking assistant. The questionnaires also intended to uncover any differences in opinion arising from different types of personality using the Myers-Briggs Type Indicator (MBTI) (Myers, 1974).

1.4.5.   Analysis and implications for design

The last step in the methodology included the statistical analysis of the data gathered during the experiment that was undertaken to assess the various humanised properties under investigation. It also determined the implication of the experimental results for the design of speech output interfaces. Aspects deserving further research were also identified.

The (preliminary) results presented in this book indicate that speech output offered benefits for information awareness, especially because it provided unobtrusive notification and reminding. The results also show that anthropomorphic characteristics, such as the proper management of interruptions and linguistic variation, contribute to a more enjoyable work environment. In fact, the experimental environment was well accepted by the participants in the experiment. Results concerning politeness are not so conclusive, but they point to the need for further research.

This research methodology is followed linearly through the book.

1.5 Summary

For many people, there is a desire for all personal information acquired over time to be stored, organised and accessed using a computer, but current interface metaphors emphasise a graphical approach to information management that is far from optimal. People wish to maintain knowledge about the status of sources of personal information, but there is a range of problems, arising from the strict application of the desktop metaphor, that limit the computer-human interface as far as personal information awareness is concerned: it is difficult to find visually hidden information, there is a lack of semantics in notification cues, designers seem to disregard the costs of interrupting the user with unimportant messages, and there is a lack of integration for notifications.

One way to address these problems is to use speech to support the provision of contextual cues that invoke the psychological processes involved in the awareness of personal information. Since people already react socially to mediated computers, and communication is a two-way channel, using speech raises social expectations that put an obligation on the designer to anthropomorphise the interface and make it follow the same social norms people use when interacting with other people. In this way, the user-interface is humanised and this book explores this arena.

Chapter 2

REINFORCING SOCIAL ACCEPTABILITY

2.1 Overview

In a humanised system, *speech output* has the potential to offer a complementary solution to the existing problems of: finding visually hidden information, the lack of semantics in alerting cues, the lack of identification and co-ordination between high priority and unimportant notifications, as well as the lack of a suitable integration of otherwise disparate notifications. Furthermore, spoken language is especially attractive because it is the "most natural, efficient, flexible, and inexpensive means of communication among humans" (Zue, 1997).

Previous research found out that people react socially to computers (Reeves and Nass, 1996). Moreover, given that the reception of speech invokes even stronger social responses (Nass et al., 1994), this fact demands that the system *reinforces its social acceptability* by complying with human expectations regarding social interaction. When using speech output at the interface, this may be achieved by making the system reflect the same social norms people employ in conversation. Therefore, the design of interfaces that employ natural language should be guided by aspects of the psychology of language, and regard language in terms of conversation and not as "disembodied grammatical sentences composed of strings of characters" (Brennan, 1990). This book suggests that to reinforce the social acceptability of a speaking system, the design should take into account at least three critical anthropomorphic aspects: proper spoken interruptions, linguistic variation and linguistic style, or politeness.

Since interruptions are inevitable in a computer-based system for notification and reminding, the first social norm that a humanised system should exhibit is that of an adequate management of spoken interruptions, by making them *relevant* and *minimally intrusive*. The design of such a mechanism needs to take into account the nature of interruptions, their effects on each person's attention and the ways people employ, and naturally accept, to interrupt each other. More specifically, when using speech output the system must at least be able to know when to interrupt,

---

and how to interrupt; that is, what to say to obtain the person's attention, and how to interrupt the audio channel.

Furthermore, interruptions are raised by the occurrence of events, either for notification or reminding of desired information, and these events are inevitably repetitive. For visual interfaces it is extremely important to maintain consistency in the presentation of information, but for speech output the repetition of the same utterance over and over will necessarily irritate, and distract, the person. So, while the semantic consistency must be maintained, the message must be conveyed with variation so as to avoid annoying the user, and diverting the user's attention from the very reason why the message was given in the first place. The types of linguistic variation people usually employ in a conversation, which have no impact in the meaning they intend to convey, include small variations of intonation and prosody, as well as variation in the words used to construct sentences, or variation in positioning of words when constructing utterances. The design of a humanised system has necessarily to take into account these phenomena in order to produce sufficiently varied spoken output.

But being interrupted can be sometimes sufficiently annoying *per se*. While the interruption may be urgent and very relevant to the person, and even conveyed in a non-repetitive way, it will still distract the attention and necessarily annoy the person. The strategy usually employed by people who are interrupting is to be polite so as to attenuate the adverse effects of the interruption. Therefore, the design of a humanised system should take this norm into account, and at least make use of typical polite expressions, particularly when getting the person's attention prior to conveying the actual message.

This chapter concentrates on this set of anthropomorphic characteristics, which reinforce the social acceptability of a system that uses speech output to maintain people's awareness of information. It discusses the importance of each characteristic and reviews a number of techniques that may be used to guide the design of humanised systems which incorporate those behaviours. The aim is to discuss the design aspects that contribute to a more enjoyable and productive work environment. Subsequent chapters apply these concepts to the design of an experimental environment that delivers humanised speech-based notifications and reminders.

2.2   Spoken Interruptions

2.2.1.   The nature of interruptions

Interruptions are commonplace in the work environment, and have been characterised in the Management Science literature as fragmented activities that occur at an unrelenting pace (Mintzberg, 1973), and as a stream of disjointed activities (Stewart, 1967). Recently, the concept of interruption has been characterised as "an externally-generated, randomly occurring, discrete event that breaks continuity of cognitive focus on a primary task" (Speier et al., 1997). By its very nature, an interruption "requires immediate attention" and "insists on action" (Covey, 1989).

This characterisation implies that an interruption is a disruptive event, the timing of which is beyond the control of a person. It forces people to shift their attention away from their primary activity, and having handled the interruption, re-focus attention on that primary activity. It has been found that what makes an interruption disruptive is the complexity of the new task rather than the duration of the interruption (Gillie and Broadbent, 1989). Previous research into the effects of task interruption on individual decision-making has identified two broad classes for categorising the characteristics of interruptions (Speier et al., 1997):

1. Characteristics that affect the *cognitive processing*, such as complexity, content, frequency, duration, and timing of the interruption.

2. *Social characteristics* that influence how the person *responds* to the interruption, such as the form of the interruption, the person or object generating the interruption and existing social expectations regarding responsiveness to the interruption.

This book suggests that these parameters can be used to help the system decide *when* to interrupt, as well as to determine *how* the system should interrupt. For example, interruptions should happen more frequently at opportune moments, should convey relevant content, and should be less distracting than human-inspired interruptions.

Regarding the decision of "when to interrupt", it has been said that: "one way of coping with depleted *attentional* reserves is to set priorities for use of attention, giving priority to information pertinent to one's own goals and neglecting less pertinent cues that carry information about the mood and needs of others" (Kirmeyer, 1988). This observation suggests that the attribution of priorities to interrupting events, by setting higher priorities to information relevant to a user's current activity, or long-term interests, and lower priorities to information not directly related with a person's own goals, is desirable.

A recent study about the nature of interruptions in the workplace has evaluated the effect of interruptions on the activities carried-out there (O'Conaill and Frohlich, 1995). One of the interesting suggestions is that preventing interruptions is not necessarily ideal because it would also prevent beneficial interactions from occurring. The study suggests that a way to deal with interruptions would be to have "light-weight" filtering of interruptions. The light-weight nature of the filtering mechanism is required so as to ensure that it would not become as disruptive as the interruption itself. The study also suggests what forms the interruptions should take. This is based on asynchronous messaging with a combination of audio and written messages that can be stored for later notification (O'Conaill and Frohlich, 1995).

There has been substantial research directed towards handling incoming interruptions that affect the concentration of users, and reduce their productivity. For example, Horvitz et al. (1998) take the perspective that "human attention is the most valuable and scarcest commodity in human-computer interaction". They are concerned with environments where a number of executing applications raise a variety of notifications with the associated cost of potentially distracting the user from a primary task at the focus of attention. Similarly, Sawhney and Schmandt (2000) point out that current solutions in mobile environments overwhelm users with intrusive messaging and ambiguous notifications. They discuss interaction techniques developed for wearable computing platforms, which manage voice and text-based messages that are delivered to users when they are engaged on other tasks requiring their primary attention. Both papers highlight the fundamental problem of finding a way to ensure that users remain aware of significant events, while minimising the prejudicial effects that interruptions have on the user's focus of attention.

Undesirable interruption is a key problem that must be addressed by any humanised system that aims to allow users to feel comfortable in their work environment. But users still need to be alerted to the occurrence of important events that relate to their personal information space, such as, for example, calendar entries, line printer messages, the arrival of e-mail messages, or other to-do items. One way to approach the problem is to try to find out *when* and *how* to interrupt in order to minimise disruption and cognitive overload.

2.2.2.   When to interrupt: a context-based approach

It is necessary to consider a number of techniques designed with the specific aim of alleviating the negative impact of interruptions on the user's attention. Deciding the time to interrupt the user is a critical function when the objective is to minimise the user's vulnerability to undesirable interruptions.

To address this problem, a review of the relevant literature suggests endowing the system with knowledge of the context surrounding any interruption. This context should be based on two distinct, but equally important, pieces of information: the inferred *level of attention* towards current activity, and the *value* associated with the information underlying the interruption itself. The decision to interrupt can then be based on weighting the components of both pieces of contextual information, by considering the costs of disrupting the user's attention against the benefits associated with interrupting and conveying the information.

For example, Sawhney and Schmandt (2000) consider the problem of delivering spoken e-mail and voice messages in nomadic environments, and suggest developing a model that dynamically selects a suitable "notification strategy" that is based on three pieces of contextual information: the priority of an e-mail message, the usage level of the wearable device and the environmental context. Sawhney and Schmandt (2000) argue that such a system must infer the level of the user's attention through monitoring current activities such as interactions with the device and conversations in the room. Their approach is based on calculating a notification level through a weighted average for those three contextual cues. The value obtained is then used to decide whether an interruption should be generated. This value is also used to decide how the interrupting message should be delivered to the user (as discussed in section 2.2.3).

While this strategy proved to be sufficient in the nomadic domain, it is this author's opinion that another critical piece of contextual evidence is missing in the approach suggested by Sawhney and Schmandt (2000): the *urgency* associated with the message being conveyed. However, while the priority of a message can be directly obtained for example from the e-mail message header, an indicator of the urgency of the message can only be obtained by having prior knowledge about what each user considers to be urgent. This knowledge can for example be part of a user model maintained by the system, and can either be introduced directly by the user or learnt by the system through observation of each user's actions on each message.

In another example, focussed on the need to mediate the flow of potentially distracting alerts and communications to users, Horvitz et al. (1999) suggest a similar context-based approach. They relied upon a set of "inferencing procedures" that balanced the costs of interrupting a user's attention against the costs of deferring alerting messages. This model is based on exploring "utility-directed notification policies" that support an automated "attention manager". More specifically, the approach suggested by Horvitz et al. (1999) concentrates first on using Bayesian models[3] as a means for *inferencing* the user's focus of attention under uncertainty. These inferences are used to predict the expected cost of transmitting an interrupting alert or notification to the user. At the same time, the model dictates that the informational benefits associated with alerts must also be inferred. The difference between the expected costs of interrupting and the informational benefits of the alerting message provide a measure of the utility of the alerting action to be performed by the system.

But a deeper analysis of this model reveals that a critical aspect lies in the first step: determining the user's focus of attention and the user's involvement in the current task. This is accomplished through monitoring the context surrounding the user in order to identify the user's "state of attentional focus" (Horvitz et al., 1999). The objective is to obtain a measure of the cost of interrupting given a probability distribution over the states of a user's attention. Moreover, the set of contextual elements used to characterise the user's attention is richer when compared with the model suggested by Sawhney and Schmandt (2000). Horvitz et al. (1999) suggest that a user's current attention is influenced by elements such as the user's scheduled appointments, the time of the day, the proximity of deadlines, the status of ambient acoustical signals in the user's "office", the status and configuration of software applications, and the ongoing stream of user activity built from sequences of mouse and keyboard actions.

Because alerts can take the form of audio, visual, or a combination of audio and visual messages, the expected cost of interrupting the user must include not only the cognitive cost of the interruption, but also the cost of obstructing the graphical content being accessed and referred to as part of the user's current task. Horvitz et al. (1999) suggest combining both costs into a single measure, and then calculating the overall expected cost of alerting by considering both (1) the probability of the user being in a specific cognitive state of attention given the evidence gathered

---

[3] Bayesian models are graphical models that encode probabilistic relationships among variables of interest. These models are mainly used to enable a system to learn causal relationships among the variables, and therefore to enable the system to predict the consequences of changes in the variables (Heckerman, 2001).

from the contextual elements, and (2) the combined cost associated with a specific alert that occurs when the user is in that attentional state.

In contrast, the informational value of an interrupting message depends on a careful analysis of the contents of the message that causes the interruption. In this respect, the approach suggested by Horvitz et al. (1999) includes a richer variety of evidence than the model developed by Sawhney and Schmandt (2000). Horvitz et al. (1999) describe their approach using an example in the e-mail domain. With the ultimate objective of identifying the "criticality" of e-mail messages (as a measure of their informational value), the authors suggest considering the following pieces of information: the sender, the recipient, the time criticality inferred from the language used in the message, the presence of past and future tenses used to refer to events mentioned in the message, the presence of language suggesting coordinative tasks, the presence of phrases associated with personal requests for help or assistance, the importance of the message as given by priority flags, the length of the message, the presence of attachments, the time that the message was composed, and finally the presence of signs of junk e-mail. While these elements are clearly oriented towards the specific domain of e-mail management, they still provide a useful source of meta-information that could be used to infer the "criticality" of other types of interrupting messages, such as for example diary related reminders and notifications.

Of course the final decision regarding the timing of an interruption is one of the following alternatives: interrupting immediately, delaying the interruption, or abandoning it definitively. In order to make this decision, Horvitz et al. (1999) suggest that the system should go ahead and interrupt only when a positive value is obtained when subtracting the expected cost of interrupting from the informational benefits of alerting. If this difference is negative, the system should delay the interruption until a later time when the cost of interrupting is smaller; or simply avoid the interruption altogether.

This review indicates that context plays a crucial role in the decision of when to interrupt. However, it is necessary to ponder whether there is a significant advantage in using richer, but more complex, sets of contextual evidence, as suggested by Horvitz et al. (1999), over more constrained, but lighter, sets of contextual elements, as suggested by Sawhney and Schmandt (2000). Necessarily, the number of context elements, and the associated procedures, must always depend on the kind of environment being addressed. This book identifies a set of elements designed to support the generation of interruptions concerning information awareness in the e-mail, printing and diary domains, and describes a system that uses these elements to decide when to interrupt the user. The elements include the urgency and the priority users assign to the various items of personal information.

2.2.3.   How to interrupt: forms of interrupting

While it is important to decide when to interrupt, it is equally critical for the system to decide how the interruption should be conveyed for minimal disruption.

Some interruptions can be very short and have a negligible impact upon a user's current activity because they do not require any overt response. Others, however, may have longer durations requiring a response from the user. In these cases, a difficulty arises when the user resumes the initial activity. This difficulty is twofold: either "remembering where you were before being interrupted, or remembering to resume the activity at all" (Dix et al., 1995). Consequently, as far as the form of the interruption is concerned, it should ideally be as short as possible and require no overt response, in order to minimise the impact on the user's attention.

The length of the interruption is not the sole characteristic to be considered when structuring the interruption. The system should also ensure that the user is aware of imminent relevant messages, as well as ensure that sufficient information is conveyed, which allows the person to decide what to do concerning the interruption. The final requirement relates to the visual intrusiveness of the interruption: ideally, the system should avoid superimposing graphical information on top of the working area being accessed by the user – a common technique that in any other medium would simply be regarded as rude.

One approach that addresses these requirements involves the design of a form of interruption that exploits the aural channel: speech-based messages can be short, can be designed to convey sufficient semantics, and allow the user to remain aware of potentially interesting messages without interfering with the visual channel. However, the speech-based approach does have an adverse impact in the cases where the user is accessing audio, or multimedia, presentations as part of the current task. In these cases, interruptions will be disruptive. Therefore, the system has to ensure that the interruption of the audio channel follows the conventions that are commonly accepted. In the particular case of interrupting the audio channel, a common technique is to fade out the source of the existing aural information, while fading in the source of the interrupting information, and performing the reverse functions at the end of the interruption.

Since any form of humanised interruption also requires getting the person's attention before conveying the actual contents, the exploitation of the audio channel offers advantages in that the person's visual workspace remains unaffected. However, it does require a careful design of the aural attention-getters, and it may require the person to switch attention away from the visual channel. An aural strategy that does not use speech for interrupting and obtaining a user's attention is that based on *earcons* - "non-verbal audio messages that are used in the computer/user interface to provide information to the user about some computer object, operation or interaction" (Blattner et al., 1989). In fact, earcons have been shown to be an alternative means of communicating information in a human-computer interface (Brewster et al., 1993).

The literature on aural-based interruptions presents additional suggestions. For example, a model based on "scaleable auditory presentation" (Sawhney and Schmandt, 2000) allows the delivery of sufficient information to minimise the interruption on the human listener. This model involves categorising the presentation of interrupting messages according to seven levels of disruption, ranging from subtle auditory cues to full foreground spoken presentations. The category that the system selects depends on the inferred priority of the message, as well as on the user's context.

From the point of view of the form of the interrupting message, the method proposed by Sawhney and Schmandt (2000) relies on structuring, and assembling, increasingly intrusive aural messages. Starting from complete silence, Sawhney and Schmandt (2000) suggested a method that applies a scale in which the second level presents subtle changes in ambient sounds playing in the background. These alert the user to events and ensure that the user is continually aware of the on-going status of the system. The next level prescribes the presentation of distinct auditory cues (audio only), which aim to provide feedback, priority or identification information. At the fourth level, the method summarises the message and conveys it using synthetic speech. The final three levels include increasingly longer and more disruptive messages using speech synthesis to convey an overview in the background, the full body, or the complete interrupting message in the foreground.

The system described in this book takes an approach to structuring interruptions that is based on a two-phase process. Initially the system cues the user through speech-based attention-getters in order to signal that it is ready to deliver spoken information. Subsequently, the system modulates the audio channel to present the interrupting message. These messages were designed to convey sufficient information about the interrupting event in the foreground.

2.3 Linguistic Variation

2.3.1. The need for linguistic variation

Having discussed some of the more salient features that a humanised system should exhibit when it is about to interrupt a user to convey a spoken message, the discussion now turns to ways of humanising the spoken message itself.

In the context of speech interfaces, the degree of linguistic variation is a major problem. If these interfaces are truly to be perceived as a satisfying companion, they must exhibit the same level of *fluency* as that available from a human companion. Fluency can be improved by enabling the system to *vary* the words used to express a concept (Reiter and Dale, 1995), and to vary the way the words are spoken, in order to provide variety.

If the computer regularly speaks a word in the same irritating manner then it will distract users from their activity; they will anticipate every word, phrase or sentence to be spoken as soon as the system signals a new message. For example, if the system detects a new e-mail message shortly after a previous e-mail alert has been conveyed, then the new message should not sound identical to the previous notification. Similarly, if the user requests the repetition of a notification of work carried out by the system, the message should not be repeated in the same way. Furthermore, while the meaning must remain the same, care must be taken to avoid distracting interactions between the two varied messages. For example, if the message is "one to go before your job is printed" and is repeated as "your print job is second in the queue" the immediate subconscious interpretation is that someone has jumped in front of you, despite the fact that the meaning is actually the same.

Witten (1982) emphasises the importance of "varied speech" when designing the speech output part of a human-computer dialogue in order to obtain "natural interaction". Furthermore, he points out that successive utterances with identical intonations should be avoided, and suggests applying small changes in the speaking rate, pitch range and pitch level to add variety to synthetic speech.

Of course, a perfectly humanised system should possess the same levels of linguistic knowledge as those of a human. It should not only be able to "speak" fluently, but also to understand every word, sentence and meaning spoken by the user. However, the representation, and the manipulation of those representations in natural language is a large and difficult problem, both in terms of allowing a computer-based system to understand and to generate language. A common way to approach this problem is to restrict the application domain, and develop specific techniques that address the requirements imposed by that domain. In this book, the main focus is on the *generation* of appropriately varied *spoken language* to create notification and reminder messages that concern personal information.

There are two main methods for enabling the computer to speak: synthesised text-to-speech (TTS) and concatenated text-to-speech[4] (Schmandt, 1994). Speech synthesisers normally accept text as input and analyse the words in order to determine their phonetic pronunciations. These phonemes are then fed into an algorithm that tries to simulate the human vocal tract, and outputs the sounds corresponding to the phonemes. Prosodic features, such as intonation, pauses and stress, may be included in the model and controlled on the basis of "prosody markers" (Bernsen et al., 1998). While this method allows the speech synthesiser to speak any word, making it easy to generate new phrases at any time, it generates a voice that, for many languages, has little naturalness or quality.

In contrast, concatenated text-to-speech analyses the input text and looks-up pre-recorded words and phrases from an existing audio library. These digital audio recordings are then concatenated and replayed to produce a spoken version of the initial text. This method generates a more natural voice, but it makes it very difficult to get the prosody right, and requires a huge amount of effort in predicting and recording the audio snippets that compose the audio library. Thus, maintenance of the audio library may be difficult and costly (Bernsen et al., 1998). Moreover, the addition of new snippets to the library requires that the original speaker is available, or all words and phrases have to be re-recorded. However, the main disadvantage of this approach is that, if the original text includes a word that is not part of the library, the system will not be able to speak it at all.

This book focuses on synthesised text-to-speech because it allows the system to have a richer vocabulary (an essential requirement for linguistic variation) whilst minimising the development effort.

The degree of variation adopted in this book mimics the variation people employ in normal conversation; "the same intention may be expressed by different linguistic means" (Blum-Kulka, 1997). But the semantic meaning must remain unchanged. The literature suggests that, to sound "natural", this variation should span various levels of human communication. It is not sufficient simply to vary the words used to assemble a message. There must also be some variation at the speech synthesis level, more specifically in the way in which each word is spoken and in the prosody of the utterance. Some progress on providing this variation at the concatenated text-to-speech level is reported by (Cook and Benest, 2001).

2.3.2.   Types of linguistic variation

In order to make a computer-based system exhibit human-like linguistic variation, it is appropriate to take an analytic approach to human speech communication, uncovering what really happens when we speak. Schmandt (1994) presents a hierarchical structure that decomposes the human communication process into a stack of linguistic layers. The lower layers consider speech from an acoustic perspective, while the higher layers focus on the meaning and intention of what is spoken.

This approach provides advantages in that it allows for a systematic identification of the sources of human linguistic variation, which are enabled by the possibility of choosing among two or more equivalent (or near-equivalent) forms to express a given idea, or to achieve a certain communicative goal. This variable nature of human language affects all linguistic levels as well as the rules governing linguistic behaviour and communicative interaction. In this context, the hierarchy of eight linguistic layers described by Schmandt (1994) is particularly useful in that it highlights the processes that humans employ to communicate verbally. Schmandt's (1994) specific layers are as follows.

1. Discourse: refers to the regulation of human conversation for pragmatic purposes. It includes for example the processes for taking turns in conversation, the history of referents in a conversation that allow pronouns to refer to words spoken earlier, and the process of introducing new topics in the conversation.

---

[4] Synthesised text-to-speech is sometimes referred to as parametric speech, while concatenated text-to-speech is sometimes denoted as coded speech, such as for example in (Hansen et al., 1993).

2. Pragmatics: designates the intent or motivation with which an utterance is spoken. Pragmatics is about how language is used both in terms of the ways in which speech is used to achieve an action, as well as in terms of its effects on the conversants. Thus, this layer includes the processes that relate to the underlying reason an utterance is spoken.

3. Semantics: denotes the meaning of each word, and their meaning when combined in sentences.

4. Syntax: refers to the rules that control the combination of words in a sentence, and their forms such as case and number. Syntax provides structure in a language by constraining the way in which words may be combined, according to a set of rules.

5. Lexical: designates the set of words that are included in a language, the rules for forming new words, and the stress of syllables contained in the words.

6. Phonetics: refers to the series of sounds that convey the words contained in any sentence.

7. Articulation: designates the configuration of the vocal tract that produces the phonetic sounds.

8. Acoustics: denotes the realisation of the string of phonemes in the sentence as vibrations of air molecules so as to produce sound.

This analytic framework makes it possible to identify and characterise the sources of linguistic variation. To meet the requirement for preserving the semantic meaning of varied messages, the interesting sources of linguistic variation include the phonetic, lexical, and syntactical variation.

Phonetic variation may be achieved at the speech synthesis level and includes the variation in the *prosody* with which utterances are spoken. Prosody refers to the patterns of stress and intonation in a language[5]. Thus, the prosody of an utterance includes many of the features of speech other than just the sounds of the words being spoken. Such features are the *pitch contour* or intonation (the melody obtained through the rise and fall of the fundamental frequency of the sound wave), the *stress pattern* or rhythm (the series of stressed and unstressed syllables that constitute a word), the

---

[5] Source: WordNet 1.6, Princeton University, 1997.

speaking rate (the speed at which speech is produced), the *pausing*, and the *emphasis* on words (Jurafsky and Martin, 2000; Schmandt, 1994; Witten, 1982; Sagisaka et al., 1996).

Providing support for variation at the phonetics level allows the system to include subtle changes that affect the global sounding of the utterance and eliminate the annoyance caused by repetitive sounds. However, because the prosody of an utterance is related to the specific words that compose it, an incorrect prosody might adversely alter the meaning of the utterance. Therefore, there must be a close relationship between the system component that generates the text sentences and the component that synthesises the speech corresponding to those sentences. In the system described in this book, there is a close relationship between text generation and the corresponding speech synthesis in the sense that the prosody is adjusted prior to sending the text to the speech synthesiser.

Lexical variation refers to the cases where different words are used to represent the same meaning. This phenomenon occurs when people choose semantically related terms, or synonyms, to refer to the same entity. However, since the choice of semantically related terms depends on the context in which the word is used, it is often not sufficient to vary just one word, without varying the other words that constitute its context. Since several words have to be changed, the lexical variation is often accompanied by a syntactical variation; that is a change in the structure of the phrases that make up sentences. This is a common phenomenon that occurs when people re-word their utterances in order to express the same message in different words, for example for the purpose of clarification, through paraphrasing.

2.3.3. Generating linguistic variation

The generation of spoken language is typically achieved in two steps: first the information is converted into well-formed sentences, which are then fed to a text-to-speech (TTS) system that generates the corresponding utterances (Zue, 1997). The first step handles the generation of the sentences that constitute the message. The second step then involves the generation of the utterances that correspond to those sentences.

From this arrangement, it follows that the lexical and syntactical types of variation should be generated during the first stage, whereas the phonetic variation should be generated at the TTS level. However, rather than looking at these processes as completely independent, it is beneficial to integrate them as parts of a single process for generating spoken language (Zue, 1997).

2.3.3.1.   Generation of linguistically varied language

Natural Language Generation (NLG) is a field of research that aims to design computer systems that generate grammatically and stylistically correct texts, in English or other human languages, "from some underlying non-linguistic representation of information" (Reiter and Dale, 1995). Essentially, these computer systems aim to present information in a manner that people find easy to understand.

The two main areas of language generation include *single-sentence generation*, often called realisation or tactical generation, and *multisentence generation*, achieved with text planning or strategic generation (Hovy, 1996). Hovy distinguishes the *tasks* of generation from the *processes* of generation, and points out that a language generator can address one or more tasks, and normally includes one process. The tasks identified by Hovy (1996) include text planning, sentence planning and surface realisation. A thorough description of these language generation tasks falls beyond the scope of this book, but the reader might wish to see for example (Hovy, 1996), and (Reiter and Dale, 1995).

These generation tasks can be segmented into two parts: deciding "what to say" and "how to say it" (Dale et al., 1990). First, a generator determines the content of text and its degree of detail, and creates a text structure (text planning). Then, it determines what words to use in the sentences, and in what order or style, to present the content (sentence planning). Finally, each generated sentence is converted into a grammatically correct sentence (surface realisation) (Hovy, 1996).

The language generation process can range in sophistication and complexity, starting with the simpler and less flexible method of canned sentences and templates, to heavier and more flexible combination methods. Figure 1 illustrates the continuum of language generation methods. For each point on this range, there may be various types of suitable algorithms (Hovy, 1996).

Figure 1. Continuum of Natural Language Generation methods

According to Hovy (1996), the simplest approach to language generation is based on canned methods. This approach, which the author points out is used in the majority of software, is based on including fixed strings of words that become the output of the system, as required by the particular application (e.g. for error messages, warnings, status messages or for composing letters). Furthermore, this method can be used equally well for single-sentence and for multi-sentence generation. It is simple, but from the point of view of the generation of linguistic variation, it is quite inflexible in that it requires all messages to have been previously created and stored in a library.

A more appropriate method for generating linguistic variation is through templates. These are generally used when a message has to be produced several times with slight changes (Hovy, 1996). In essence, templates are fixed natural language expressions that contain variable slots. Whenever a template is activated, there is the need to determine both the values of the template variables, and an appropriate natural language expression that describes them. The application using templates is then responsible for (1) determining the required data that must be part of the message to be conveyed according to the message type and user's preferences, and (2) determine the templates, which contain the variables that can be substituted with instances of the selected data, to be activated. Thus, template-based generation can also be applied equally well to single-sentence and multisentence generation.

From the perspective of the NLG framework of tasks introduced in Figure 1, the content selection that occurs during text planning is performed by the application using the templates. Subsequently, the selection of a template according to their constraining conditions can be seen as a simple kind of sentence planning. Then, the task of surface realisation is reduced to a lexical mapping of the instances into the template slots. Typical template applications include the generation of form letters and reports where the text is quite regular in structure (Geldof and Velde, 1997; Reiter et al., 1999).

Given the nature of templates, this method seems to offer some advantages for the specific purpose of generating linguistically varied sentences. In fact, the template-based approach is not as computationally demanding as more complex natural language generation methods such as "phrase-based systems" or "feature-based systems" (Hovy, 1996), and it can be made more flexible by creating categories of templates and using these categories on a conditional basis. A category of templates can easily be made to include several templates that cover frequently used phrases that convey a specific content. Thus, it is quite straightforward to create a set of linguistically varied templates that apply to each type of message to be conveyed.

Moreover, the template-based approach provides the designer with an attractive degree of freedom for creating as much variation as required for each intended message or text. To achieve the lexical and syntactical variation, it is just a matter of constructing key sentences, and then varying the words and expressions as appropriate. Of course, this is not a completely automated process, but it couples the capturing of domain knowledge and the experience of the application designer during template construction. This in turn results in the generation of more natural, and domain appropriate, sentence variations.

2.3.3.2.   Generation of linguistically varied speech

The speech synthesiser is the component responsible for converting written text into spoken language. The text to be synthesised is constructed by the language generator, and is then analysed in order to obtain the correct pronunciation of the words - the phonetic representation of the written text. Often this initial analysis involves pre-processing the text to identify special constructs of the language (in English there is the need to expand, for example, abbreviations, acronyms, dates, times, e-mail addresses, currency amounts and numbers), and determine the precise locations where paragraphs and sentences start and end, according to punctuation. Further analysis is then required to decompose each word into its constituent parts, called phonemes (morphological analysis), and determine the pronunciation of each phoneme from the combination of the surrounding phonemes[6]. Then, a syntactic and semantic analysis has to be performed in order to determine where both the word occurs in the sentence and the correct meaning of the word. Finally, the sentence structure, the words and the phonemes are processed in order to determine the correct prosody of the utterance (Sagisaka et al., 1996; Dutoit, 1997; Schmandt, 1994).

The inclusion of phonetic variation may be achieved by controlling these processes that occur during the analysis. This functionality is often provided so that the designer can improve on the quality of the speech synthesis. For that purpose, designers have the possibility of using special markers to annotate the text in order to mark the start and end of paragraphs and sentences, and to specify the correct pronunciations for the words and the other special constructs mentioned above. But, when including phonetic variation, the most important aspect to be controlled is the one that relates to prosody. For this purpose, it is possible to use the markers to specify precisely how the

---

[6] The fact that the pronunciation of a phoneme, which is a unit of sound in a language, depends on the surrounding phonemes is known as co-articulation.

text should be spoken in terms of the emphasis on words, pauses, pitch, speaking rate and loudness. Thus, a particular sentence can be made to sound different in two different occasions, by slightly adjusting the values of its prosodic elements.

The resulting phonetic representation of the initial text includes special markers that describe how the text should be spoken. This phonetic string is then fed to the synthetic speech generator, which produces the audio waveform that corresponds to each sentence. The main methods for synthesising speech have already been briefly mentioned, the description of which falls beyond the scope of this book. Comprehensive introductions to the methods of speech synthesis technology may be found for example in the following texts (Dutoit, 1997; Sagisaka et al., 1996; Schmandt, 1994; Witten, 1982).

2.4   Politeness

2.4.1.   The need for politeness

In pursuing the goal of reinforcing the perception that the system deploys the social norms expected of a work companion, the linguistic style adopted by the system is as important a factor as linguistic variation. In this context, the choice of a particular linguistic style should enable the system to be perceived as sometimes being overly polite and sometimes more neutral in politeness.

It has been demonstrated that the linguistic style exhibited by life-like computer characters leads people to make specific inferences about personality and character (Nass et al., 1994). In a similar vein, Walker et al. (1997a) argue that it is very important to devise mechanisms for endowing the system with linguistic style in any domain where the system speaks to the user. Walker et al. (1997a) claim that the stylistic choices made by people, whenever they communicate their intentions, express their character and personality, and that these choices *influence* the way in which listeners infer the personality and character of the speaker (Walker et al., 1997a). For example, people might be more willing to accept advice conveyed politely by an "introvert" system, or heed warnings presented in a more serious tone, giving the impression of a "firm" system. By incorporating such linguistic styles, the system appears to users as possessing a personality, and its social presence might be better accepted by users (Huhns and Singh, 1998a). Since the person interacting with the speaking system will inevitably be affected by the linguistic style exhibited, it is important to incorporate polite behaviour in the design.

There are, however, other compelling reasons for the need to take politeness into account. First, since the system is taking the social role of a work companion, it is likely to be the "agent" that interrupts the user. These interruptions may produce a negative reaction (e.g. irritation) on the person being interrupted. To reduce this reaction it is proposed that the system adopts a polite behaviour so as to maintain a measure of harmony with the user.

The other reason for desiring a system that is able to express different degrees of politeness is related to familiarity. In fact politeness, positiveness and flattery can help to cement relationships, or to destroy them, but in this case can help to reinforce the perception of a helpful assistant, and lead the user to become more familiar with the system.

There is a danger, however, that polite behaviour may strengthen the impression that the system is able to take responsibility for its actions, and that it will act rationally. This is a serious ethical issue, which must be taken into account by ensuring that no attempt is made to deceive users into thinking that they are in the presence of a thinking machine. In fact, the system must be carefully designed in order to ensure that the attempt to facilitate the interaction through anthropomorphism does not become a "cheap fraud" (Boy, 1997).

Moreover, by giving the illusion of possessing a personality, the design of politeness is confronted with issues such as what roles must the system assume and in what situations. For example, should the system take the tone of an expert? In what situations is this appropriate? When is it preferable to adopt the more familiar tone of a team mate? Would it be necessary to make the personality exhibited by the system adaptable to the specific preferences of users? Will users find politeness totally unnecessary? These are issues that must be addressed by research, and the study described in this book sheds some light on to these questions.

2.4.2.   Politeness as a choice of linguistic style

By choosing the precise linguistic form, people are able to moderate their politeness during a person-to-person dialogue. This means that, depending on the context, people often choose different verbal strategies (also know as politeness strategies) for accomplishing communicative goals (Blum-Kulka, 1997).

People use language to achieve specific goals, such as for example making statements, asking questions, apologising, giving directions and showing gratitude. These are categories in a set of *speech acts*, which constitute the fundamental units of human communication. The basic idea is that linguistic expressions have the capability to perform communicative acts (Austin, 1962; Searle, 1969). According to Austin (1962), any utterance simultaneously performs at least two types of act[7]:

- A *Locutionary act*, which is the act of constructing a sentence with a specific sense and reference. The locutionary act refers to *what is said*.

- An *Illocutionary act*, which is the performance of a communicative function, such as asking a question, stating a fact, commanding or promising. The illocutionary act refers to what a person does in uttering a linguistic expression; that is, what is implied when it is said, as amplified below.

Based on Austin's theory, Searle (1979) proposed that illocutionary acts could be grouped into five main categories, which are based on the purpose of the acts (Searle, 1979):

- *Representative*: an utterance that describes the state of the world regarding a specific entity, for example by asserting or concluding. Thus, a representative is a speech act by which a person conveys a belief that a given proposition is true, for example: "You have five new e-mail messages".

- *Directive*: an utterance whose purpose is to get the listener to do something, for example by ordering, requesting or asking. Thus, a directive is an attempt by the speaker to get the listener to perform some action. There are several ways to perform a directive, some more indirect than others. For example, "Check your e-mail inbox" is a more direct form of a directive than "It would be important if you checked your e-mail inbox", or even "Would you mind checking your e-mail inbox?"

---

[7] Austin (1968) also defined a third type of speech act, the *perlocutionary act*, which represents the *effects on other people* caused by uttering a given expression.

- *Commissive*: an utterance that commits the speaker to doing something in the future, such as promises, contracts or guarantees. For example, "I will alert you whenever you receive new messages from this mailing list" is a promise that commits the speaker to alert the listener whenever there is new information.

- *Expressive*: an utterance that intends to express the psychological state of the speaker, such as thanking, apologising or congratulating. An example of an expressive might be "I'm sorry to interrupt you".

- *Declaration* (also known as a *performative*): an utterance whose purpose is to effect a change in some state of the world, such as firing an employee or declaring peace.

The main interest of the taxonomy suggested by Searle (1979) is that it classifies almost any utterance that might be produced, and it highlights the different kinds of functions that may be achieved using speech. From the point of view of politeness, the illocutionary acts must also satisfy *social goals* (Ardissono et al., 1999). In this context, *indirect speech acts* (Searle, 1975) play an important role since people often use them whenever the more direct forms appear impolite. According to Searle (1975) an indirect speech act is a means of accomplishing a communicative act that is expressed in an oblique fashion. Searle (1975) has identified four fundamental ways of communicating indirect requests:

- Asking or making statements about *abilities* – questioning about a person's ability is an indirect request to get the listener to perform some action, for example "Can you check your e-mail?"

- Stating a *desire*, such as "I would be grateful if you checked your e-mail".

- Stating a *future action* – inquiring about another person's future actions is another way to state an indirect request, for example "Would you please check your e-mail?"

- Citing *reasons* – the utterance implies that there are good reasons to comply with the request, for example "I need to know your opinion about the subject of this e-mail message".

It is true that indirect speech acts may prevent people from offending those to whom they are speaking, and thus they play a central role in exhibiting polite behaviour. However, as Ardissono et al. (1999) argue, there is still no formal explanation of how indirect speech acts contribute to the phenomenon of politeness. To date, the most prominent theory of politeness, which was proposed by Brown and Levinson (1987), is an informal explanation of the politeness strategies adopted in various natural languages in terms of social goals and means-ends reasoning.

According to Brown and Levinson's theory, politeness is considered to be an intentional and strategic behaviour, which is meant to present and preserve their public image (dubbed as *face*) in case of threat. This behaviour is performed through positive or negative linguistic styles. Brown and Levinson (1987) claim that preserving *face* is one of the basic motivations of human interaction. Furthermore, they argue that there are two dimensions: (1) *positive face*, which denotes people's concern that they have the approval of others, and (2) *negative face*, which designates people's wish to preserve their autonomy from the impositions of others.

In Brown and Levinson's theory, social interaction is seen as a process where a person keeps balancing the satisfaction of their own positive and negative face needs, with the face needs of other people with whom they interact (Brown and Levinson, 1987). Thus, according to this view, politeness strategies can be seen as the means by which individuals defend and compensate risks to face. This means that people normally find themselves between wanting to achieve their own goals and the desire to avoid affronting the face of others. So speakers often plan their actions so as to put the other person's face at the same level. In the case of indirect speech acts, this behaviour focuses on the imposition conveyed through a request.

Given that the computer-based system is perceived to be performing acts of communication whenever it conveys a spoken message, and, as stated above, given the fact that most of these acts are inherently imposing, or *face threatening* (Brown and Levinson, 1987), it is suggested that the system should take into account the face needs of its users. For example, whenever a system provides a *directive*, such as an instruction to perform an action, or a notification about a new piece of information, it will challenge the user's need for freedom of action (the user's negative face). On the other hand, whenever the system provides a *warning*, such as a reminder to prevent forgetting some action, it will be challenging the user's positive face, for example by implying a weakness on the person's ability to remember their important commitments.

However, two aspects must be noted at this point of the discussion. First, this assumes that users will perceive the computer as a social partner, and therefore will be influenced by its communicative acts. Previous research has concluded that people readily form team relationships with computers and that, when they do so, they are more open to influence from the computer (Nass et al., 1996). Second, because the computer is being perceived as a social partner, it could then exhibit a personality in that it would also be perceived as possessing a "face", and would be trying to satisfy this perceived face needs. For example, the adoption of an apologetic tone often constitutes a threat to the positive face of a person. Similarly, an apologetic computer would be perceived as possessing a weak personality.

According to Brown and Levinson (1987), the politeness strategies employed by people fall into four main categories. Blum-Kulka (1997) provides a good explanation:

- *Direct Strategies*: when the risk is minimal, speakers realise their communicative act in the most direct way possible. This may be achieved, for example, by providing a command such as "Check your e-mail".

- *Positive Politeness Strategies*: these strategies enhance the positive face needs of the listener, for example by attending to the hearer's interests or needs, displaying a common point of view or showing optimism. These are often seen as approval orientated strategies, in that they orientate the realisation of the communicative act to the hearer's desire for approval. An example of this kind of strategy might be as follows: "There's a new e-mail message about the Eurospeech conference. I think you might want to check your e-mail", or "You'd like to check your e-mail, wouldn't you?", or even "Let's check our e-mail".

- *Negative Politeness Strategies*: these strategies are intended to satisfy the hearer's negative face, that is their freedom from having other people's perspectives or wills imposed upon them. In this context, they are seen as autonomy orientated strategies because they orientate the performance of the act to the hearer's desire for autonomy. This is often accomplished for example by asking about co-operation, or giving options to the hearer not to do the intended act. The use of conventional indirect speech acts to convey a request is a prime example of a negative politeness strategy. For example, saying "Could you check your e-mail?", "You might consider checking your e-mail", or "You wouldn't want to check you e-mail, would you?" are all different possibilities for employing autonomy orientated strategies.

- *Off-the-Record Strategies*: sometimes risks to face are estimated as being very high. In these situations, the speakers can perform a communicative act in a way that leaves the maximum number of options for denial. That is, people perform the act in such an indirect way that the speaker cannot be made responsible for any communicative intent. The use of unconventional indirect speech acts[8] (Blum-Kulka, 1997) is a good example of this strategy. For example, by employing utterances such as "I can see that you haven't checked your e-mail this morning", or "It seems that there is a lot of new e-mail messages", the speaker cannot be said to have requested that the listener checks the e-mail, nor can listeners be made responsible if they do not check their e-mail.

2.4.3.   Incorporating politeness in the design

Of course, endowing a computer-based system with such a repertoire of strategies must take into account the context in which these forms are to be used, and develop a model that specifies the most appropriate strategies to use in each possible situation. For example, if the kind of personality that the designer wishes the user to perceive is one of a sober assistant, the strategies that could be considered include the negative politeness and the off-the-record strategies. However, if it is intended to promote the perception of a cheerful assistant, more like a group member or a team mate, the direct and positive politeness strategies seem more appropriate for this purpose.

Basically, there are two methods for incorporating polite behaviour, such as the strategies given in section 2.4.2, in the design of a spoken language system. First, it is possible to use pre-defined utterances, which must be anticipated during the design. These are especially developed for the specific domain where the system will be operating, such as the ones used by Nass et al. (1994). Alternatively, it is possible to consider the creation of an automatic generation mechanism, based on existing theories of social interaction, such as the one described by Walker et al. (1997a), which has the potential of producing polite utterances appropriate for more than one target domain.

However, before stating that politeness is an indispensable characteristic of a spoken language system, it is imperative to perform evaluative studies, designed to uncover the need for a polite system, and the degree to which a polite system contributes to an enjoyable work environment. From this perspective, the pre-defined method for introducing the politeness in the design seems more appropriate. In fact, using pre-defined utterances allows the designer to control, and evaluate,

---

[8] Unconventional indirect speech acts are another indirect form where the interpretation that is given to the act is much more open-ended than for conventional indirect speech acts.

just those aspects being considered, such as for example the appropriateness of polite behaviour when getting the user's attention. Moreover, the adoption of pre-defined utterances in the system design is well suited to the template-based approach described earlier for the generation of linguistic variation.

As far as the automatic generation of polite strategies is concerned, an interesting model developed by Walker et al. (1997) combines the speech act theory with Brown and Levinson's (1987) theory of linguistic social interaction to produce an algorithm that generates utterances in different linguistic styles. Walker et al. (1987) argue that their model enables a computer-based system to exhibit Linguistic Style Improvisation (LSI).

On a final note, politeness can also be thought of as yet another factor contributing to the achievement of linguistic variation, but at a more pragmatic level of communication. While the discussion of linguistic variation concentrated on the phonetic, lexical and syntactical aspects of linguistic variation, the polite behaviour promotes the perception of variation at the level of intentions.

2.5   Summary

The possibility that a computer can alter social perception is a conclusion of previous research. When the cues a computer makes available to a person's perceptual systems are sufficiently similar to those people are used to notice, then people apply the same social evaluations that they make in real life. Thus, when a computer is made to comply with human social expectations, and designed to reinforce its social acceptability, it makes users feel more comfortable with the interaction. As far as the speech output is concerned, this reinforcement may be achieved through the careful design of spoken interruptions, varied spoken messages and appropriate linguistic styles.

This chapter has highlighted some of the most important design requirements for creating humanised interrupting messages. Having first gained the person's attention, the interrupting message should be short, but provide sufficient content so as to allow the user to appreciate the meaning of the interruption, and decide whether to stop performing the current task or carry on with it. Using spoken messages enables the exploitation of the non-visual intrusiveness of the aural channel. This chapter has reviewed a range of possible forms for delivering interrupting speech-based messages.

In order to avoid irritating the user, it is proposed that a certain degree of variation is required that mimics the natural human linguistic variation. This variation may be expressed at the phonetic, lexical and syntactical levels of spoken communication. One possible approach would be to endow the system with a pre-defined number of templates that express the same meaning for each possible situation, and then have the system select a different template each time the corresponding situation occurs.

In order to reinforce the perception that the computer has the role of a work companion, it is important to consider the linguistic style that the system exhibits. The polite behaviour achieved through different linguistic styles may help to attenuate the adverse effects of interruptions, while promoting the perception of a consistent character. Politeness strategies may be designed to address specific communicative acts, and they can be included in the design using the template-based approach. However, the importance, and the need, of politeness must first be evaluated through carefully designed user studies.

Chapter 3

INFORMATION AWARENESS

3.1 Overview

The research contained in this book is the result of exploring the anthropomorphic aspects of future personal information environments. It is assumed that in the future each user will have (effectively) infinite storage space and infinite processing speed in a computation engine that may be physically distributed. Such devices would be used to store and manage a user's lifetime collection of personal information. This information will be derived from various sources such as the World Wide Web, television, electronic mail, camcorder video recorders, digital cameras, and document scanners. The activities and processes involved in managing these personal repositories can be very complex, because of the heterogeneous nature of personal information and because of the problems that arise when the user needs to become aware of new information or forgets the content of previously stored information.

Research in personal information management suggests a range of solutions that take advantage of human cognitive capabilities. The central idea is to provide memory aids, such as a *"memory prosthesis"* (Lamming et al., 1994) or a *"guardian angel"* (Bell, 1997), designed to exploit the fact that this kind of information belongs to the user's information repository in which each data item is subconsciously tagged with a recognisable context. In order to design such a memory aid there is the need to identify and automate the context-dependent *cues* that enable people to re-discover the information they need, including that material lost from conscious memory.

Personal information awareness refers to that part of personal information management, which deals with the acquisition of knowledge about new information (through notifications), and knowledge in support of the remembering of existing information (through reminders). Thus, information awareness refers to a process which enables people to appreciate the significance of sets of desired information.

In order to understand how better to support the awareness of personal information, it is necessary to review first the existing body of research work developed to address personal information management issues. Existing work highlights both the psychological processes involved, and the problems people face while managing personal information with current computer-based systems. However, little research work has explored the issues involved in effective support for information awareness (McCrickard, 2000).

This book argues that psychological principles should be exploited by the interface to enhance the provision of notifications and reminders resulting from personal information events. This may be achieved by identifying the kinds of *cues* that provide the support required by human memory to bring information to awareness. This chapter presents and discusses a set of key elements that contribute to the design of the contents of humanised notifications and reminders.

3.2   Personal information management

3.2.1.   Characteristics

The main objective of a personal information management system (PIMS) is to provide uniform and seamless access to any relevant information for a task being undertaken. This goal can be expressed more pragmatically through the following requirements.

- An appropriate way of organising and structuring the information.

- An efficient way of retrieving and displaying information at the user interface.

Barreau (1995) considers a personal information management system to be an information system that has been created for an individual, or developed by an individual, for personal use, and it includes:

- the set of methods and rules which the person uses for acquiring information;

- the mechanisms used for the organisation and storage of information;

- the rules used for system maintenance;

- the mechanisms that allow retrieval of information; and

- the procedures needed to produce the required outputs.

Personal information can be defined as all the information that is handled by individuals, be it organisational data or private data. Concerning this information, two different processes can be identified:

- *Information handling*, involving tasks such as the creation, collection, viewing, manipulation, analysis and annotation of information;

- *Information storage and retrieval*, involving the organisation, search and retrieval of information.

Data contained in a personal information management system typically includes all appointments and to-dos in a user's diary, a set of private and organisational e-mail and newsgroup messages, and the ever-growing collections of World Wide Web bookmarks and personal documents of various types such as letters, reports, photos, spreadsheets, manuals, annotations, electronic books, papers, statements, videos, graphs, and other types of digital document. The common, and distinctive, characteristics of all these different kinds of personal information are: (1) they belong to the user's *information repository*, and (2) each data item is part of a *personal context*, which can be used to add semantics to data fragments.

These characteristics have a *fundamental* implication for the design of personal information systems. Since the information existing in a user's repository has been manipulated, categorised or entered by the user, human memory plays a crucial role in personal information management, both in the processes of information handling, and information storage and retrieval. Thus, the general strategies used by people when manipulating information, together with relevant psychological facts, can, and should, be used to guide the technology for enhancing information management.

3.2.2.   Problems in personal information management

Some research has investigated the problems people face while managing personal information. These problems can be roughly divided into two main categories:

- *Information organisation* problems, including the *categorisation* (creation of category labels), and the *classification* (the act of placing an item under a specific category) of information;

- *Information awareness* problems, including *being aware of new information*, which is raised by the occurrence of unpredictable events, or relates to upcoming scheduled events, and *remembering existing information*, which is related with past events.

Silverman (1997) argues that a surprisingly little amount of work has been dedicated to the issues related with personal information awareness. In fact, given that notifying (alert to upcoming events) and reminding (alert to past events) are such basic functions, it is surprising that there are still some unanswered research issues (Silverman, 1997), which include:

- how little is understood about the forgetting and reminding processes;

- how often reminding and notifying are ignored or misunderstood in existing systems;

- how existing interfaces inadvertently make reminding and notifying more complex; and

- how difficult it is to design better user interfaces to overcome obstacles to effective reminding and notifying.

Given the distinctive nature of personal information, both organisation and awareness problems can be better addressed by paying special attention to the psychological processes that deal with human memory (Williamson, 1998). In considering the particular requirements of information awareness, it is helpful to first review the issues and proposed solutions to the information organisation problems, and then to consider ways to address the unresolved issues of information awareness.

3.3   Information organisation

3.3.1.   Problem characteristics

The creation of category names, and the placement of information under these categories, poses important problems as far as information management is concerned, because normally information falls within several overlapping but distinct categories. This problem acts as an important impediment for filing information since people are not certain that they will be able to retrieve the information at a later time because they will fail to remember how it was classified. People usually organise information in two ways.

- *Active information*, which includes items that are frequently accessed, is the less formally organised, and manifests itself in the form of real piles of paper-based documents in non-computerised environments. These documents are browsed.

- *Archive storage*, where information must be formally organised (categorised and classified), and which has a very low frequency of usage over long periods of time. This information requires access through a search engine.

3.3.2.   Strategies to address information organisation problems

One strategy that has been suggested to overcome the problem of organising computer-based active information is the creation of *electronic piles* (Mander et al., 1992) of documents where information is organised using a spatial arrangement, but information remains unclassified.

Even though the kinds of information, and the processes used to manage them, differ across the active information and archive storage levels, both can benefit from a personal information management system that exploits the human cognitive abilities, and more specifically that complements the human memory capabilities, by taking advantage of the fact that a personal workspace is constituted by familiar information. After all, searching an unfamiliar space of information in order to find one specific item is a difficult task since users do not know in advance what is going to be found. In contrast, searching a personal workspace involves human memory processes because the information that is going to be found has already been seen, though may be temporarily forgotten. For example, while a keyword search may be one of the most appropriate strategies for searching an unfamiliar space, it does not seem to be the most suitable solution for information that has already been manipulated by users. In fact, a keyword search suffers from the same fundamental problem that complicates the categorisation of information: words have several meanings, and also several synonyms, which can be used interchangeably to categorise the same information fragments.

When considering the cognitive aspects of personal information management, Williamson (1998) points out that the help which can be offered by technology falls into two categories: assistance with information categorisation and classification, and help with subsequent retrieval. Thus, to facilitate the storage process it is necessary to automate the categorisation and classification of information by associating characteristics that later will aid memory in recalling that information. In fact, the majority of documented human memory problems are related to recalling stored information. It is accepted that people store most facts in long-term memory (LTM) (Pashler and Carrier, 1996), but it is also true that people have difficulties in finding them, and it is believed that the problem lies in the way memories are encoded and stored. Therefore, if memories are not encoded properly, the stored items cannot be easily found. Memory can therefore be aided by prompting if people are given the proper *cues* (Roediger and Guynn, 1996).

3.4   Issues with information awareness

3.4.1.   Problem characteristics

Due to the increasing volumes of digital information, and considering the limitations of the human biological memory, it is only natural that people turn to computer-based notifications and reminders to increase their efficiency.

On the one hand, people need to be *notified* of new relevant information, or timely information, such as the arrival of important messages, upcoming appointments, unpredictable events, critical announcements concerning their current activity, key status messages, or other events that are in the eminence of occurring or have just occurred, which concern a person's information space.

On the other hand, people need to be *reminded* of existing information, such as due or missed appointments, due to-do items, actions, important procedures, methods to be applied to a task, or other events that have already started or occurred. Furthermore, people depend on these notifications and reminders to be able to stay productive, and both types of function put a heavy cognitive burden on people.

However, existing interfaces do not alleviate this burden, because they merely remind a user that time is up, not what to do when the alarm sounds. In cases where more information is provided, often in a graphical-based window, it is visually intrusive, obscuring other information being displayed and accessed, and requiring an overt action to dismiss the alerting window, which causes further disruption to the person's attention. Because current interfaces do not pay sufficient attention to the importance of notifications and reminders, there is always the risk of lowering human performance with *under-reminding*, or overloading the person with *over-reminding*.

3.4.2.   Strategies to address information awareness problems

Relatively few strategies have been explored for desktop-based environments that enable users to maintain awareness of the contents of personal information sources which produce information that is updated at frequent intervals, or which disclose information that should be conveyed to users in a timely fashion.

Existing research efforts have explored visual techniques, such as "constant and cyclic animations" (McCrickard, 2000), or "adjusting windows" (Bailey et al., 2000) in an attempt to communicate information in the periphery and allow a person to focus on the primary task. While these techniques may reduce the visual disruptiveness by avoiding superimposing information on top of a user's workspace, the use of graphical animation techniques and additional display windows still distracts the user's attention and contributes to cluttering the workspace.

Other research efforts have investigated the use of background audio techniques to assist in awareness. For example the "Audio Aura" (Mynatt et al., 1998) system exploits non-speech audio to create a peripheral display of auditory cues. However, while the cues conveyed through different auditory signals may signal the occurrence of distinct events, they are not reliable in that they do not convey sufficient information so as to enable the user to appreciate the full meaning of an event.

A potentially better solution to the information awareness problem involves using *speech output* as an unobtrusive complement to the graphical presentation of information, and provide what are the indispensable *cues* that support the user's own memory processes. This is an important requirement because it is not sufficient just to use speech-based messages. If these are not properly designed to convey sufficient information about an event, they will not enhance the awareness of information that is hidden from view. For example, a message might alert the user that "the deadline is about to expire", but not tell the user when this will actually happen.

So, in order to assist human memory, the design of notifications and reminders to be conveyed at the interface must provide the right information about the event that caused them. These cues must both allow for the *recognition* of the importance of the event, as well as facilitate subsequent *retrieval* of event-related information.

However, the literature provides little insight into the appropriate strategy for delivering notifications and reminders. The problem is that there is *no* accepted theory about what kind of *content* provides the most beneficial notifications and reminders (Silverman, 1997) - unresolved issues concern questions such as what is the best medium, the appropriate message length, the contents of the message body and its attributes, that should be used to design appropriate notifications and reminders.

This book proposes that what users need are "*Forward Cues*" that at any given time provide a *clear* indication of what is going to be found if users take the initiative to interrupt what they are doing and turn their attention to an event that occurred in their personal information space.

3.5 Psychological principles and implications for design

3.5.1. Human memory characteristics

Research on human memory indicates that there are two broad categories of memory (Pashler and Carrier, 1996): short-term memory (STM) and long-term memory (LTM). Short-term memories can be seen as the *active* contents of the mind that result from perceptual analysis (Nairne, 1996). The term "working memory" (Baddeley and Hitch, 1974; Baddeley, 1986) is used to refer to the "internal machinery that collectively selects short-term memories and maintains them in an active state" (Nairne, 1996). Working memory can be broken down into two distinct slave systems: the *phonological loop* (or articulatory loop), which is responsible for temporary retention of *verbal* material and *semantic* meaning, and the *visuo-spatial scratchpad* (or *sketchpad*), which is responsible for temporary retention of *visual* and *spatial* material (Baddeley and Hitch, 1974; Logie, 1995). Furthermore, it is believed that the phonological loop and the visuo-spatial scratchpad function independently of each other (Baddeley, 1986). Because these systems are independent, they are prone to interference from different kinds of concurrent tasks. For example, performing two spatial tasks might require more memory resources than performing one spatial task and one verbal task. Thus, if two tasks employ different parts of the working memory, they will be performed more effectively (Wickens, 1992). Moreover, Wickens (1992) showed that spatial tasks were disrupted less when the phonological loop was used in concurrent information processing tasks.

The implication of this finding for the design of notifications and reminders is as follows. While users are performing normal tasks at their computer screen, they will be using both the visuo-spatial sketchpad and the phonological loop. Thus, a graphical-based alert would also require using both systems to locate and to interpret the information presented on the screen, causing an interference with the original task. However, listening to a concurrent speech-based notification or reminder would only require using the phonological loop. While this still interferes with the phonological loop resources being used in the original task, it may attenuate the adverse effect of the interruption and increase the efficiency of the whole memory system, by eliminating the interference with the visuo-spatial scratchpad resources, given that no information is presented on the screen.

Retrieval is the means of *using* information stored in long-term memory (LTM). This process is intimately related to that of *encoding* and *storage* of information in memory. The way an event is encoded and stored determines how well it can be retrieved later, and what retrieval cues[9] will effect its retrieval. Retrieval difficulties may be responsible for much of the forgetting that occurs in human memory. So information may be available (stored) that is not accessible (retrievable) without the proper cues. Thus, an understanding of the psychological principles governing long-term memory should be useful to guide the design of alerts.

For example, previous research indicates that what is retained in long-term memory from a linguistic message is its *meaning* and *not* its exact wording (Anderson, 1995). This fact has two immediate implications as far as the design of notifications and reminders is concerned. First, employing spoken notifications and reminders at the interface appears to be a suitable means of conveying the *meaning* of the information items that originated the messages. Secondly, varying the words used to assemble a message does not appear to be detrimental to the understanding of the meaning of the message. This is an important observation as far as the use of linguistic variation is concerned.

---

[9] The retrieval cue is the information present in the individual's cognitive environment when retrieval from memory occurs.

Furthermore, research also indicates that "recognition is superior to recall"[10] (Houston, 1986). This means that personal information systems should allow for an initial recall-directed function, in order to bring information to awareness, followed by a recognition-based scanning whenever users search their personal information repository. In terms of design, this suggests exploiting speech to support the recall-directed function, leaving the recognition function (the presentation of details) for the most suitable graphical presentation.

The *encoding-specificity* principle states that "recollection of an event, or a certain aspect of it, occurs if and only if properties of the trace of the event are sufficiently similar to the retrieval cue" (Tulving, 1983). Thus, according to cue-dependent forgetting theorists, "memory for an event is always a product of information from two sources": (1) the memory trace, and (2) the retrieval cue. The fundamental idea is that both the traces of past experiences and the information (or cues) in the cognitive system during recall are critical determinants of remembering (Roediger and Guynn, 1996). Thus, the greater the match between encoding activities and retrieval activities, the greater the "positive transfer" (measured as the performance in a memory test) will be (this is why the encoding-specificity principle is also known as the transfer-appropriate processing principle).

Therefore, according to the *encoding-specificity* principle, maximising the similarities between a *study* (the occasion in which information is learned) and a *test* (the occasion in which there is an attempt to retrieve learned information from long-term memory using some sort of retrieval cue), benefits retention of information in long-term memory. However, it must be noted that the physical similarity of study and test events is *not* the crucial determinant of retention; rather, psychological similarity (between encoding and retrieval processes) *is* critical. This suggests that if the psychological *context* of users can be reproduced, it may improve recall.

3.5.2.   The importance of context

Context is an important factor in personal information management (Barreau, 1995). The suggestion is that the context of a person's activities plays a major role in recalling forgotten information. Moreover, reconstructing the context under which information has been handled is a very important factor for recall. The interest in context as a key factor in personal information management derives

---

[10] Recognition refers to the awareness that something perceived has been perceived before, while recall refers to the process of summoning back to awareness, a subject or situation to hand, i.e. the process of

from Tulving's (1983) findings about episodic memory: (1) a person's life can be thought of as being a series of successive episodes; (2) precise data about an episode is not usually remembered, but temporal relations between episodes are remembered very well; and (3) presenting partial information about an episode helps people remember more about it.

Moreover, it has been demonstrated that, for autobiographical (personal) events, the activity, the people involved, the place and the time are typically well remembered (Larsen et al., 1996). Furthermore, all these elements except time are remembered explicitly, and time is reconstructed from temporal cues afforded by the event, providing reference intervals within which an event can be placed (Larsen et al., 1996). For example, a person may remember that an event occurred early in the day, while the exact day and year of this event may not be remembered at all.

This means that humans have a "poor memory for details" (Houston, 1986). Knowing that people interpret information in the context in which it appears, rather than storing information in memory exactly as it has been acquired, means that systems which provide, and require users to remember, details such as file names or category names, will inevitably provoke very low levels of recall. Thus, there is a need to provide recallable and recognisable attributes that, when attached to information, will improve their retrieval, and these characteristics, including activity, people, time and place, may be found in the context where the information items are manipulated.

However, for personal information management, the context of the information access task is different from the context that is assumed by traditional information retrieval tasks. In general, users already know most of the information they need and where it is stored (Mathe and Chen, 1998). Furthermore, contextual factors such as the relative relevance to a task, individual user preferences, and frequency of access have been shown to be very important to organise, categorise, classify and retrieve information from an individual point of view (Barreau, 1995); work is viewed as a "highly situational context-based process" (Barreau, 1995) that requires users to accomplish their tasks subject to the constraints of their working environment. Therefore, the context in which a particular item of information is created or acquired may influence the way it is classified, stored and, most importantly, retrieved.

Barreau (1995) defines context as "the situation in which an event occurs and includes all aspects of a person's experience". However, this definition is a little too vague to be of pragmatic use to guide

remembering, bringing back or restoring a piece of information.

the design process. An alternative definition states that context is "any information that can be used to characterise the situation of an entity. An entity is a person, place or object that is considered relevant to the interaction between a user and an application, including the user and the application themselves" (Dey and Abowd, 1999). This later definition makes it easier to characterise the context elements for a given application scenario since it includes in the context only those pieces of information that *affect* users as they perform the task, and the pieces of information that can be used to *characterise* the user's situation.

Consistent with cue-dependent theories, Barreau (1995) suggests using retrieval cues available in a person's own system to "jog a person's memory to locate an item or retrieve a fact". These retrieval cues are in essence context clues from the user's situation at the time the item of information was created, acquired or last used. According to Barreau (1995), the context in which users work includes: the nature of tasks, the subject matter, the software tools, the addressees of the work, temporal information such as dates of last use, acquisition or creation of information, and the intended use for the information.

Consistently with autobiographical memory research findings, Dey and Abowd (1999) argue that the most important contextual clues are location, identity, activity and time, and that these constitute the primary context types. According to their framework, location refers to *where* the situation is located, identity refers to *who* are the entities present in the situation, activity refers to *what* is occurring in the situation, and time refers to *when* the situation occurred.

The main implication of these findings for the design of notifications and reminders is that these factors are in play at the time an information item is created, acquired, classified, categorised, stored or retrieved. Therefore, a humanised system for information awareness should accommodate situational factors such as the ones described above to notify and remind users.

3.6   Supporting information awareness

3.6.1.   Design requirements

The design of humanised notifications and reminders is fundamentally a problem of identifying the right sort of cues that enhance the awareness of personal information, and mitigate the limitations of human memory. Memory research emphasises that successful retrieval largely depends on the presence of the original context surrounding a particular event. Thus, the general requirements for the design can be stated as follows.

First, it is important to maximise the psychological similarity between the situation in which information is acquired and the situation where it has to be remembered. This means that the properties of the retrieval cues must match those of the memory trace for the information items.

Second, human memory stores the meaning of any information item, both in terms of how relevant and important it is from the perspective of a person's tasks, interests and preferences. Thus, the context that surrounds the event of creating or acquiring a specific item of information constitutes the ideal source for extracting the cue attributes that are most likely to aid human memory in retrieving the required information at a later time. Moreover, elements such as people, activity, place and time are remembered very well.

For notifications and reminders, which may or may not be dealt with by the user immediately, the specific cue design requirements can be stated as follows:

1. To provide sufficient attributes (the cues) about an item of information, which allow the user to appreciate the meaning of the item in terms of the individual's interests.

2. To present a set of attributes (the cues) characterising the information item that matches what the person is likely to find when looking for the same item later on. Since the design is intended to create a speech-based mechanism that complements the graphical-based presentation of information, these attributes must match the ones that the graphical display of information items presents to the user. For example, e-mail messages are often graphically characterised through sender, date/time and subject attributes.

In summary, the contextual cues must provide the *semantics* the person associates with each item of personal information. For example, when people enter an appointment in their personal diary, the key elements that characterise this item are the subject, the relation of the event to personal tasks, the other persons involved, and the place where it will take place. Therefore, the global meaning of this particular appointment depends equally on each of these contextual elements. The implication is that a system that notifies the user of the imminence of this appointment should convey more cues than just the type of scheduled task (appointment).

3.6.2.   Forward cues

Given that the system is intended to enhance the awareness of personal information, in this book the cues that the system presents when conveying notifications and reminders are designated as *Forward Cues*. The central idea is to provide enough information to allow the person to appreciate what will be found ahead. This is accomplished by making use of the cues people normally use to assign meaning to their information items, and which they remember about that information.

Combining the contextual elements suggested in the literature, and adapting them to the design of humanised notifications and reminders, this book proposes the following key elements to be conveyed through speech-based messages:

- KIND - the kind of personal information *domain* that is the source of the information to which a notification or reminder refers, such as for example e-mail, diary, or printing.

- TIME - the *temporal restrictions* that apply to any notification or reminder, such as for example how long until a task is due, how long until the beginning of an appointment, or the time elapsed after the arrival of new information.

- QUANTITY - the *number* of specific items to which the notification or reminder message refers, such as the number of new e-mail messages, the number of due to-dos, or the number of new newsgroup articles.

- PEOPLE - the *name* of the person, group or entity that originated the specific item, such as the name of the person who sent an e-mail message, the name of the group with which the appointment is made, the author of a news article, or the addressee of a to-do.

- NATURE - the *type* of the task to which a specific item of information belongs, such as for example the type of an e-mail message (e.g. on-going correspondence, to read, pending, or junk mail), the type of appointment (e.g. seminar, meeting, lecture, or dinner), or the type of a news article (e.g. opinion, critique, political, sports, or leisure).

- DESCRIPTION - the *title* or a *summary* of the *subject* of the specific item of information, such as the subject of an e-mail message, the description of a to-do or appointment, or the title of a news article.

- PLACE - the physical location where the specific item of information was generated, such as the institution where an e-mail message came from, the place where an appointment is due, or the magazine where a news article appears.

3.7 Summary

A range of problems in personal information management arises due to the increasing volumes of information that have to be handled, stored and retrieved. While information organisation problems have been addressed by previous research, information awareness is equally critical and has not received sufficient attention. Information awareness refers to a process which enables people to appreciate the significance of sets of desired personal information, and it can be better supported through the proper design of notifications and reminders to be conveyed to the user.

The characteristics of personal information suggest using psychological evidence to guide the design of systems that alleviate both information organisation and awareness problems. Given that human memory plays a central role in these processes, it is of fundamental importance to understand how it processes different kinds of perceptual information and how these kinds of information can be presented in a manner more compatible with human cognition. Context plays a central role in memory recall, and it influences the way a person perceives information. Given that context has the potential to provide the most powerful retrieval cues, it is important to include contextual elements in the design of notifications and reminders. Essentially, context cues provide the means through which people appreciate the semantics of an event.

This book proposes the notion of *Forward Cues* as the building blocks of humanised notifications and reminders, which allow a person to appreciate what will be found ahead. These cues were defined in terms of the specific context elements they convey, and include: kind, time, quantity, people, nature, description and place.

Chapter 4

TECHNOLOGIES FOR DEVELOPING SPEAKING SYSTEMS

4.1 Overview

In order to explore the hypothesis that a humanised computer-based system is perceived as a satisfying work companion, and therefore constitutes a more enjoyable work environment, there is the need to design and implement a suitable experimental environment. More specifically, it is necessary to create a speaking system that allows for the testing of the *importance* of using *speech output*, conveyed with *anthropomorphic characteristics*, in *reinforcing the social acceptability* of the computer, when it is *assisting* users in being *aware of personal* information.

The creation of such a humanised environment requires a *background technology* that allows for the inclusion of a number of features. First, the background technology should enable the application of social science theories in computer-based systems, so as to allow the system to be perceived by its users as a competent *social partner*.

Secondly, the background technology must facilitate the creation of a *co-operative* computer-based environment based on *delegation*. This is an important requirement because the experimental environment must be unobtrusively monitoring the sources of potentially interesting information without requiring constant user intervention. More specifically, the system needs to operate autonomously and concurrently with the user, sense important changes in the environment constituted by the personal information sources of interest, and react accordingly, by notifying or reminding the user. Furthermore, the experimental environment also needs to maintain an updated profile of the user's interests, in order to provide only relevant and purposefully tailored information. The combination of these characteristics promotes the perception of the environment as a personal assistant.

Finally, given that there are multiple sources of information to be monitored, the background technology should allow for the design and development of a complex environment comprising various specialised, independent and concurrent software components that will be monitoring the different sources of information, and conveying messages at unpredictable occasions. Such architecture also requires that the components communicate by passing messages to another software entity responsible for coordinating the delivery of spoken information to the user.

4.2   Background to the speaking system

4.2.1.   Software agents

An emergent paradigm for developing software applications, which fulfils the requirements given above for a background technology, is that of *software agents* (Bradshaw, 1997; Jennings and Wooldridge, 1998). Considering the first requirement, the agent-oriented development of software has been described as a paradigm based on a "cognitive and societal view of computation" (Shoam, 1997). The immediate implication is that, through the agent paradigm, specific ideas from social theory can enter into the design of computer-based systems.

Similarly, the creation of an experimental environment that emphasises a co-operative interaction between users and computers is another aspect that may be achieved through the agent paradigm. Software agents have the potential to promote an "equal partnership" (Jennings and Wooldridge, 1998), in which the computer co-operates with users to achieve their goals, mainly through the delegation of tasks (Millewski and Lewis, 1997). In fact, there is a strong view that "the future of computing will be 100% driven by delegating to, rather than manipulating computers" (Negroponte, 1995). From the point of view of providing the adequate functionality required by the experimental environment, the delegation metaphor is especially useful in that it potentially promotes the perception of a personal assistant by supporting the design and development of software systems through software abstractions (agents), which exhibit the following characteristics:

1. Environmental awareness and reactivity: software agents are sensitive to changes in the environment and to changing user needs, and respond in a timely fashion in order to satisfy their design goals (Jennings and Wooldridge, 1998; Wooldridge, 1999).

2. Autonomy: software agents typically operate on behalf of their users without their constant guidance, and independent of other software systems. Agents control both their own internal

state and their behaviour, according to the goal they were designed to attain. (Griss and Pour, 2001; Jennings and Wooldridge, 1998; Wooldridge, 1999).

3. Adaptation: software agents adapt their behaviour according to their user's preferences, learning either by their own observation or through user feedback, in order to tailor the interaction to reflect their user's interests (Jennings and Wooldridge, 1998; Maes, 1994).

Finally, considering the third requirement for the experimental environment, the software agent paradigm provides an effective way for dealing with the challenges posed by the design of complex computer systems (Jennings, 1999; Jennings and Wooldridge, 1999). It is suggested that agent technology "can provide a better means of conceptualising and/or implementing a given application" (Jennings and Wooldridge, 1998), in particular by providing a "natural way" (Jennings and Wooldridge, 1998) of modelling problems in terms of a set of autonomous entities, which are able to communicate between themselves in order to facilitate the design and implementation of architectures for software-based systems.

Jennings and Wooldridge (1998) argue that thinking about the design of computer-based systems in terms of agents benefits the identification and the description of the different *roles* that exist within the system, and that it benefits the characterisation of the *relationship* existing among those roles. Moreover, after identifying the various agent roles in the system, designers may adopt, or adapt, existing internal agent architectures[11] (see (Wooldridge and Jennings, 1995) for examples of common agent architectures), so as to deliver the required functional characteristics inherent in each role. Additionally, thinking about the design of the architecture for a software environment in terms of a collection of agents might address its inherent complexity by taking advantage of the agents' interactions through the exchange of asynchronous messages.

Of course, such a paradigm for software design, which is based in the allocation of function, is likely to distract the designer from the task of creating an integrated, fluid and humanised user-interface. However, the work described in this book demonstrates that such a functional approach offers a suitable foundation for the design and development of a humanised system.

---

[11] An agent architecture is a particular methodology for building software agents that specifies how the agent can be decomposed into a set of component modules and how these modules should be made to interact (Maes, 1991a).

Although there is no universal definition of agents, the most common view is that an agent is a "system situated within and part of an environment that senses that environment and acts on it, over time, in pursuit of its own agenda and so as to effect what it senses in the future" (Franklin and Graesser, 1996). This definition implies that an agent may be regarded as a software component that interacts with its environment, and with other agents and reacts to changes in the environment, serving as a surrogate for its users. Therefore, what fundamentally distinguishes a software agent from traditional software is the capability of acting without human intervention (Shoam, 1997), and there is a general agreement that autonomy is central to the notion of agency (Wooldridge, 1999). However, because the various attributes associated with agency differ in importance according to the application domain, there is little agreement beyond the notion of autonomy (Nwana, 1996). For example, Wooldridge (1999) considers that a software agent is an "intelligent agent" when it is capable of not only autonomous, but also *flexible* actions. By flexible, Wooldridge (1999) means environmental awareness and reactivity, pro-activeness (goal directed behaviour that enables a software agent to take initiative in order to fulfil its design goals) and social ability (the capability of interacting with other software agents in ways beyond simple message passing).

In terms of the desirable characteristics for the experimental environment, intelligence in this sense is not a requirement. However, autonomy, environmental awareness, reactivity, and adaptation are desirable characteristics for the purposes of the experimental environment, which are afforded by the agent paradigm. Thus, while there is not yet a consensus about the attributes of a software agent, the agent abstraction is still useful as a technological basis for the design and implementation of an experimental environment that is aiming at testing the importance of speech induced anthropomorphism in reinforcing the social acceptability of the computer, and testing whether it enhances the awareness of information that is hidden from view.

The problem of information awareness is closely related to the problem of *information overload* (Maes, 1994): we have already become literally inundated with personal information - everyone has to read, filter, sort, store, answer and discard growing volumes of digital information as part of their daily activities. Research points to strategies involving the utilisation of autonomous and learning software components capable of acting on behalf of their users. So far, these software agents have been able to address information overload problems mainly by filtering various types of incoming information, and recommending resources based on user preferences. Thus, it seems likely that the techniques behind software agents can also be exploited to support the provision of systems that deliver information in ways more compatible with human cognition.

Research in this direction is based on psychological principles of human memory retrieval processes, and is addressing the need to provide easy-to-use interfaces to dynamic and unstructured information. For example, a recent approach has investigated the use of software agents that act as *memory enhancers*, exploiting the user's own memory and the various contexts surrounding the user's activities, in order to collaborate, and assist, in retrieving the required information (Rhodes and Starner, 1996; Rhodes, 1997).

As additional examples, systems based on the delegation metaphor have been deployed through agent-based architectures to address information management problems such as filtering e-mail and newsgroups messages (Maes, 1994), helping in meeting scheduling and calendar management tasks (Kozierok and Maes, 1993; Kautz et al., 1998; Mitchell et al., 1994), assisting in travel planning (Rich and Sidner, 1998; Ndumu et al., 1998), and assisting in other tasks as diverse as tracking stocks in portfolios, advising on how to use software products or suggesting shopping products (Huhns and Singh, 1998c).

In summary, a software agent is a high-level software abstraction. Designing a complex software environment following agent-based techniques requires the specification of a solution in terms of these abstractions, both by identifying the required agents and their behaviours. The motivation for an agent-oriented approach is well argued by Jennings and Wooldridge (1999) when they suggest that agent-oriented techniques are well suited to designing and developing software systems for the following reasons.

1. Agent-oriented decomposition constitutes an effective means of dividing the problem space associated with a complex system.

2. The abstractions used in agent-oriented approaches constitute a natural means of modelling complex systems.

3. The agent-oriented methodology for the identification and management of organisational relationships is appropriate for dealing with the dependencies and interactions existing in complex systems.

4.2.2.   Delegation-based environments

The delegation model for user-interfaces, which is based on software agents, differs from the traditional user-interface model where users perform tasks through computer-based *tools*. Delegation is the process of entrusting responsibility for a task to subordinates by providing them with authority to act on one's behalf, but without giving up ultimate control (Jenks and Kelly, 1985). Thus, applying the delegation model to user-interfaces implies that users entrust tasks to autonomous software entities, which should be capable of attaining their design goals without further intervention from the user. This model is based on delegation of authority (Shoam, 1997) and delegation of work, rather than commanding the software to perform tasks (Maes, 1994); thus it is well suited to *support* environments that are designed to experiment with the inclusion of anthropomorphic characteristics in the user-interface.

In fact, because delegation is a typical interpersonal activity, people may find it easier to interact with an anthropomorphic-based experimental environment. Thus, basing an environment on delegation is likely to promote the perception that there is a *personal assistant* at the interface, acting to provide knowledge support that "augments human cognitive abilities" (Maes, 1997b). The co-operation between humans and computers afforded by delegation is stressed by Maes' suggestion that computers should act as automated personal assistants whose responsibility is to gather information and provide support to typical human activities such as understanding, reasoning, problem solving and creativity, as depicted in Figure 2.

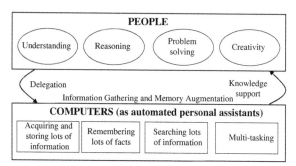

Figure 2. Computers as automated personal assistants (Maes, 1997b)

An environment that emulates the behaviour of a personal assistant should exhibit the properties of a typical human assistant. Human assistants can be time-savers whenever they are allowed to act independently and concurrently. Thus, allowing a software agent to be executed in parallel while people are directing their attention at other activities is critical to enable users to truly delegate tasks to their agents (Lieberman, 1997). Hoschka (1996) suggests that the required properties of a good human assistant, which should be employed to model computer-based personal assistants, are as follows.

- Domain competence: knowledge of the areas in which they assist, in order to be capable of solving problems in those areas.

- Competence assessment: they must know their own limitations and capabilities and make them very clear to their users.

- Adaptive behaviour: they must be able to adapt their behaviour and functions to a user's particular needs, and also learn from their users.

- Processing imprecise instructions: they must be able to interpret incomplete and ambiguous instructions.

- Explaining abilities: they must be capable of explaining their actions, conclusions and suggestions in a straightforward way.

- Co-operation support: they must support both individual users and groups of users working together.

The set of attributes suggested by Hoschka (1996) refers to an ideal assistant whose behaviour has not yet been achieved with current agent technology, but it helps to identify the desirable set of traits that software agents should exhibit in order to support delegation effectively.

While delegation seems to be a useful metaphor for the experimental environment infrastructure, there are pitfalls associated with the delegation model that should be taken into account when designing an agent-based environment. Millewski and Lewis (1997) suggest that delegation is often an unnatural activity, which may be cognitively costly, requires sophisticated communication and control mechanisms, and, most importantly, requires trust. Millewski and Lewis (1997) state that software agents may be more appropriate for some tasks than for others. For example, agents should be limited to tasks that take much time to do or are distracting (e.g. monitoring sources of dynamic information or performing complex searches). These are tasks that are too tedious to perform, or that involve skills which are not worth the user learning. Moreover, users should always have the option of performing the tasks themselves whenever they do not wish to delegate them (Millewski and Lewis, 1997).

4.3   Environmental awareness and autonomy

An autonomous software agent is a system, which is embedded in an environment, capable of interacting independently and effectively with the environment through its own *sensors* and *effectors* to accomplish a given set of tasks (Russel and Norvig, 1995). Because software agents are embedded in a software environment, they need a software architecture that describes their data structures, the operations that may be performed on these data structures and the flow of control between these data structures (Wooldridge, 1999). The *agent architecture* is a map of the agent's internals that stipulates how the agent *senses* its environment, how it makes *decisions* on what to do with sensed information, and how it executes its *actions*.

Figure 3 illustrates the general architecture of autonomous software agents. The *sensors* receive input from the environment and model the agent's ability to observe its environment. The observed data is passed on to an *action* component that represents the agent's "decision- making process" (Wooldridge, 1999) that includes deciding which actions to perform and commanding the agent's *effectors* to carry out those actions on the environment.

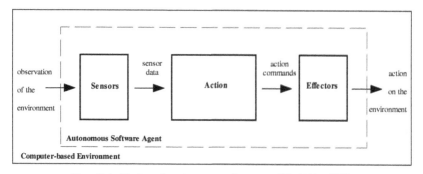

Figure 3. Architecture of an autonomous software agent (Wooldridge, 1999)

This basic architecture illustrates the agent's attributes of environmental awareness, reactivity and autonomy. Environmental awareness is provided by the agent's sensors, which allow the agent to model the environment in which it operates, to track it and to react to changes in it. The agent's input can be a piece of information raised by the occurrence of an event in the environment (e.g. the arrival of new e-mail messages), a message sent by another software agent, or an internal event defined by the agent (e.g. a reminder set by the agent to wait five minutes for a reply to a message or for the occurrence of a particular event in the environment).

Autonomy is achieved by making the agent observe the environment by itself (i.e. without the intervention of the user or other software agents), turn the observations into descriptions suitable for the decision-making process, interpret the results of this process in terms of appropriate actions to perform in the environment, and finally execute these actions through the effectors (e.g. sending a message to another software agent, or conveying a message to the user). Thus, an autonomous agent is essentially a program that "operates in parallel with the user" (Lieberman, 1997), and is always running. For example, if the agent discovers a condition that may interest the user, the agent may independently "decide" to alert the user.

There are currently two main approaches for designing autonomous software agents based on this basic architecture: the *reactive* and the *deliberative* approaches. These approaches differ mainly in the way the design regards the agent. The reactive approach is based on a bottom-up perspective, while the deliberative approach is based on the more traditional top-down perspective (Brooks, 1991). According to the bottom-up approach (reactive architecture), the designer starts by implementing a simple behaviour, covering the entire range from observation to action, and then proceeds by incrementally adding more complex behaviours. In contrast, the top-down approach (deliberative architecture) is based on modularising the abilities of the software agent, such as the observation of the environment, modelling the environment or planning actions to be carried out. According to this approach, the designer starts by specifying the overall architecture of the agent, and then develops the range of required components separately (Brooks, 1991).

The speaking assistant (acting as an experimental environment) described in this book uses both approaches to the design of the software agents that constitute the system. The software agents that monitor the user's environment are based on the reactive approach, while the design of the software agent that communicates with the user is based on a number of functional components that represent the different abilities of the agent, as described in Chapter 5.

4.3.1.   Reactive architectures

The reactive architectures for software agents are inspired by the idea that most of a person's daily activities consist of routine actions, rather than abstract reasoning. Thus, according to this perspective, modelling a software agent is a matter of designing a system that simply *reacts* to an environment, without having any concerns related to reasoning about the environment (Wooldridge, 1999). Such a software agent must possess a collection of simple behavioural procedures, which react to changes in the environment in a "*stimulus-response* basis" (Wooldridge, 1999). This results in a simple architecture where the action component performs a mapping between perceptual stimuli and action commands, as Figure 4 illustrates.

The reactive architectures, sometimes referred to as behavioural[12], are based on the original Brook's "Subsumption Architecture" for modelling robots (Brooks, 1986), and have two distinctive and defining characteristics. First, the agent's decision-making that occurs in the action component of the architecture is achieved through a set of "task accomplishing behaviours" (Wooldridge, 1999). Each one of these behaviours can be regarded as an individual action that takes perceptual stimuli and maps them to actions to be performed by the software agent. Thus, each behaviour is intended to achieve a particular task (Wooldridge, 1999). Furthermore, the set of behaviours may be implemented as a set of simple rules of the form: one situation implies one action.

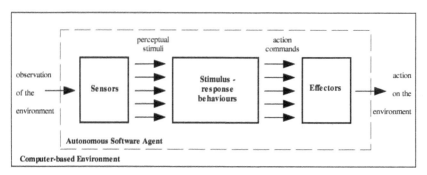

Figure 4. Generic architecture of a reactive agent (Wooldridge, 1999)

The second defining characteristic of reactive architectures is that it is possible for many behaviours to become appropriate at a given instant (Wooldridge, 1999). Thus, there is the need for a

---

[12] The reactive architecture is sometimes referred to as *behavioural* because the central idea is that of designing and combining individual behaviours.

mechanism that allows the agent to select a specific action to be performed among the set of possible actions. Brooks (1986) proposed arranging the behaviours into a "subsumption hierarchy" where they are arranged into layers: the lower layers in the hierarchy would have higher priorities and inhibit the higher layers. According to this standpoint, higher layers would represent increasingly abstract behaviours. For example, an e-mail agent may detect a set of unread e-mail messages in the user's inbox. Some of these messages are newly arrived, while the remaining messages have been received a while ago. If the agent is first to notify the user about the new messages, before reminding the user about unread messages, it is possible to encode the notification behaviour in a low-level layer, and the reminding behaviour in a higher-level layer. This would be giving priority to notification behaviour over reminding actions.

The motivation behind Brooks's (1986) approach, which is based on behavioural decomposition rather than functional decomposition, is that neither the functional components nor the appropriate interfaces between them are known in advance. Thus, Brooks (1986) adopts an engineering approach to the development of reactive agents, and proceeds to their development in an incremental way: starting with the simplest behaviour, and making it work before adding more advanced behaviours.

Wooldridge (1999) suggests that there are obvious advantages to such reactive architectures, which include simplicity, economy, computational tractability and robustness against failure. However, a reactive architecture is not versatile in the sense that it does not assume that the software agent builds a model of its environment. The implication of this is that the agent must possess enough environmental information available for observation, in order to enable the agent to determine an appropriate action.

Furthermore, a reactive agent does not seem to be well suited to stimulus-free tasks that require a response to events beyond the agent's sensory limits, such as for example predicting the behaviour of another agent. Moreover, because most reactive agents are often *hard-wired*, it is difficult to understand how they can be designed to learn from experience and improve their performance over time (Wooldridge, 1999). Finally, while effective software agents can be designed that possess a small number of behaviours (e.g. normally less than ten layers), it becomes much more difficult to build software agents that include many layers because the "dynamics of the interactions among the various behaviours become extremely complex to understand" (Wooldridge, 1999).

While Brooks' "subsumption architecture" is the best known reactive architecture, other reactive approaches have been suggested and implemented, such as the "Agent Network Architecture" (Maes, 1991b) or the "PENGI system" (Agre and Chapman, 1987).

4.3.2.   Deliberative architectures

Deliberative architectures are designed by means of a top-down process. It is becoming common for system designers and users to attribute "beliefs, desires and intentions" (Rao and Georgeff, 1991) to software agents, especially because humans tend to think and speak using cognitive terms such as these. Thus, it becomes more natural to use the same cognitive expressions when designing software agents and their behaviours. Additionally, the attribution of such "mentalistic attitudes" to software agents provides for a stronger notion of agenthood (Nwana, 1996; Wooldridge and Jennings, 1995).

Since a software agent operates in some computational environment, there is the view that, for the agent to operate properly in a changing environment, it is necessary to *model the environment* rather than just react to it. Defenders of this perspective suggest that it is necessary to represent the information the agent possesses about its environment through some combination of its data structures and its processing. This information, which reflects the state of the environment, can be called the set of *beliefs* that the agent is said to possess (Huhns and Singh, 1998b). Furthermore, agent designers also use the term *desires* to express the state of the environment the agent prefers, and the term *intentions* to describe the state of the environment the agent is trying to achieve; the intentions should be a subset of the agent's desires, and connect directly to the agent's actions (Huhns and Singh, 1998b).

Thinking in terms of these cognitive concepts enables designers to build their agent architectures by determining the agent's beliefs, desires and intentions in a particular environment, and to relate them to the agent's perceptions (through the agent's sensors) and actions (through the agent's effectors).

The class of deliberative architectures for agents is based on these cognitive concepts and has its roots in *practical reasoning* - "the process of deciding, moment by moment, which action to perform in the furtherance of our goals" (Wooldridge, 1999). Wooldridge (1999) believes that practical reasoning involves two key processes: *deliberation* (deciding *what* goals we want to achieve), and *means-ends reasoning* (deciding *how* to achieve those goals).

To date, two main approaches have been defined for implementing cognitive concepts in the context of deliberative architectures. These approaches are reflected in two possible kinds of agent architecture: *logic-based* and *procedural* (Huhns and Singh, 1998b). Logic-based architectures use cognitive concepts to model an agent's reasoning: beliefs, desires and intentions are represented in modular data structures, which are then manipulated to perform means-ends reasoning. Furthermore, these cognitive concepts are defined formally and the manipulations are achieved through the application of a theorem prover (Wooldridge, 1999). One example, which employs a logic-based architecture, is the "Artimis" system, designed to operate in a spoken-dialogue interface for information access (Breiter and Sadek, 1996).

Procedural architectures also employ representations of beliefs, desires and intentions, but these concepts are processed procedurally, rather than through theorem proving (Huhns and Singh, 1998b). These architectures exhibit better performance than logic-based approaches, and most of the practical deliberative agent architectures fall into this category. The most representative example of procedural architectures is the Belief-Desire-and-Intentions (BDI) architecture (Wooldridge, 1999; Wooldridge and Jennings, 1995), which is illustrated in Figure 5.

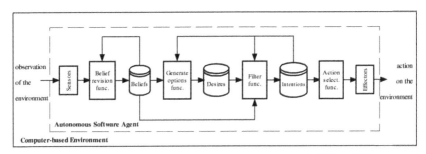

Figure 5. Generic architecture of a Belief-Desire-Intention agent (Wooldridge, 1999)

According to Wooldridge (1999) there are seven main components in a BDI agent, which enable the following process to be applied, as Figure 5 illustrates. Initially, the agent has a set of *beliefs*, which represent the information the agent possesses about its current environment. The component called *belief revision function* takes the agent's perceptions of the changing environment acquired through its sensors and the agent's beliefs, in order to determine a *new* set of beliefs. Using this updated set of beliefs and its *intentions*, the agent then employs an *option generation function* that determines the set of options available for acting - its *desires*. Thus, the set of desires represents the possible course of action available to the agent at any given instant.

The *filter function* represents the agent's deliberation processes, and it is used by the agent to determine a new set of intentions based on existing beliefs, desires and intentions. This new set of *intentions* corresponds to the agent's commitments, which are taken by the *action selection function* in order to determine a concrete action to be performed by the agent in its environment.

It is clear that BDI architectures attempt to mimic the process of deciding what to do, which people appear to use in their daily activities. The basic components of this architecture, as illustrated in Figure 5, are data structures that represent the agent's deliberation (the agent decides what intention to have in the face of a changing environment), and means-ends reasoning (the agent decides how to execute these intentions). Wooldridge (1999) argues that the BDI architecture is especially useful to model a deliberative agent mainly because it is intuitive and it provides designers with a clear functional decomposition that allows them to understand what kinds of subsystems may be required to build a specific agent.

4.4   Adaptation

Given that the experimental environment is serving the purpose of notifying and reminding the user about timely and relevant pieces of personal information, it is desirable that the environment generates *tailored presentations* of that information, *adapted* to the particular *interests* and *preferences* of each user. Furthermore, information delivery should be tailored both in terms of *content* and in terms of *form*.

Another reason that justifies the need for a user-adaptive environment is related with anthropomorphism. The main purpose of the experimental environment is to test the benefits and effects of humanised spoken messages. Since humans typically adapt to other humans, an environment that adapts to users may reinforce the perception of a consistent humanised system.

The benefits of such an adaptive behaviour are readily apparent: it enables the agents comprising the computer-based environment to enhance information awareness to deliver exclusively relevant information.

Adaptation refers to an important attribute of software agents, which enables them to adapt their behaviour, over time, to suit the *preferences*, and the particular behaviour, of individual users (Shoam, 1999). Thus, adaptation is a relevant property of agents whenever there is the need to *personalise* their services, and promote the perception of a personal assistant.

4.4.1. User profiles

The key data structures that support computer-based personal assistants are termed personal *profiles* (Huhns and Singh, 1998c), which constitute the most important part of *user models*. According to Benyon and Murray (1993), a *user model* represents the preferences, characteristics and knowledge that a system believes the user possesses. Benyon and Murray (1993) state that user models contain one or more of three types of structures: (1) a *user profile* (data related to a user's background and interests), (2) a *psychological model* (cognitive skills and personality traits of the user), and (3) a *student model*[13] (data concerning what the system "believes" the user knows about the domain in which the system operates). The process of gathering information about users of a computer-based system, and of using that data to provide information adapted to the specific requirements of users has been termed *user modelling* (McTear, 1993).

Profiles allow software agents to gather knowledge about the user and to tailor their subsequent interactions with the user, most notably to tailor the information they present to users. Therefore, the user profile constructed by the agent should ideally reflect accurately the true requirements and needs of the user (Soltysiak and Crabtree, 1998). User profiles typically contain explicit assumptions on those characteristics of the user that are relevant to the behaviour and appearance of a system, and they normally exist as separate repositories to enable its use by different system components.

Figure 6 illustrates the general schema for a user-adaptive system that is based on user profiles, highlighting the typical processes required to achieve personalised system behaviour. First, there is the need to consider what kind of inputs concerning the user will be used to develop the user profile. Typical attributes and properties of the user that are often used include such elements as personal characteristics, general interests, proficiencies and current goals. However, since the nature

---

[13] The term "student model" was chosen because of the similarity of the data contained in this model to that held by intelligent tutoring systems (Benyon and Murray, 1993).

of the adaptation has necessarily to vary according to the context of the task, it is necessary to identify more precisely the profile elements that will be useful for the specific tasks for which the adaptive environment will be providing assistance. This means that the *content* of the user profile is specific to the task (Soltysiak and Crabtree, 1998), and that the profile should only include the characteristics of the user that have an effect on the adaptation.

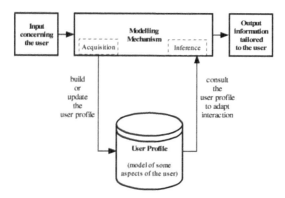

Figure 6. General schema for user-adaptive systems (adapted from (Jameson, 2001)).

After identifying users' attributes that will make up a user profile, it is necessary to consider how the system will construct the profile, i.e. the *modelling mechanism* the system will employ to acquire users' characteristics and represent them in a suitable profile. Because the modelling mechanism has an impact on how the information is represented in their profile, the same mechanism should subsequently be used by the user-adaptive system to consult the profile and tailor the presentation of information according to users' preferences represented in their profile.

There are two fundamental approaches to acquiring profile information, each with its own advantages and drawbacks:

- *Explicit* techniques, whereby profiles are constructed *directly* by the user supplying relevant information;

- *Implicit* techniques, which enable the user-adaptive system to *learn* users' interests and preferences by automatically *monitoring* and *inferring* users' characteristics.

The explicit techniques for user profiling rely on the direct intervention of the user, and collect information through general questionnaires, ratings of representative sample data or detailed, but lengthy, surveys (Crabtree et al., 1998). These methods may allow gathering precise information about the characteristics of the user being modelled, but they only provide a static view about the individual, and may place a heavy burden on the user, especially if it is frequently necessary to track changing interests.

In contrast, implicit techniques enable agents to learn a user's set of interests and preferences in a more autonomous fashion, involving minimal feedback from the user, and allowing the computer-based environment to adapt more easily to changing user needs over time (Crabtree et al., 1998). However, it is much more difficult, and error prone, to identify preferences from users' behaviours than to ask users directly.

Of course, the modelling mechanism depicted in Figure 6 stipulates both the way the information is represented in the user profile, and the way in which this information will be subsequently used. For example, according to the Open Profiling Standard[14] (OPS), a profile is defined as a "hierarchical collection of personal profile information, the features and corresponding values describing an end user" (Hensley et al., 1997). The kind of profiles defined in the OPS allow for multiple *feature-value* pairs to model the specific users' characteristics such as personal and demographic data, preferences and interests. Additionally, these *feature-value* pairs may be grouped together to form sections, and sections may contain other sections, just like a generalisation hierarchy structure.

Thus, explicit techniques may be employed to gather the required information, which can then be stored by the modelling mechanism in the user profile as *feature-value* pairs. The modelling mechanism may then be used later by a software agent for example to make inferences about the appropriateness of delivering a piece of information to the user.

The main disadvantage of explicit techniques is that they provide *static* user profiles; that is, in order to be able to adapt over time, the system needs explicit user input to update the profile according to changing user's interests. Implicit techniques address this issue by automatically monitoring a user's behaviour and updating the appropriate values associated with a user's attributes contained in the user profile. This learning behaviour is typically achieved through statistical keyword analysis or through machine learning techniques (Soltysiak and Crabtree, 1998). Although the experimental environment described in this book relies on explicit techniques, the

---

[14] The Open Profiling Standard has been proposed to provide a standardised method for acquiring, storing and utilising user profiles (Hensley et al., 1997).

following paragraphs provide a brief overview and a number of examples related to the application of machine learning techniques to learning of user profiles.

Machine learning techniques (Mitchell, 1997) attempt to produce a specific learned model that accurately *classifies* new cases, given a set of already classified examples and a type of model for classifying individual cases. Pazzani and Billsus (1997) describe and compare examples of machine learning techniques, such as decision trees or probabilistic classifiers, applied to the problem of learning user interests. As an example, Bayesian classifier algorithms were found to produce the best results among the methods evaluated (Pazzani and Billsus, 1997).

Applying machine learning techniques to software agents is exemplified by Maes (1994), who describes a number of interface agents, such as one for handling electronic e-mail (Maxims), an agent for Usenet News filtering (Newt) and an agent for recommending books and music (Ringo). All three employ learning techniques to detect patterns in user's actions, in order to improve their behaviour over time without imposing too great a burden on the user.

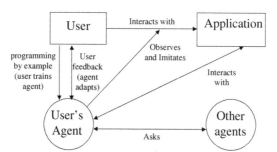

Figure 7. Possibilities for software agents' learning behaviour (Maes, 1994)

As Figure 7 illustrates, Maes (1994) suggests four ways in which an agent can learn information about user's preferences and habits: (1) agents can learn by "looking over the shoulder" of their users, observing and imitating their interaction with other applications; (2) agents also learn through direct and indirect feedback from the user on the agent's actions; (3) agents may also learn from examples and explicit training instructions provided by the user; and (4) agents may ask for advice from, and share expertise with, other agents.

4.4.2.   Issues with user-adaptive agents

A design based on user-adaptive agents that employ user profiles raises important issues related to information *privacy* and user's *trust*. Since adaptive software agents have access to much personal information about users, they have necessarily to *trust* such an agent-based environment. According to Crabtree et al. (1998), users have to trust that the agents will operate correctly and that the agents will not make improper suggestions. However, even more importantly, users have to trust that the software agents will present information in an appropriate and timely manner, such as the notification of important e-mail messages as soon as possible, but leaving other unimportant messages for users to consult at their discretion. Above all, users must trust the agents *not to disclose* any personal or sensitive information to a third party (Crabtree et al., 1998).

Additionally, users should be aware of every piece of personal information that exists in the user profile, and should be granted unconditional access to the stored information in order to alleviate the perception of a privacy intrusive system (Kühme, 1993).

4.5   Communication and scalability

An experimental environment that enhances information awareness has to deal with a variety of different sources of personal information. Decomposing the problem into various software components helps to assign specific functionalities to each component, which address the particular requirements of the information source being monitored. Furthermore, it is necessary that the observations obtained by each component are communicated to the user through speech-based messages.

It has already been argued that agent-based technology provides a suitable means for designing the functionality of each component as autonomous software entities. Thus, the experimental environment might be constituted by a set of software agents, specialised by source domain; that is, each specialised agent is responsible for monitoring a different source of desired information, and for preparing alerting reports (notifications and reminders) to be communicated to the agent which is responsible for delivering them to the user.

Huhns and Stephens (1999) argue that it is possible to analyse, describe and design computer-based environments in which a set of software agents can operate and interact with each other productively; agent-based technology provides the required protocols for software agents to *communicate* and *interact*. *Communication protocols* enable agents to exchange and understand messages, while *interaction protocols* enable the agents to have "conversations", which are defined as "structured exchanges of messages" (Huhns and Stephens, 1999). The experimental environment described in this book makes use of a communication protocol.

In general, the communication protocol specifies the *types of message* that can be exchanged between the two agents. For example, a communication protocol might stipulate the following types of message to be exchanged: (1) *assert* a piece of information, (2) *request* for a piece of information, and (3) *reply* with a piece of information.

The existence of an inter-agent communication protocol enables the designer to map a particular problem into a multi-agent environment, in which particular agents are specialised according to their task, and communicate information among them. In this way, it is possible to distinguish the part of the environment that is in charge of interacting with the user (e.g. conveying spoken messages and listening to spoken instructions), from the parts of the environment that carry out the specialised monitoring tasks.

The division of tasks, and the communication based on a common protocol, allow for the development of a *scalable* environment. This means that extending the functionality of the environment only requires the creation of additional specialised agents whose sole imposition is to adhere to the common protocol.

Usually, the part of a software architecture for an agent-based environment that is in charge of interacting *directly* with the user is termed the *interface agent*. For example, Maes (1994) defines an interface agent as a computer program that acts as a "personal assistant who is *collaborating with the user* in the same work environment". Similarly, Sycara et al. (1996) suggest an architecture for agent-based environments that includes interface agents as the components which interact with the user by receiving user specifications and delivering required information. Normally, interface agents also acquire, model and utilise user's preferences that are used to "guide system co-ordination in support of user's tasks" (Sycara et al., 1996).

Thus, from the user's perspective, the interface agent is the software entity that represents the experimental environment, and that mediates between the user and the other components of the environment. From the point of view of the whole system architecture, the interface agent is not the experimental environment, but the part that communicates with the user.

In terms of a software agent's architecture, the ability to communicate is situated both in the agent's sensors (receiving messages) and effectors (sending messages). It is the communication ability that enables the software agents to *co-ordinate* their actions and behaviour, in order to allow the multi-agent environment to be more "coherent" (Huhns and Stephens, 1999). Moreover, and of special interest to the design of the experimental environment, the degree of co-ordination is the extent to which the agents co-operate to perform a required task. For example, in order to enhance information awareness, some agents are responsible for monitoring specific sources of the user's personal information, another agent monitors the user's presence, and yet another is responsible for assembling spoken messages and communicating with the user through speech (the interface agent). In this context, the agents co-operate by making use of another agent's services in order to maintain the users' awareness of their personal information.

4.5.1.   Communication roles

It is clear by now that it is important for software agents of differing capabilities to be able to communicate. Huhns and Stephens (1999) suggest that agents might assume one of four different roles in a dialogue according to the communication capabilities they possess. Figure 8 illustrates the suggested classification of agents according to their communication capabilities for two fundamental *message types*: *assertions* and *queries*. An assertion is an informative message that pre-supposes acceptance. A query is an interrogative message that assumes a reply.

			Role of the agent in the dialogue			
			Basic agent	Passive agent	Active agent	Peer agent
Communication capability of the agent		Receives assertions	X	X	X	X
		Receives queries		X		X
		Sends assertions		X	X	X
		Sends queries			X	X

Figure 8. Classification of communicative agents (Huhns and Stephens, 1999)

According to Huhns and Stephens (1999), a *basic* agent is one that at least is able to receive assertions. A *passive* agent is one that is able to receive both assertions and queries, and also reply to questions with assertions. In order to assume an *active* role in the dialogue, an agent must be able to send queries and assertions, and receive assertions. An agent that is capable of making and accepting both assertions and queries is seen as a *peer* to other agents.

Beyond the basic message types of assertions and queries, other types of messages have been defined which are based on work undertaken in speech act theory (Austin, 1962; Searle, 1969). The main idea is to use human spoken dialogue as a model for communication between software agents. Table 1 lists the most common types of messages defined for inter-agent communication.

Message type (communicative action)	Intended meaning (illocutionary force or performative)	Suposition (expected result)
Assertion	Inform	Acceptance
Query	Question	Reply
Reply	Inform	Acceptance
Request	Request	
Explanation	Inform	Agreement
Command	Request	
Permission	Inform	Acceptance
Refusal	Inform	Acceptance
Offer / Bid	Inform	Acceptance
Acceptance		
Agreement		
Proposal	Inform	Offer / Bid
Confirmation		
Retraction		
Denial		

Table 1. Types of message for inter-agent communication (Huhns and Stephens, 1999)

4.5.2.   Communication protocols

Usually, communication protocols for software agents are specified at three distinct levels (Huhns and Stephens, 1999):

1. The *method of interconnection*: this is the lowest level of the protocol, and specifies the way in which information is transported by means of a transport mechanism, such as TCP, SMTP or HTTP (Finin et al., 1997).

2. The *format of the messages*: this is the middle level of the protocol, and specifies the syntax, or the structure, of the information being transferred.

3. The *meaning of the messages*: this is the highest level of the protocol, and specifies the semantics of the information being transferred. This level includes both the *meaning* of the *contents* of the messages, as well as the *type of message*, i.e. the meaning of the message itself, which should be domain independent.

In order to specify a protocol, Huhns and Stephens (1999) suggest a possible message *format* (or message syntax) as a data structure containing the following five fields: *sender*, *receiver*, *language*, e*ncoding* and *decoding* functions, and *actions* to be taken by the receiver.

Ideally, the communication protocol should be universally shared by all agents comprising a computer-based environment. For that purpose, the communication protocol should fulfil three different requirements:

1. The protocol should be *concise*.

2. The protocol should *separate* the message *type* (meaning of the message) from the *semantics* of the enclosed message (meaning of the contents of the message), which often depends on the particular domain in which the agents operate.

3. The protocol should have a *limited* number of message types, i.e. of primitive communication acts.

The best-known example of a protocol for exchanging *information* and *knowledge* between software agents is the Knowledge Query and Manipulation Language (KQML) (Finin et al., 1997). KQML was designed so that all the information required for understanding the content of a message *is* included in the communication protocol.

In KQML, the method of interconnection was called the *communication layer*, the message types were called *performatives*, and were defined in the *message layer*, the meaning of the message contents were defined in the *content layer*, and the basic *format* for KQML messages was defined by the following structure (Finin et al., 1997):

(KQML performative   - Type of message (message layer)

  :Sender <word>   - ID of the sending agent (communication layer)

  :Receiver <word>   - ID of the receiving agent (communication layer)

  :Language <word>   - Language used to express the content (message layer)

  :Ontology <word>   - Ontology for the domain of content (message layer)

  :Content <expression>)- The message content (content layer)

4.6   Summary

This chapter has identified the main requirements for the design and implementation of an experimental environment that aimed at testing the importance of exploiting speech output, conveyed using anthropomorphic characteristics, in reinforcing the social acceptability of the computer, and in enhancing information awareness.

The requirements for a suitable foundation for the experimental environment have been presented and included the following. The background technology for the experimental environment must (1) enable the application of social science theory to computer-based systems, (2) facilitate the creation of a co-operative computer-based environment founded on the delegation metaphor, and (3) allow for the design of a complex computer-based environment that comprises a number of specialised software components which monitor disparate sources of personal information, and communicate among themselves and with the user. It was argued that agent-based technology provides the required background through its provision of a delegation metaphor for specifying and designing computer-based environments that are constituted by autonomous, reactive, adaptive and communicative software entities.

When designing any agent-based system it is important to determine how sophisticated the agents' reasoning will be, by specifying the agent's internal architecture. Reactive agents simply retrieve a set of pre-defined behaviours (like a reflex reaction) without maintaining any internal state. In contrast, deliberative agents behave as if they possess mental attributes normally associated with human thinking, by searching through a space of behaviours, maintaining internal state, and predicting the effects of their actions. This is the basis for the class of BDI architectures.

Taking a fully agent-oriented perspective for the design of the software architecture for the experimental environment involves, first the identification of the tasks the environment is required to provide, and then the assignment of each task to different software agents. Finally, it involves the specification of a suitable protocol that enables the agents to communicate among.

Chapter 5

DESIGN OF A SPEAKING ASSISTANT

5.1 Overview

The objective of this chapter is to describe the design and the prototype implementation of the experimental environment that enables the importance of speech induced anthropomorphism in reinforcing the social acceptability of the computer to be evaluated. This experimental environment also enables evaluating whether speech-based alerts enhance the awareness of dynamic information that is hidden from view. Thus, the experimental environment appears to users as a *speaking assistant* which helps them to maintain awareness of desired personal information that is visually hidden.

The work described in this chapter helps in *understanding* the main design considerations that should be taken into account when creating an assistant-like system which aims to humanise the interface (1) by employing speech output, conveyed following social norms, and (2) by supporting information awareness through the provision of adequate cues as part of those messages which are designed to notify and remind users about the occurrence of events.

Designing a computer-based environment following an assistant-focussed perspective involves addressing such issues as the following.

- How to *split* the environment into a number of separate software agents that perform specific monitoring tasks.

- How to develop a *software architecture* that is based on a collection of software agents.

- How to design the *internal architecture* of each software agent, in such a way that it collects the contextual information required to cue the user in a manner compatible with human cognition.

- How to *communicate* collected information between the software agents.

- How to *transform* collected information into appropriate spoken messages to be delivered to the user.

- How to *present* the spoken information following typical social norms such as knowing when and how to interrupt, speaking with a degree of linguistic variation, and adopting a number of politeness strategies so as to exhibit an appropriate linguistic style.

5.2   A speaking assistant for information awareness

5.2.1.   System objectives

The main objective of the speaking assistant for information awareness is to provide a suitable experimental environment that allows for evaluating users' perceptions and reactions to anthropomorphised spoken notifications and reminders.

A second objective of the system is to provide an adequate experimental environment to evaluate the extent to which exploiting speech as part of a complementary mechanism to the existing graphical presentation of information offers advantages over purely graphical-based approaches as far as information awareness is concerned.

The third objective of the system is to provide an experimental environment that allows for evaluating the suitability of agent-based techniques for designing and implementing speech-based anthropomorphic systems for information awareness.

In order to meet these objectives, the practical requirements of the system design are as follows.

1. The system must be designed in a way that *complements* the graphical presentation of information with speech output.

2. The system must be designed so that it supports a user's continued *awareness* of dynamic personal information which is hidden from view, by extracting selected contextual information as the *cues* required for the human cognitive system, and presenting those cues as part of the spoken notification and reminding messages.

3. The system must be designed so as to follow typical conversational norms (including appropriate interruptions, linguistic variation and politeness) when speaking to the user.

4. The system should be designed as an architecture of communicative software agents.

5.2.2.　Design considerations

5.2.2.1.　Selecting information sources to be monitored

The first decision to be taken in the design of the experimental environment concerns the specific *source domains* of personal information that are to be monitored by the system. The criteria used for selecting the appropriate information sources included the identification of:

1. a set of typical tasks that users have to carry out on a daily basis;

2. a set of tasks for which graphical-based information awareness support is too intrusive;

3. a set of sufficiently different tasks that covers a complex set of design issues;

4. an initially small, but representative, set of tasks that enables a realistic empirical study to be carried out.

Based on these criteria, the set of source domains monitored in the experimental environment includes those of e-mail, printing and diary.

5.2.2.2.　Mapping monitoring tasks into specialised agents

The second design decision concerns the allocation of specific system functionalities to different software agents. Given the initial set of chosen tasks, there is a corresponding set of *specialised agents*, one agent for each information source being monitored.

The e-mail agent is responsible for monitoring the user's e-mail inbox, and providing notifications and reminders concerning e-mail messages. Similarly, the printing agent monitors the user's printing activity, checking the appropriate printer queues, and provides notifications and reminders concerning printed documents. The diary agent monitors the user's diary, checks diary entries, and provides notifications and reminders concerning appointments and to-do*s*.

When designing a specialised agent's architecture, not only has account to be taken of *what* the agents must sense, but also *how* they process sensed information, and *how* they will act on the basis of that processing. As described, the specialised agents are responsible for monitoring changes in the particular domains they observe, and are also required to analyse the pieces of information they observe and to extract the contextual elements compatible with human cognition. For example, when the diary agent senses that there is an upcoming appointment, it should assemble a notification message containing the sort of explicit cues described in chapter 3, such as the type of appointment, who will attend, and where it will take place.

This kind of processing is also valid for other specialised agents: each agent should identify the contextual elements describing a piece of information, such as quantity, people type, description and place, and assemble appropriate notification and reminding messages. Since the specialised agents are *not* responsible for communicating directly with the user, these messages must be further formatted according to a common communication protocol, and delivered to the interface agent that manages all direct interactions with the user.

The kind of processing just described indicates that a *reactive* architecture for agents is well suited to the kind of functionality required of the specialised agents: the occurrence of some event monitored by each specialised agent triggers the analysis of the item of personal information, and causes the agent to extract contextual cues and to assemble a notification or reminding message that is then sent to an interface agent.

Of course, other tasks may also be identified that involve personal information, the awareness of which might be supported through the speaking assistant described here. For example a Usenet *Newsgroups agent* could be looking for new postings on interesting threads, and checking for replies to messages posted by the user. Similarly, a *Birthdays agent* could issue notifications about upcoming dates, along with gift suggestions, and remind the user when the important date arrives. A *Tannoy agent* could be monitoring general announcements and notify the user as soon as a new announcement is broadcast. There could also be an *Auctions agent* that would be looking for bids at a certain price, for a number of products, and that would notify the user as soon as the conditions stipulated by the user were met. Further examples include a *Finances agent* (monitors user's accounts, looks for cheques to clear, issues low-balance warnings), a *Generic Searches agent* (looks for specific information requested by the user, on the local network or on the Internet, and notifies the user whenever promising results are found), and an *Investments agent* (monitors share prices and associated headlines).

5.2.2.3.   Incorporating a user profile

Beyond the specialised agent's attributions, the experimental environment should support other important functionalities. First, it is necessary to maintain an updated profile of the user, containing user's preferences concerning the set of personal information sources monitored by the system. There are two possible alternatives: (1) centralising the profile as part of a *User profiler agent*, or (2) having each specialised agent maintain the part of the user profile that is relevant to the task the agent is supporting.

The first alternative has advantages in that it makes the architecture of each agent much simpler, but it requires a more complex communication protocol since the updates and queries to the user profile have to be communicated between the *user profiler* and the other software agents. Thus, the second alternative, which involves the existence of a number of separate profiles, maintained by each specialised agent, seems to be an attractive possibility, although it may involve some repetition of a number of attributes that may be common to the set of information sources being monitored, such as a user's personal background information. However, for the specialised agents operation, the most important attributes contained in the user profile is information regarding the *urgency* and the *priority* values that users assign to specific items of information being monitored by the specialised agents. Thus, because the specialised agents maintain a local user profile including these attributes, it becomes their responsibility to decide *when to interrupt* the user. They achieve this behaviour by incorporating a *precedence* value in each message, and the message precedence is obtained based on priority and urgency information contained in user profiles.

5.2.2.4.   Sensing user's presence

Another important functionality the system must support concerns updated information about the user presence. For example, on a desktop environment users are often away from their workstation's physical location. In this case it makes no sense to speak to the user. It makes more sense to store a number of potentially interesting messages, and to deliver them as soon as the user logs in again. As is clear, the events that notifications refer to may expire, and they must be delivered *at later times* in the form of reminders. For example, if at any given time there are two new e-mail messages of interest, but the user is not present, the e-mail agent should be informed of the unavailability of the user, and instead of conveying an immediate notification, it should *remind* the user at a later time to check for new e-mail messages (given that while the user was away, two new important messages arrived).

This functionality of maintaining updated information about the user's availability can be provided by a *user presence agent*, which continuously checks the proximity of the user, and broadcasts updated information about the user's presence to the specialised agents whenever the user leaves or returns to the proximity of the workstation. For example, it could use information acquired through an infra-red device that detects emissions from a wearable transmitter that the user is carrying.

5.2.2.5. *Defining a communication protocol*

As stated above, the design of the experimental environment has also to consider a suitable communication protocol, and has to include an interface agent that receives messages from the specialised agents and communicates them to the user by using speech output.

As far as the communication protocol is concerned, it is essential to specify a structure (format) for the messages, as well as to specify the meaning associated with each message. This meaning involves both the specification of the *types of message*, and the specification of the *meaning of the information contained* in the messages, as explained in chapter 4.

Since the specialised agents act as purely reactive agents (that is, they are not defined as possessing any reasoning capability), and given that they do not need to negotiate with other software agents, it does not seem necessary to employ a full-blown agent communication protocol such as KQML. In fact, the specialised agents' communication capabilities correspond to those of a simple passive agent (see Section 4.5 for a definition of agents' communication roles).

In the context of the experimental environment, the only categories of message that have to be supported by the communication protocol are (1) *assertions*, which enclose messages carrying notifications and reminders about the occurrence of events, messages carrying user presence information and messages subscribing to services; and (2) *acceptances*, which enclose messages acknowledging the receipt of other messages.

5.2.2.6.   Interacting with the user

As far as the interaction with the user is concerned, the design of an interface agent (the Speaking Agent), which is responsible for *co-ordinating* the delivery of spoken information to the user, involves the consideration of four major issues. First, received messages need to be prioritised according to their precedence value (that is according to the value obtained by weighting their priority and urgency values). Second, the contents of received messages, whether notifications or reminders, has to be transformed into appropriate English-language sentences. However, it is not sufficient just to produce the sentences, as it is also necessary to include linguistic variation and politeness. Finally, it is necessary to modulate the multimedia channel. This means that the speaking agent has to appropriately interrupt possible on-going multimedia presentations before delivering the spoken message to the user.

The following paragraphs explore in more detail the design considerations just presented. First, the software architecture of the speaking assistant that serves as the experimental environment is presented. This is followed by a discussion of a number of categories for structuring the delivery of spoken information to the user. This discussion aims to highlight a number of design issues and the way they were tackled in the experimental environment.

5.2.3.   System architecture

The software architecture of the speaking assistant is illustrated in Figure 9. As shown, the speaking assistant for information awareness is constituted by three main types of software agent: the *specialised* agents, which are personal information monitoring agents, the *service* agents, which provide environmental information required by the specialised agents, and an *interface* agent – the speaking agent.

Several remarks must be made concerning the software architecture of the speaking assistant presented in Figure 9. First, the architecture emphasises the flow of information towards the user, as the main objective of the experimental environment is to allow for testing user's perceptions and reactions to anthropomorphised presentations of spoken information.

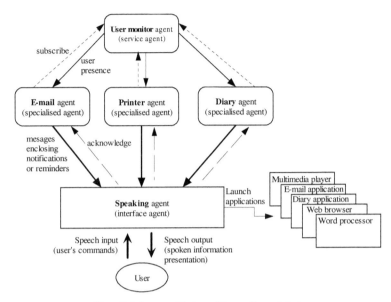

Figure 9. Software architecture of the speaking assistant.

Second, the software agents comprising the architecture are not defined as having learning abilities. Instead, the system relies on users manually updating their profiles, which are then read by each specialised agent, as Figure 10 illustrates. This is a deliberate design decision, justified by noting that learning users' profiles involves user interaction with the learning agents over an extended period of time. Since the main objective of the experimental environment is to allow for the evaluation of humanised spoken information delivery in a single experiment, and not to evaluate an agent's learning capabilities, the software agents only have the capability of consulting a user's profiles.

However, it is possible to extend the software architecture depicted in Figure 9 to include learning agents. For this purpose, each specialised agent should be made to observe the user's interactions with their e-mail, printing and diary applications, and update the corresponding profiles automatically, although users would always have the possibility of consulting and modifying the information being gathered by the specialised agents.

Additionally, all communications occurring among the agents comprising the architecture are defined as being *asynchronous* communications. This is required in order to prevent the specialised agents, the user monitor agent and the speaking agent having to block their execution, wait for the acknowledgement messages, and lose new information associated with the occurrence of a new or unpredictable event, such as the arrival of new e-mail messages, users leaving their physical location, or messages sent by other specialised agents.

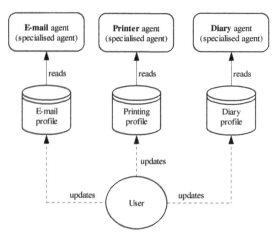

Figure 10. Framework for updating and reading the user profile.

Finally, the architecture depicted in Figure 9 also highlights the role of the speaking agent as an interface agent. The speaking agent is responsible for communicating with the user, conveying spoken information or listening to user's spoken commands, and for modifying the interface as appropriate (e.g. by interrupting other on-going presentations to convey a spoken message or by launching applications at the user's request). The design of the spoken information delivered by the speaking agent is described next, and the following sections explore in more detail the design of the agents' internal architectures, and the design of the messages comprised in the communication protocol.

5.2.4.   Spoken information delivery

The spoken information that can be generated and delivered by the speaking assistant has been divided into four main categories (illustrated in Table 2): attention-getters, monitor reports, reportages and the interactive guide.

Attention-getters are messages designed to interrupt the user and indicate the system's readiness to deliver some information. These messages might be created as simple auditory sounds, but designing them to be polite expressions, such as for example "excuse me", potentially enhances the social acceptability of the system, and should promote the perception that the system behaves as a work companion. Given that the contents of these messages are independent of the personal information domains monitored by the experimental environment, they can be generated at the speaking agent level.

Categories of information presentation	Type of spoken message	Personal information domain	Examples
Attention-getters	Interrupters	Any domain	Polite interrupting expressions (e.g. "Excuse me!", "Sorry to interrupt but...")
Monitor Reports	Notifications (alerts to the imminence or to the occurrence of new events)	E-mail	Arrival of new e-mail messages
		Printing	Printing in process / finished
		Diary	Imminent starting of scheduled events (e.g. appointment, seminar, lecture, meeting)
			Scheduled events now starting (e.g. appointment, seminar, lecture, meeting)
			Upcoming personal dates (e.g. birthdays, holidays, anniversaries)
			Upcoming to-do items
	Reminders (alerts to events that have already occurred)	E-mail	Replies to received e-mail messages
		Printing	Printed documents ready in the printer tray
		Diary	Started or overdue scheduled events
			Personal dates (e.g. birthdays, holidays, anniversaries)
			Due to-do items
Reportages	Structured Linear Presentation	Any domain	Video clips, on-line lectures
Interactive Guide	Structured Non-linear Presentation	Any domain	Interactive Presentations

Table 2. Categories of spoken information presentation

Monitor reports are short messages designed to support the user's awareness of personal information through the provision of cues that make the alerts convey more semantics about the events to which they refer. There are two distinct types of message within this category: notifications and reminders. As stated earlier, notifications refer to alerts concerning the imminence or start of new scheduled events, or the occurrence of unpredictable events, while reminders refer to alerts concerning past events of which the user needs to be reminded. Monitor reports are viewed as non-interactive messages - once their delivery starts it is not to be interrupted, either by the user or by other monitor reports. Additionally, monitor reports do not offer the user the opportunity to navigate through, or to choose, the contents being delivered. Given that the contents of monitor reports depend on the personal information source domains monitored by the experimental environment (e.g. e-mail, diary and printing), and given that the contents must cue the user as to the occurrence of events, the corresponding spoken messages generated by the speaking agent must be created on the basis of information received from the specialised agents.

Reportages constitute the next level of complexity associated with the presentation of spoken information. They are viewed as structured linear multimedia presentations of information requested by the user. Reportages are also viewed as non-interactive messages, though users may decide when to receive them and when to pause them or terminate their presentation. Reportages may also be interrupted by monitor reports. This kind of presentation of spoken information may for example take the form of a video clip, or an *On-Line Lecture* (Benest, 1997). The contents of these messages correspond to overview reports created by the specialised agents concerning a number of events that occurred, or that are scheduled to occur, over a certain period. For example, the e-mail agent might create periodic reportages summarising the activity of the user's e-mail inbox over one day. The diary agent may create a reportage summarising the events scheduled for a given day, and the printer agent can create a reportage describing the printer traffic generated by the user during the day. Additional examples include the generation of search reports that highlight information found with snapshots of that information, or the creation of investment reports concerning the movement of specific shares during one business day.

Finally, the interactive guide constitutes the most complex kind of spoken information delivery that might be generated by the speaking assistant. It is intended to present sufficient information about a search requested by the user, guiding users while they navigate through complex spaces. These complex messages may be interrupted by monitor reports and provide the user with the opportunity to engage in a dialogue with the system.

The design of the experimental environment has concentrated on the first two categories of information presentation because: (1) they provide sufficient material to meet the experimental environment objectives, and (2) they allow a number of conclusions to be drawn concerning the delivery of spoken information, which might then be used to guide the design of more complex delivery types such as the reportages and the interactive guide.

5.3   Specialised agents

5.3.1.   Specification

5.3.1.1.   Generic architecture

The specialised agents operating in the experimental environment are the e-mail agent, the printer agent and the diary agent. These software agents are concerned with observing a particular source of personal information, and with generating appropriate monitor reports that correspond to the occurrence of events. These messages are subsequently communicated to the speaking agent that is in charge of conveying them to the user.

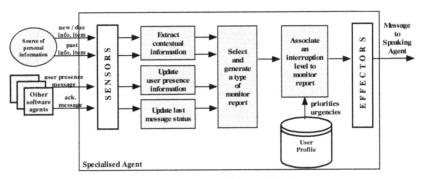

Figure 11. Generic architecture of the specialised agents.

In terms of the internal architecture, the functionality just described corresponds to a *reactive* behaviour, as illustrated in Figure 11. The specialised agents continuously monitor the relevant source of information located in the user's desktop environment, and this information acts as a trigger to a set of condition-action rules that cause the agent: (1) to extract the contextual elements from the relevant piece, or pieces, of information being monitored, (2) to select a type of monitor report to be generated (either a notification or a reminder), and (3) to associate an interruption level to the monitor report, according to user defined priority and urgency information existing in the user profile. The effectors of the agent generate a message which encapsulates the monitor report according to the communication protocol, and send this message to the speaking agent.

The e-mail agent monitors the user's e-mail inbox and detects the arrival of *new* e-mail messages, as well as the presence of existing e-mail messages *not yet viewed* by the user. The printer agent monitors the user's printing queue and detects *new* print jobs issued by the user, as well as the *completion* of print jobs belonging to the user. The diary agent monitors the user's diary and detects *new* and *just starting* scheduled events, as well as due to-do items entered by the user that have not yet been checked off.

Before discussing in detail the design of the architecture of each specialised agent, it is important to discuss first which context elements are extracted from the information items being monitored, and second to describe the way each specialised agent associates an interruption level to the monitor report, which conceptually corresponds to making a decision about when to interrupt the user.

5.3.1.2.   Contextual cues for information awareness

The types of contextual cue required to support information awareness have already been discussed in section 3.6. The extraction of these contextual elements that characterise the pieces of personal information being monitored by the specialised agents is one of the most important functions performed by these agents. It is necessary to *map* the types of contextual cue into the specific attributes that characterise e-mail messages, print jobs and diary entries, respectively.

There are seven main types of contextual cue required to support effective information awareness through notifications and reminders: kind, time, quantity, people, nature, description and place (as described in Section 3.6). Table 3 illustrates the context elements to be extracted by each specialised agent, along with their correspondence to these seven types of contextual cue.

As soon as a specialised agent senses a trigger condition from an event occurring in the particular domain it observes, the agent immediately analyses the new pieces of information (for notifications), or the existing pieces of information (for reminders), in order to gather the contextual elements shown in Table 3.

Types of contextual cue	Context elements to be extracted to compose notifications and reminders		
[KIND] (personal information management domain)	E-mail	Printing	Diary
[TIME] (temporal information)	- time interval to check for and notify about new messages - time interval to remind about unread messages	- time at which the document entered the printing queue - time at which the document finished printing	- time interval until a scheduled event (appointment) is due - time interval to remind about started events and due to-do items
[QUANTITY] (number)	Number of new or unread e-mail messages	Number of printed documents	Number of upcoming, starting or due appointments and/or to-do items
[PEOPLE] (who is the human originator)	Name of the person who sent the received messages	Name of the user who printed the document waiting in the queue	Name of the person(s) who will attend the appointment, or who is the addressee of a to-do
[NATURE] (type, task or activity)	Type of e-mail message (e.g. On-going correspondence, to read, to-do / pending, junk mail or, indeterminate / misc)	Type of document printed (e.g. word processor, webpage, picture, e-mail message, PDF document...)	Type of appointment (e.g. seminar, lecture, meeting, lunch/dinner...)
[DESCRIPTION] (refers to a subject, a specification, or a summary)	Subject of the received e-mail message	Position where the printed document is waiting in the printer queue	Summary or description of the appointment or to-do
[PLACE] (refers to an institution, or to a physical location)	Where does the e-mail message come from? (e.g. institution/company, Internet domain)	ID of printer (identifies its physical location)	Place where the appointment or to-do is due to occur.

Table 3. Types of contextual cue to be extracted by the specialised agents.

5.3.1.3. Deciding when to interrupt

The information value of a new or existing piece of information depends heavily on each user's interests, as described in section 2.2.2. More specifically, as far as notifications and reminders are concerned, there is the need to determine the *precedence* of the message over other activities in which the user may be engaged. The precedence value may be obtained by weighting the *urgency* and *priority* that users assign to each piece of information. In the context of this book, *urgency* is viewed as the importance of a piece of information in relation to the user's short-term interests (such as the activities they are currently engaged in, or the people with whom they are working), while *priority* is viewed as the importance of a piece of information in relation to the user's long-term interests (such as a set of research topics, music genres, authors or other pre-determined interests).

For example, consider user A, who is interested in multimedia and intelligent user interfaces, and who is currently engaged in an on-going project with persons B and C. User A views e-mail messages from persons B and C as *urgent*, and considers e-mail messages containing the keywords "multimedia" and "intelligent user interfaces" to be of high priority, whereas other e-mail messages are considered to be non-urgent and possessing a null priority.

Information about user's priorities and urgencies may be stored in the user profile (for example as simple attribute-value pairs) which is consulted by the specialised agents whenever a new notification or reminder is about to be generated.

Thus, the process of deciding when to interrupt has been modelled around three basic parameters: urgency, priority and user presence. The *urgency* and *priority* parameters may assume Low or High values, whereas the *user presence* parameter assumes one of the In/Out values, as Table 4 illustrates.

Parameter	Values	Description
Urgency	Low, High	Short-term importance of the message
Priority	Low, High	Long-term importance of the message
User presence	In, Out	The user may be present or away from the physical location of the workstation at a particular instant

Table 4. Parameters for deciding when to interrupt.

The model is designed to enable the specialised agents to decide the most suitable occasion to interrupt a user with a given monitor report, and is based on calculating a value for the *precedence* of the message over other activities in which the user may be engaged. The value of a monitor report's precedence is expressed through an *Interruption Level*. These levels range from high precedence, which corresponds to highly intrusive monitor reports (IL1), to null precedence (IL4). A simple method for calculating the interruption level is proposed in Table 5.

As shown, the most intrusive interruption level (IL1) corresponds to every monitor report for which the obtained urgency and priority values are both high. Monitor reports that possess level IL1 take precedence over any activity the user may be engaged in, and cause the speaking agent to interrupt the user immediately, even interrupting other speech-based presentations in which the user may be engaged. The next level (IL2) prescribes that the user should be interrupted only when the audio channel becomes free; it corresponds to monitor reports having high urgency and low priority values. The interruption level IL3 corresponds to monitor reports with low urgency and high priority, and it dictates that these monitor reports should be conveyed to the user only when the user logs in to the workstation[15]. Finally, the interruption level IL4 is applied to all monitor reports that have corresponding low values of urgency and priority, and it prescribes that these monitor reports should never be conveyed to the user.

Interruption level	Precedence	Definition	Degree of intrusiveness	Action
IL1	High	urgency = high **and** priority = high	High (most intrusive)	Interrupt immediately (after the next break in current speech ouput)
IL2	Normal	urgency = high **and** priority = low	Medium (intrusive)	Interrupt at the next user break (end of video clip, on-line lecture, or music track)
IL3	Low	urgency = low **and** priority = high	Low (non-intrusive)	Interrupt at the next user login (with a reminder)
IL4	Null	urgency = low **and** priority = low	Null	Do not bother to interrupt

Table 5. Definition of monitor reports *Precedence* as *Interruption Levels*.

The simple model described above could easily be extended by augmenting the granularity of the urgency and priority values beyond the two basic Low and High levels. For example, if it is desirable to include a normal value for both urgency and priority, it could be specified that all monitor reports possessing normal urgency or normal priority should possess an interruption level IL2.

Given that low urgency and high priority monitor reports (IL3) should only be conveyed whenever the user returns to the physical location of the workstation, this has two implications. First, this means that the notifications with an associated IL3 level are never conveyed to the user, but the information they refer to will later be conveyed under the form of a reminder, when the user logs back in to the workstation. Second, it is necessary to endow the specialised agents with the ability to detect those occasions in which the user logs in. This service is performed by the user monitor agent, which provides updated information about the user's presence to the specialised agents.

There is an additional consideration to be incorporated in the design. Whenever there is a new piece of information, this raises the need to convey a notification. However, if the user is not present, or if the notification has low precedence (IL3), it will not be conveyed, but there is still the need to alert

---

[15] The computer system adopted automatically logs out the user after a set period of inactivity (no mouse movement or keyboard use).

the user to the piece of information at a later time using a reminder. Therefore, the specialised agents need to maintain a *record* that describes the monitor reports concerning pieces of information that have already been sent to the speaking agent (and conveyed to the user), and the pieces of information that were not yet conveyed to the user, but were scheduled to be conveyed at a later time through a reminder.

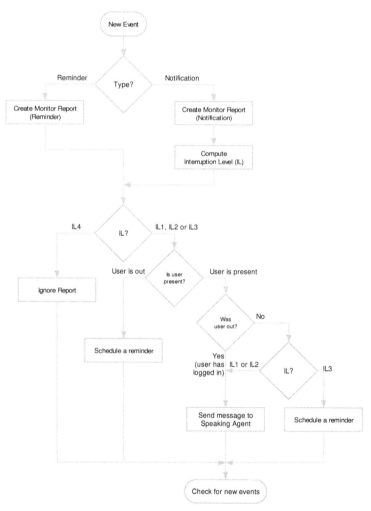

Figure 12. Deciding when to interrupt with notifications and reminders.

The process of deciding when to convey notifications and reminders is illustrated in Figure 12. As shown, whenever there is a new event (which corresponds to the detection of a new piece of information, or to a scheduled reminder) the specialised agent first checks whether this corresponds to a notification or a reminder. If this is a notification, the agent creates a new monitor report assuming the form of a notification and computes its interruption level according to the contents of the new piece of information. If this is a reminder, there is no need to calculate the interruption level since it has already been computed at the time the new piece of information was first detected. Then, the specialised agent enters a decision process that first eliminates the monitor reports with both low urgency and priority (IL4).

For the remaining reports (with levels IL1, IL2 and IL3), the agent decides what to do based on the user's presence, If the user is not present, the agent schedules a reminder and waits for new events. If the user is present, then the agent has to check whether the user just logged in. If the user has just logged in, then the agent may convey any notification or reminder regardless of its interruption level, and does this by sending a message to the speaking agent. However, if the user has been logged in for some time, there is the need to check the interruption level of the monitor report. If the monitor report has an associated IL1 or IL2 level, then the monitor report can be sent to the speaking agent to be delivered to the user. But if the monitor report has an associated level of IL3, it should only be conveyed at the user's next log in, and the agent schedules a reminder to be conveyed at that time.

The decision process just described can be regarded both as a scheme for determining when to interrupt the user, which acts as a filtering mechanism, and as an interruption model that adapts to each user's preferences in terms of the urgency and priority values associated with new pieces of information. It also demonstrates that deciding when to interrupt must attend to two different criteria: (1) the predicted precedence of a monitor report, and (2) the user's context, which has simply been modelled as the user's presence.

The general decision process illustrated in Figure 12 must however be slightly refined for each specialised agent in order to meet the specific requirements associated with reporting about e-mail messages, print jobs and diary entries. The specification of the decision process associated with each specialised agent is described in the following sections, along with examples that illustrate the resulting spoken messages that are conveyed to the user.

5.3.2.   E-mail agent

The specialised e-mail agent builds notifications concerning newly arrived e-mail messages and builds reminders concerning messages received that were not yet read by the user. Of course, these notifications and reminders are subject to urgency and priority values that depend on the user's preferences.

The e-mail agent continuously monitors the user's e-mail inbox and maintains an updated record of the status of the inbox. In this way, the agent is capable of determining which messages are new, and which messages remain unread or have already been read by the user.

In order to determine the notifications and reminders that should be issued, the e-mail agent maintains four different lists of messages: a list containing *old unread* messages, a list containing *new unread* messages, a *notifications* list containing new messages to be notified to the user, and a list containing messages that should be issued as *reminders*. Using these lists, the e-mail agent applies the following process.

First it fetches unread messages from the user's inbox and stores these messages in the *new unread* list. Then, for each unread message existing in the *unread* list, the agent checks if the message also exists in the *new unread* list. If the message is *not* present in the *new unread* list, it means that the user has already read the message and it is not necessary to remind the user to read it; the message can be discarded from the *unread* list. If there was a reminder in the *reminders* list about this message, then it should also be discarded from that list. However, if the unread message also *exists* in the *new unread* list, it means that the user has not yet read the message, and the agent moves this message into the *reminders* list, and discards it from both the *new unread* and *unread* lists.

Every message remaining in the *new unread* list is a candidate to be part of a notification. After determining the message's interruption level, the agent copies IL1 and IL2 messages into the *notifications* list and IL3 messages into the *reminders* list. The last step performed by the e-mail agent includes moving every message from the *new unread* list into the *unread* list.

After building these lists, the e-mail agent will build a notification concerning the messages stored in the *notifications* list, and it will check for a user login in order to build a reminder concerning the messages contained in the *reminders* list. But what happens to reminders if the user does not leave the workstation for a long period of time? In this case, the e-mail agent has a pre-defined policy concerning the issuing of reminders at specific times of the day. For example, the e-mail agent may issue reminders at fixed times such as 9:00 am, 12:00 am, and 5:00 pm. Of course, these settings may be adjusted or overridden by the user so as to enable the agent to conform more closely to a user's requirements.

When building the notifications and reminders, the agent extracts the cues given in Table 3. For example, suppose that at a given instant the e-mail agent has two e-mail messages in the *notifications* list, one from Dr. Benest and the other from the Agent-news distribution list. The spoken message that could be delivered concerning the notification issued by the e-mail agent might be one of the following:

"You've got two new e-mail messages."

"There are two new e-mail messages from Dr. Benest and Agent-news."

"You've got two new e-mail messages, including ones from Dr. Benest and Agent-news. Subjects of these messages include: conference paper and news for the agent research community."

Now, suppose that the message was not conveyed to the user, so that it needs to be conveyed at a later time under the form of a reminder. The possible alternatives include:

"Don't forget you have two unread e-mail messages in your inbox."

"You've still got two unread e-mail messages from Dr. Benest and Agent-news."

"Did you remember to check the two e-mail messages you left in your inbox? They were sent by Dr. Benest and Agent-news. The messages cover: conference paper and news for the agent research community."

5.3.3.   Printer agent

The specialised printer agent keeps track of the user's printed documents by continuously monitoring the printer queues for print jobs belonging to the user. The agent builds notifications concerning the position of the user's documents in the printer queue as soon as the user prints them. The agent also builds reminders whenever the printer finishes printing the documents. As far as the urgency and priority values are concerned, by default the printer agent considers all documents to be urgent, unless the user specifies a different urgency value for each type of document. For example, printed word processor documents and Portable Document Format (PDF) documents might be assigned with high urgency, whereas e-mail messages might be assigned with low urgency.

In order to determine the notifications and reminders that should be issued, the printer agent can follow a list-based approach similar to the one described for the e-mail agent. In this case, the printer agent maintains two different lists describing print jobs: the *middle* list contains print jobs issued by the user where the position in the printer queue is greater than one, while the *printing* list contains the print jobs issued by the user, which are currently in the first position, and are being printed on one of the system default printers.

The printer agent keeps checking the user's printer queues and whenever it detects a new print job issued by the user (identified through the username) it reads the position of the print job in the queue. If the position is greater than one, the agent verifies the *middle* list to check if the print job was already printing. If not, this means that it is a new document, and the agent builds a notification reporting its position in the particular queue.

If the position of the print job is equal to one, it means that the document has started printing. In this case, the document might have been waiting in the queue and it just started printing, or it may have entered an empty queue. This is an important distinction because the agent should *not* notify the user that a document is printing if it has been waiting in the queue and the user has already been notified that it is there. However, it is important to notify the user when a new print job entered the empty queue directly to the first position.

In order to achieve this behaviour, the agent first checks if the print job that is in the first position of the queue is mentioned in the *middle* list. If it is in the *middle* list, then this means that the print job finally started printing, and there is no need to notify the user about it. The agent removes this job from the *middle* list and adds it to the *printing* list. However, if this job is not in the *middle* list, it means that it corresponds to a new print job, and the agent adds it to the *printing* list and builds a notification reporting that the document has started printing.

The agent also keeps comparing its own *printing* list with the relevant printer queues it monitors. Whenever the agent detects that there is a print job in the *printing* list, which no longer appears in the printer queue, it means that the printer has finished printing the document, and the agent removes the job from the *printing* list and builds a reminder to alert the user for a document that can be collected from the printer tray.

When building the notifications and reminders, the printer agent uses the cues described in Table 3, which are extracted from the information existing in the printer queues. For example, if at a given instant the printer agent detects one word processor document in the third position of the printer whose ID is pp07, the spoken message that could be conveyed to notify the user might be one of the following:

"Your document is waiting to be printed."

"The printer is quite busy at the moment."

"Your word processor document is waiting in the printer queue."

"Your word processor document is waiting behind two others."

"Your word processor document is waiting for another two on printer pp07."

Supposing that this document entered the first position of the printer's queue, the appropriate spoken messages for the notification include the following:

"Your document has started printing!"

"Your word processor document is printing right now."

"Your word processor document is about to be printed on printer pp07."

Finally, when this document finishes printing, the reminder could be conveyed through one of the following alternatives:

"Your document has just finished printing."

"The document you sent to the printer is now ready."

"Your word processor document is finally printed."

"The word processor document you printed is now ready on printer pp07."

5.3.4.   Diary agent

The specialised diary agent keeps track of appointments and to-dos entered in the user's diary. The agent builds notifications concerning the imminence of scheduled appointments (issued a pre-defined amount of time before the appointment is due, which is adjustable by the user), and notifications concerning the start of scheduled appointments (issued at the start time entered in the user's diary). The agent builds reminders concerning past appointments (in the cases where the user has missed the notifications when away from the workstation), and reminders concerning to-do's entered in the diary (which by definition do not possess a start time, nor a duration).

In order to determine the notifications and reminders that should be issued, the diary agent has to apply a decision process similar to the one illustrated in Figure 13. As shown, the diary agent checks the user diary for the occurrence of scheduled appointments and triggers a new event at a pre-defined time before the appointment is due, and another event at the time the appointment is due. In the first case, the agent checks for the user's presence. If the user is present, the agent issues a notification about the *imminence* of the appointment, in order to allow the user to have sufficient time to prepare to attend the event. If the user is not present, then the agent records that the user missed this notification.

As soon as the due time triggers the occurrence of a new event, the agent checks if the user is present, and if so it builds a notification alerting the user for the *start* of the event, as recorded in the user's diary. In this case, it is no longer important to keep a record that the user missed the imminence notification, and the agent clears the missed record before waiting for the occurrence of new events. However, if the user is not present at this time, there are two possibilities: either the user did not miss the imminence notification and is already away for the appointment, or the user missed the imminence notification, in which case the agent is unsure of whether the user remembered the appointment. In the first case, the agent does not need to issue another notification since the user is already away, and it waits for the next event.

In the latter case, the agent will check for the user's presence until either there is a new event or the user is back. If there is a new event, this means that the last appointment is no longer valid (because there is a new one in the user's diary), and there is no point alerting the user about it. In this case the agent resumes the normal operation for a new event. Of course, this corresponds to a simplification of the problem in that it does not cater for the cases where there are overlapping events.

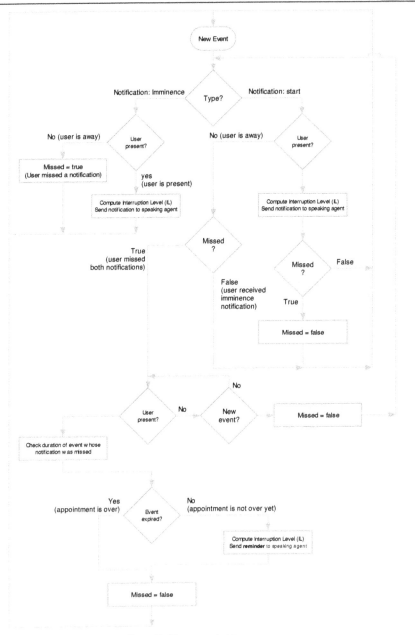

Figure 13. Diary agent decision process.

Returning to the discussion, if the user is back before a new event is triggered, the agent has to decide whether it is still important to remind the user about an appointment that has already started, which the user may have forgotten to attend. In this case, the agent checks for the duration of the missed appointment in the user's diary, and if the appointment is not over yet, the agent issues a *reminder* to alert the user that the appointment has already started but still valid. If the appointment is already over, then the agent clears the missed record and waits for a new event without interrupting the user with another message.

When building the notifications and reminders, the diary agent uses the cues described in Table 3, which are extracted from the entries in the user's diary. For example, if at a given instant the diary agent detects the *imminence* of a seminar about software agent architectures in the user's diary, it may issue a *notification* that results in the speaking agent conveying one of the following spoken messages:

"Your seminar starts in less than 5 minutes."

"You have a seminar starting in less than 5 minutes in CS105."

"You have a seminar starting in less than 5 minutes in CS105. It is about software agent architectures."

The corresponding notifications that may be issued at the due time include for example:

"Your seminar is due to start at this moment."

"You have a seminar starting right now in CS105."

"Seminar is due to start at this moment in CS105. Don't forget it is about software agent architectures."

In case the user missed the notifications, but the seminar is not over yet, the reminders that could be delivered include the following:

"Don't forget your seminar started a few minutes ago."

"Your seminar has already started in CS105."

"Did you remember your seminar that started a few moments ago in CS105? It is about software agent architectures."

5.4   Communication protocol

5.4.1.   Message structure

The communication protocol establishes the rules for communication between the specialised agents comprising the experimental environment. The protocol defines the format, or structure, that a message must take, the meaning of the message, the meaning of the information enclosed in the message, and the way in which the software agents exchange messages.

As far as the structure is concerned, the messages exchanged within the experimental environment are composed by a collection of data fields sent and received together. All messages contain a header constituted by four fields and a payload, which encloses the contents of the message, according to the following format:

messageType

    :senderID <string>

    :receiverID <string>

    :contentType <string>

    :content <string expression>

The **messageType** field identifies the type of communication action the sending agent is trying to achieve with this message. As stated earlier, within the experimental environment there are two possible actions: either an agent is trying to *assert* some information that it wants the other agent to possess, or trying to *confirm the acceptance* of some information that it has received.

The **senderID** identifies unequivocally the sending agent while the **receiverID** has the same purpose for the receiving party. The IDs have the following form <agentType>#<xxxx>, where <xxxx> represents an integer with four digits. This format was designed so as to ensure that similar types of agent could co-exist in the experimental environment. For example, if the designer decides that there should be two specialised e-mail agents in the environment, one to interface with E-mail application A and another for application B, the designer might associate respectively the IDs email#0001 and email#0002 to each agent.

The **contentType** field allows the receiving agent to know how to interpret and process the message contents conveyed in the **content** field. Thus, the **contentType** string describes the intended meaning of the message contents enclosed within the **content** field.

5.4.2.   Message types

The message types define the meaning of the messages exchanged between the software agents that comprise the experimental environment. As stated above, there are two fundamental categories of messages: *assertions* and *acceptances*.

Within the assertions category, there are two different types of message: *inform* and *subscribe*. The *inform* type is used by the specialised agents to enclose notifications and reminders, which are sent to the speaking agent that converts them into spoken language and conveys them to the user through speech output. The *inform* message type is also used by the user monitor agent to enclose user presence information that it sends to the specialised agents. Examples of this type of message include:

inform

  :**senderID** email#0001

  :**receiverID** speaking#0001

  :**contentType** NOTIFICATION

  :**content** <string expression>

inform

  :**senderID** userMonitor#0001

  :**receiverID** email#0001

  :**contentType** USER_PRESENCE_UPDATE

  :**content** <string expression>

The *subscribe* type of message is used by the specialised agents to subscribe to services provided by service agents such as the user monitor agent. For example, the printer agent might subscribe to the user presence information service by sending the following message to the user monitor agent:

subscribe

> :**senderID** printer#0001
>
> :**receiverID** userMonitor#0001
>
> :**contentType** REQUEST_USER_PRESENCE
>
> :**content** <string expression>

Currently, the protocol only includes one type of message within the acceptances category – the *acknowledge* type. Any agent that receives a message from a sender agent uses the *acknowledge* type of message to reply and confirm the acceptance of the original message. For example, the speaking agent might confirm the reception of an *inform* message sent by the diary agent using the following message:

acknowledge

> :**senderID** speaking#0001
>
> :**receiverID** diary#0001
>
> :**contentType** CONFIRM_RECEPTION
>
> :**content** <string expression>

5.4.3.   Message contents semantics

The message contents enclose all the information an agent wishes to communicate to another agent that exists in the experimental environment. From the point of view of the meaning of the message contents, the most important and complex messages are the ones that convey notifications and reminders generated by the specialised agents.

Beyond these complex messages, there are simpler messages for requesting user presence information, conveying user presence information and for confirming message reception. The types of message content defined in the communication protocol are illustrated in Table 6.

contentType (string)	Purpose
NOTIFICATION_IMMINENCE	To communicate cue information required to assemble a spoken message concerning the **imminent occurrence** of an event.
NOTIFICATION	To communicate cue information required to assemble a spoken message concerning the **occurrence** of an event.
REMINDER	To communicate cue information required to assemble a spoken message concerning the **past occurrence** of an event.
USER_PRESENCE_UPDATE	To communicate the **instant** at which the user presence changed, and the **current status** of the user's presence.
REQUEST_USER_PRESENCE	To communicate the **instant** at which the user's presence service was **requested**.
CONFIRM_RECEPTION	To communicate the **instant** at which the original message was **received**.

Table 6. Types of message content.

contentType (string)	content (expression fields)	Data Type	Example
NOTIFICATION_IMMINENCE NOTIFICATION REMINDER	Interruption Level	string	IL1, IL2, IL3
	Kind	string	EMAIL, PRINTER, DIARY
	Time stamp	date/time	25-02-2001 10:35
	Quantity	integer	3
	People	string list	(Dr. Benest, Nuno)
	Nature	string list	(picture, webpage, PDF document)
	Description	string list	(conference paper deadline, news from PT)
	Place	string list	(University of York, CEREM)
USER_PRESENCE_UPDATE	Time stamp	date/time	25-02-2001 10:35
	User present	Boolean	0,1
REQUEST_USER_PRESENCE CONFIRM_RECEPTION	Time stamp	date/time	25-02-2001 10:35

Table 7. Description of message contents.

The first three types of message illustrated in Table 6 are designed to convey the contextual cues gathered by the specialised agents, while the remaining messages merely convey status and temporal information. The message contents that correspond to the content types defined above are illustrated in Table 7.

As shown, the most complex content types, which correspond to the notifications and reminders, include up to eight expression fields that accommodate the interruption level associated with the monitor report and the context cues extracted by the specialised agents.

In order to illustrate the way in which the protocol is used by the agents to communicate, it is important to analyse some examples. For example, suppose that the diary agent detects the imminence of a seminar about agent architectures, which is scheduled to occur in CS105 at 2:00 pm. The full message generated by the diary agent has the following aspect:

inform

      :senderID diary#0001

      :receiverID speaking#0001

      :contentType NOTIFICATION_IMMINENCE

      :content IL1; DIARY; 15-05-2001 14:00; 1; Null; seminar; agent architectures; CS105

This message informs the speaking agent that there is a diary event about to start (it starts at 2:00 pm), the notification of which should interrupt the user immediately. The event refers to a seminar about agent architectures, which will occur in room CS105. Note that unused expression fields carry the Null value.

The corresponding spoken message that might be created by the speaking agent might be:

   "You have a seminar starting in less than five minutes in CS105. It is about agent architectures"

The notification that corresponds to this event is quite similar, but the **contentType** is changed to NOTIFICATION, and this changes the meaning of the spoken message that should be conveyed to the user. The full notification message has the following aspect:

inform

      :senderID diary#0001

      :receiverID speaking#0001

      :contentType NOTIFICATION

      :content IL1; DIARY; 15-05-2001 14:00; 1; Null; seminar; agent architectures; CS105

The corresponding spoken message might be:

   "Your seminar is starting right now in CS105. It is about agent architectures"

Revisiting the example given before for the e-mail agent (see section 5.3.2), suppose that it detects two new messages in the user's inbox: one from Dr. Benest and the other from the Agent-news distribution list. The message assembled by the e-mail agent appears as follows:

inform

> **:senderID** email#0001
>
> **:receiverID** speaking#0001
>
> **:contentType** NOTIFICATION
>
> **:content** IL1; 03-12-2001 15:40; mail; 2; (Dr. Benest, Agent-news); Null; (conference paper, news for the agent research community); Null.

The corresponding spoken message conveyed by the speaking agent might be:

> *"You've got two new e-mail messages, including ones from Dr. Benest and Agent-news. Subjects of these messages include: conference paper and news for the agent research community."*

One final example illustrates a message sent by the user monitor agent to the printer agent informing it of the user's logout at 6:37 pm:

inform

> **:senderID** userMonitor#0001
>
> **:receiverID** printer#0001
>
> **:contentType** USER_PRESENCE_UPDATE
>
> **:content** 03-12-2001 18:37; 0

5.5   Speaking Agent

5.5.1.   Architecture

The speaking agent acts as an interface agent: it is responsible for managing the interaction between the user and the experimental environment.

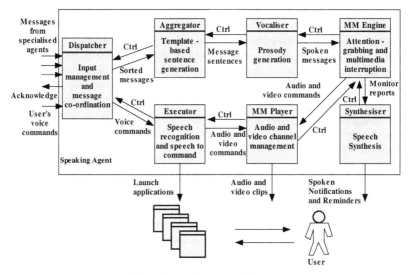

Figure 14. Speaking agent architecture.

The speaking agent receives messages from the specialised agents, conveys the corresponding spoken monitor reports, and controls the delivery of multimedia presentations. It also listens to the user's spoken commands, and modifies the interface as appropriate; for example by interrupting other on-going multimedia presentations to convey a spoken message. Spoken commands may cause multimedia clips to be played or might launch other requested applications. Essentially, the speaking agent is the experimental environment's component that is responsible for realising the humanisation of the interaction.

The internal architecture of the speaking agent is depicted in Figure 14. As shown, the internal components perform the various functions associated with message input management and co-ordination (*dispatcher*), humanised spoken language generation (*aggregator* and *vocaliser*), humanised interruption management (*multimedia engine*), and output generation (*executor*, *multimedia player* and *synthesiser*). The following sections detail the design of each of these components.

5.5.2.   Receiving and co-ordinating messages

The speaking agent's sensors are embedded in the first component: the dispatcher. Conceptually, the dispatcher acts as the speaking agent's action *co-ordinator*: it is responsible for receiving all external communications, either messages from the specialised agents, or the user's spoken commands, and for distributing these messages to the appropriate internal components.

The communication between the specialised agents and the speaking agent is based on an asynchronous method. Following this method, messages that arrive at the speaking agent do not block its execution. The dispatcher is responsible for monitoring an *incoming queue* of messages, sorting the messages according to their *interruption level* and for replying to the sender agent with an acknowledge signal as soon as its message has been processed.

All the specialised agent's messages processed by the speaking agent end up as monitor reports that are spoken to the user. However, it must be noted that messages arrive at an unpredictable rate from the specialised agents, and that there is an important distinction between messages with high precedence (IL1), normal precedence (IL2) and low precedence (IL3)- As was described in section 5.3.1.3: IL1 messages should interrupt the user immediately, IL2 messages should be conveyed the next time the audio channel is free, and IL3 messages are only conveyed when the user logs back in. In order to accommodate these distinctions, the dispatcher manages an additional *scheduling queue* that orders the delivery of spoken messages to the user. Using the queue, the dispatcher sorts and dispatches received messages according to their *interruption levels* and *time stamps*.

The dispatcher sorts messages in a way that ensures that IL1 messages always get the first queue positions, while IL2 messages wait in the queue until two conditions are met: there are no more IL1 messages and the dispatcher receives control information (Ctrl) signalling that the audio channel is free. Since the specialised agents only send IL3 messages when they receive information that the user has just logged in, IL3 messages do not differ from IL2 messages as far as the dispatcher is concerned, and thus they receive the same treatment. This ensures that, if for example an IL1 message arrives while an IL2 message is still waiting for the audio channel to be free, the IL1 message takes precedence over the waiting IL2 message and gets delivered to the user according to its precedence.

However, because messages arrive at an unpredictable rate from the specialised agents, it is also necessary to sort and dispatch messages according to their time stamps. This may happen, for example, when two IL1 messages arrive at the dispatcher's incoming queue. In this situation, it is necessary to sort the messages according to their time stamps. In this way, the dispatcher ensures that no message is lost, and avoids timing inconsistencies in the chronological delivery of messages. Additionally, a message should not be dispatched to the spoken language generation components while a previous message is being processed. Thus, the scheduling queue holds the messages until the dispatcher receives control information signalling the end of the processing of a previous message.

The dispatcher is also responsible for passing user's input voice commands to the component which controls the speech recogniser and converts user's input into appropriate commands. As before, these commands must be held and dispatched only when the processing of previous commands is finished. Note that the speaking agent does not perform any spoken dialogue management. This means that the speaking agent is not designed to maintain a conversation with the user. The main objective of the speaking agent is to provide an environment suitable for testing the assembly and delivery of humanised spoken reports, and therefore only limited user speech input was included in the design.

5.5.3.   Language generation with variation

The speaking agent's components responsible for the generation of humanised spoken monitor reports are the *aggregator* and the *vocaliser*. The *aggregator* is in charge of analysing the context cues embedded in the messages and aggregating them into a set of coherent English-language sentences. A fundamental part of this sentence generation process involves the inclusion of linguistic variation, more specifically the generation of linguistically varied sentences through the inclusion of lexical and syntactical variation, as explained in section 2.3.3.1. The *vocaliser* then takes the sentences generated by the aggregator and annotates them with prosodic information, in order to obtain more natural sounding utterances with a degree of phonetic variation, as explained in section 2.3.3.2.

The generation of linguistically varied sentences is achieved through the use of templates. Templates are fixed natural language expressions that contain variable slots. Whenever a template is activated, it is necessary to determine both the values of the template variables, and an appropriate natural language expression that describes them (see also section 2.3.3.1). The aggregator constructs sentences by first selecting a template from a template-base, whose slots are then filled-in with the appropriate context cues conveyed in the messages received from the specialised agents.

The template-base contains language templates organised by sections according to the different types of monitor reports they support. Thus, one section contains the templates for assembling e-mail notifications, another section contains templates for creating e-mail reminders, and so on for every kind of monitor report that can be generated by the speaking agent. The template-base was omitted from Figure 14 for the sake of simplicity, but Figure 15 reproduces a part of the template-base used by the aggregator for the generation of notifications and reports concerning the e-mail domain. Appendix A illustrates the full template-base that was developed for the system prototype.

Every section of the template-base is further organised according to the length of the sentences; these range from very brief to long messages. This aspect was included in the design in order to provide an additional source of variation, and to accommodate different user's preferences concerning the length of the spoken messages. For example, while for user A it may be sufficient to listen to shorter messages with fewer context cues, user B may feel more comfortable with longer, and contextually richer, spoken messages.

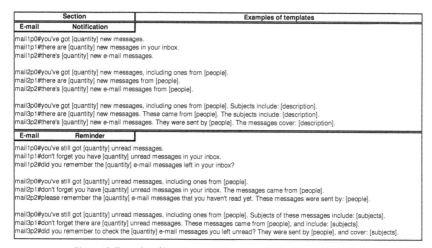

Figure 15. Examples of language generation templates for the e-mail domain.

Figure 15 illustrates that there are three possible modes for message length, the selection of which is performed by consulting a user profile maintained by the speaking agent. The shorter messages only include the *quantity* cue. The medium length messages include two cues, which depend on the monitor report being generated. For example, for e-mail reports the cues are *quantity* and *people*, for printer reports the cues are *quantity* and *description*, and for diary reports the cues include *quantity* and *place*. The longer messages include at least three cues, and may include as much information as the total number of cues gathered by the specialised agents.

For example, Figure 15 illustrates that a longer e-mail monitor report includes the *quantity*, *people* and *description*, while a longer diary monitor report includes the *quantity*, *place* and *description* cues.

Figure 15 also illustrates how lexical and syntactical variation may be achieved. The templates contained in the template-base are stored according to a simple index-based schema such as the following: <index>#<template>. By providing a number of different templates for each kind of monitor report, it is possible to assemble different sentences on different occasions whilst maintaining the meaning of the monitor report. This is achieved in the following way: whenever the aggregator is to select a template to assemble a sentence, or a set of sentences, it constructs an index that it will use to fetch one specific template from the template-base. This index identifies the template by specifying the source domain of information, the length, the number for singular or plural selection, and finally the template number.

For example, the index *mail3p0* allows the aggregator to fetch a template for an e-mail monitor report (*mail*), which corresponds to a longer spoken message (*length type 3*), refers to multiple e-mail messages (code *p* for plural), and selects template number 0. Given that there are a number of templates for each possible situation, the next time a similar message has to be conveyed, the aggregator can select template number 1 instead (index *mail3p1*).

Of course, this simple schema for including linguistic variation relies on the proper design of lexically and syntactically varied templates. However, the amount of effort involved in the creation of such templates has the potential to provide for more natural sounding messages than with a more automatic natural language generation approach.

Referring to the example given in section 5.4.3 about a notification concerning the arrival of two new e-mail messages, the definition of the content including the context cues contained in the message assembled by the specialised e-mail agent is as follows:

:**contentType** NOTIFICATION

:**content** IL1; EMAIL; 03-12-2001 15:40; 2; (Dr. Benest, Agent-news); Null; (conference paper, news for the agent research community); Null.

When the aggregator analyses this message's *contentType* and *content* fields, it uses that information to select a template from the template-base section "E-mail Notification". Furthermore, by analysing the information contained in the *quantity* field (2), the aggregator will select a template designed for generating a plural sentence. The aggregator then consults the user profile to determine the user's preferred length for spoken messages, and it then fills in the appropriate template slots with the information provided in the message's content fields. For example, suppose that the user's setting for message length is medium (message type 2), the aggregator would then have three different templates (see Figure 15) for generating the sentences corresponding to this spoken message. Given that the last time the aggregator selected template number 0, it could now select template number 1, and the resulting sentences would be the following:

"There are two new messages from Dr. Benest and Agent-news"

Note that the template does not specify any *connection particles* such as the "and" that was automatically inserted by the aggregator between the words "Benest" and "Agent-news". This was achieved because the field containing the cue *people* is defined as a list (see Table 7), so the aggregator itself included the particle "and" before the last element of the list. This processing is also valid for other fields defined as lists.

Figure 16 reproduces additional sections from the template-base, which provide examples of language generation templates for the printing and the diary domains. These additional examples illustrate the design of templates for the cases where *quantity* is one (singular).

One concern that this work addresses is that the language generation and the text-to-speech (TTS) components used in current systems are not closely coupled; that is, the same text is generated whether it is intended to be read or spoken (Zue, 1997). By integrating both components as described in this book, the speaking agent allows for the possibility of controlling both the language and the text-to-speech generation. By including the vocaliser component the speaking agent both generates language and annotates it with prosodic information in order to produce the utterances without requiring the text-to-speech component to perform linguistic analysis.

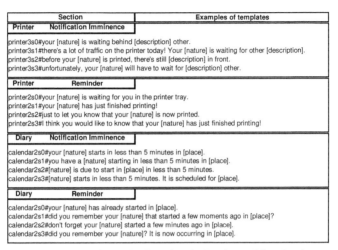

Section	Examples of templates
Printer Notification Imminence	
printer3s0#your [nature] is waiting behind [description] other. printer3s1#there's a lot of traffic on the printer today! Your [nature] is waiting for other [description]. printer3s2#before your [nature] is printed, there's still [description] in front. printer3s3#unfortunately, your [nature] will have to wait for [description] other.	
Printer Reminder	
printer2s0#your [nature] is waiting for you in the printer tray. printer2s1#your [nature] has just finished printing! printer2s2#just to let you know that your [nature] is now printed. printer2s3#I think you would like to know that your [nature] has just finished printing!	
Diary Notification Imminence	
calendar2s0#your [nature] starts in less than 5 minutes in [place]. calendar2s1#you have a [nature] starting in less than 5 minutes in [place]. calendar2s2#[nature] is due to start in [place] in less than 5 minutes. calendar2s3#[nature] starts in less than 5 minutes. It is scheduled for [place].	
Diary Reminder	
calendar2s0#your [nature] has already started in [place]. calendar2s1#did you remember your [nature] that started a few moments ago in [place]? calendar2s2#don't forget your [nature] started a few minutes ago in [place]. calendar2s3#did you remember your [nature]? It is now occurring in [place].	

Figure 16. Additional examples of templates for the printer and diary domains.

The *vocaliser* analyses the sentences passed by the aggregator and pre-processes the text to identify special constructs of the English language, such as e-mail addresses, dates, times, numbers, and a limited number of common abbreviations which it expands.

In order to include phonetic variation, the *vocaliser* then annotates the resulting sentences with special markers that operate slight changes in the prosody of the resulting utterances. These changes include emphasising particular words, varying pause time, changes in pitch and changes in speaking rate. In this way, a particular utterance can be made to sound different on two different occasions.

5.5.4.   Incorporating politeness

The incorporation of politeness is achieved both at the *aggregator* and at the *multimedia engine* levels. At the sentence generation level, the inclusion of linguistic style is determined by the design of the language generation templates, adopting the first approach suggested in section 2.4.3. For example, the e-mail notification mentioned above, might be conveyed through different politeness strategies, as the following expressions illustrate.

"There are two new messages from Dr. Benest and Agent-news" (I)

"I think you might want to check your e-mail as there are two new messages from Dr. Benest and Agent-news" (II)

"You might consider checking your e-mail, as there are two new messages from Dr. Benest and Agent-news" (III)

"It seems that there are two important messages in your inbox from Dr. Benest and Agent-news" (IV)

The politeness strategy expressed in expression I is clearly a direct strategy, as the information is communicated in a very straightforward way. Expression II illustrates a positive politeness strategy, as it is implied that the information is given according to the person's interests. Expression III illustrates a negative politeness strategy, as the information is given in a more indirect way, a style that allows people to feel they are not being forced to follow a future course of action. Finally, expression IV illustrates an off-the-record strategy, which is expressed in the most indirect way, and might lead the person to appreciate that the system is unsure about the importance of the information being conveyed.

At the *multimedia engine* level, politeness is included through the insertion of specific attention-grabbers that slightly change the style of the resulting utterance. Attention-grabbing is an important function of proper interruption, which ensures the person is aware of an imminent communication, and prevents losing the alerting content that follows, as discussed in section 2.2.3.

Continuing with the e-mail notification example given above, the spoken message might convey two very different linguistic styles when preceded by two different attention-grabbers, as the following examples illustrate:

"Excuse me, but..." + *"There are two new messages from Dr. Benest and Agent-news"*

"Attention..." + *"There are two new messages from Dr. Benest and Agent-news"*

The first expression obtains the user's attention in a more indirect way by adopting an off-the-record strategy for interrupting, while the other is a more direct strategy.

Another potentially interesting alternative would be to use small audio snippets that mimic for example airport announcements, but this was not adopted in this system.

5.5.5.   Interrupting the audio channel

It has just been mentioned that the *multimedia engine* inserts spoken attention-grabbers to alert the user to the imminence of a potentially interesting notification or reminder. However, knowing how to interrupt is not solely about properly getting a person's attention. Section 2.2.3 also discussed the need to provide a smooth transition in the user's attention from the current activity to the contents of the interruption and back to the original activity.

The *multimedia engine* was designed to explore one kind of smooth transition: that which relates to the interruption of the audio channel. The main objective is to minimise the disruption caused by a sudden interruption in the audio channel, by employing a technique based on fading out the original source, conveying the speech-based message and then fading in the original audio presentation.

In order to achieve this behaviour, the multimedia engine needs to be able control the presentation of multimedia content (e.g. audio and video clips), and to be able to modulate the multimedia output channels, especially the audio channel. This was achieved through the inclusion of a *multimedia* player component as part of the speaking agent.

There are two distinct approaches to interrupting the audio channel through fading: either the original presentation is stopped after it is faded out, or it continues to play in the background while the spoken message is conveyed through the speech synthesiser. Once the message has been delivered, the original audio presentation is gradually faded in, up to its original volume.

Both approaches pose interesting problems that might be addressed by future research. For example, suppose that the original multimedia presentation is a video clip that includes a narration, which the user is currently playing. If this presentation is stopped in order to convey a monitor report, the user's attention is necessarily deviated from the original presentation. Thus, when it is restarted after the presentation of the monitor report it is not sufficient to restart it playing at exactly the same point as when it was stopped because the user might not be able to fully recover the cognitive context which was lost because of the interruption. In this case, rewinding the original presentation to a key point might be an appropriate solution. Of course, this implies that some kind of content analysis should be performed in order to determine the location of these key points. On the other hand, if the original presentation is not stopped, but allowed to carry on playing in the background while the monitor report is conveyed, the user might lose important information that is conveyed during the elapsed time, and might not be able to follow the subsequent information presented as part of the original multimedia presentation.

A more tractable case occurs when the original audio presentation is a music track, and the *multimedia engine* was designed to address this case. It allows for testing both kinds of interruption: (1) a fade out – stop – fade in approach, and (2) a fade out to a background volume – continue playing – fade in to original volume approach.

After the insertion of the attention-grabbers, and after an appropriate fade is performed, the *multimedia engine* is ready to pass the utterances generated by the *vocaliser* to the speech synthesiser.

5.5.6.   Enhancing interactivity with speech input

The user is able to issue spoken commands to control the presentation of audio and video clips, and has the ability to invoke other applications. This is especially useful after the user has received a monitor report. For example, if the user receives a spoken notification about the arrival of important e-mail messages, the user might simply say "*Let's see the e-mail*", and the speaking agent launches, or brings to the front, the e-mail application that the user normally employs to check electronic mail. Similarly, users might like to summon the graphical presentation of the printer queues and their own diary whenever a notification or a reminder is conveyed.

The design of the speaking agent includes support for this kind of functionality. The user's spoken commands are processed by the dispatcher and routed to an *executor* component, which links to a speech recogniser, and supports a limited input grammar, which is used to associate recognised text with appropriate commands. The inclusion of this functionality may facilitate the future realisation of experiments concerning the usefulness of performing some actions at the interface following a full spoken dialogue style.

5.6   Prototype implementation

This section describes the speaking assistant prototype that has been implemented to accomplish the objectives of this research. The prototype is based on the design described in the previous sections. The implementation details presented in this section concern the specific platform chosen to deploy the prototype, the way in which the prototype components were implemented, and the storage structures used to hold user profiles and the template-base. Examples from a typical working session with the prototype are presented as a mean of illustrating the way the prototype may be used to support the implementation of experiments with end-users.

The prototype is meant to demonstrate the applicability of the speaking assistant design, and to provide a concrete experimental environment that allows evaluating the importance of anthropomorphic characteristics in reinforcing the social acceptability of a spoken language approach to information awareness.

5.6.1.   Rationale for development platform

The speaking assistant prototype was implemented with the empirical study in mind, and it implements the experimental environment architecture described above on a Windows NT platform. Windows was chosen because of its widespread presence both in the workplace and in home-computing environments, providing users with a familiar environment. Windows was also chosen because it provides only limited information awareness; searching for hidden information is distracting, it has only semantically poor notification cues, it superimposes notification windows on the top of the user's current workspace, and often presents dialog boxes with unimportant information. These current limitations make it an attractive environment to be complemented with a speech-based humanised assistant for information awareness. However, the design concepts and the architecture presented in the previous sections of this chapter could probably be implemented equally well in any other computer-based environment.

The experimental environment prototype encompasses the three specialised agents (the e-mail, printer and diary agents), one service agent (the user monitor agent), one interface agent (the speaking agent) and the inter-agent communication protocol.

The prototype is designed to be used in any Windows NT-based computer that is running the Microsoft Agent (Microsoft, 2001a) extensions, and suitable text-to-speech (TTS) and speech recognition engines[16]. Microsoft Agent is a software development kit (SDK) that enables the creation of animated characters for Windows environments. In essence, these characters can be seen as the physical representation of interface agents. Microsoft Agent enables the creation of interface characters via two distinct functionalities: a server for controlling the characters and a client Applications Programming Interface (API) for creating client applications that use the characters.

In concrete terms, the specialised agents and the service agent have been implemented as autonomous Windows applications. The speaking agent is also an autonomous Windows application, but it was implemented as a Microsoft Agent client. This enables the speaking assistant to use one of the Microsoft Agent characters as its physical presence at the interface. Figure 17 illustrates the character ("Merlin") used by default to represent the speaking agent at the interface. Microsoft Agent also enables animating the character, including synchronisation, but these features were not included in the objectives of the experimental environment.

Figure 17. The Microsoft Agent character (Merlin) used in the experimental environment

One advantage of providing the system with a graphical presence at the interface is that it helps the user to conceptualise the system as that particular interface object, and immediately attribute to it the spoken reports conveyed at the interface. Another advantage is that it may help the user to make sure that the system has not crashed, and that it is still actively monitoring the information sources it is supposed to observe.

The graphical character may however have the same adverse effects application windows cause, the elimination of which is precisely one of the objectives of this system: it may obscure other graphical information that is being accessed by the user as part of the current task. Therefore, the graphical character can be made to disappear from the graphical interface, without losing any of the system's alerting functionalities.

---

[16] The TTS engine provided as part of Microsoft Agent is based on the Lernout & Hauspie (L&H) TruVoice technology, which uses formant synthesis. The speech recogniser provided is the Microsoft Speech Recognition Engine, which offers such features as continuous speech recognition, speaker-independence, dynamic vocabularies and input grammars (Microsoft, 2001a).

5.6.2.   Specialised agents

All the specialised agents possess their own configuration windows, which enable the developer both to configure the agent and to monitor the agent's activities. Obviously, when the experimental environment is run, none of these windows appear in the graphical interface, and the only visible sign that the system is executing is the graphical character, which may be invoked by the user at any time.

Additionally, since the agents were designed as autonomous software components, it is possible to have any number of specialised agents at any given instant. So, if the user does not employ a diary, it is possible to execute just the e-mail and the printer agents.

E-mail agent

The e-mail agent is a software application that monitors the e-mail inbox defined by default at the operating system level, using the Mail Application Programming Interface[17] (MAPI). This enables the agent to use the e-mail application with which the user is most familiar. However, presently the e-mail agent is only capable of detecting new messages that arrive in the e-mail application's inbox.

This means that in the cases where the user has set up a number of e-mail filters within the e-mail application, which route new messages directly into storage folders, the e-mail agent will not be able to detect them. This limitation could be addressed in future versions of the e-mail agent.

Figure 18 depicts a typical working session with the e-mail agent, and it highlights its configuration window (not normally displayed).

It may be observed that at the instant Figure 18 was captured the e-mail agent had detected three new messages in the user's e-mail inbox, extracted the relevant context cues from those messages, and it had assembled a notification message (according to the protocol defined in section 5.4) that was sent to the speaking agent. All the messages possessed the highest precedence (interruption level IL1). The text box at the bottom of the configuration window in Figure 18 provides a visual indication of the context cues extracted from the e-mail messages, which were used to assemble the communication sent to the speaking agent. The remaining interface elements shown in the e-mail

---

[17] The Mail Application Programming Interface (MAPI) is a set of core system components that connect any mail-enabled application to MAPI-compliant information services. Additional information about the MAPI may be found in the MSDN Library (Microsoft, 2001b).

agent configuration window were only included for development purposes and are not normally visible to the user.

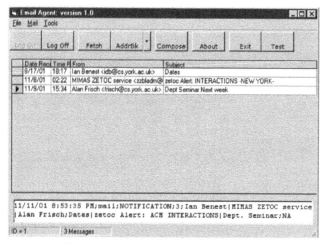

Figure 18. The E-mail Agent configuration window

Diary agent

The diary agent is an application that monitors the user's diary, which in the current implementation is simulated through a text file created by the prototype developer. This enables the developer to create an arbitrary number of appointments and to-dos in order to accommodate the different times at which the experiment may occur. The diary agent reads the simulated diary entries, and its configuration window presents them in separate text boxes for quick inspection. As with the e-mail agent, the text box at the bottom of the diary agent's configuration window exhibits the context cues extracted from the diary entries, which the diary agent included in the message sent to the speaking agent. In the instant Figure 19 was captured, the diary agent had just detected the imminence of a user's appointment (a seminar) and issued a notification concerning the imminence of the appointment.

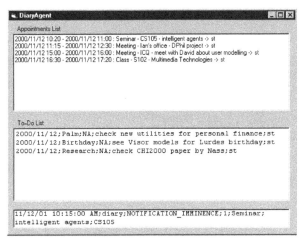

Figure 19. The Diary Agent configuration window

It will be seen from Figure 19 that the diary agent issued the notification exactly five minutes before the seminar's due time. Of course, this value may be adjusted by modifying an application parameter. Future work on the implementation of the diary agent might include this element as part of a user profile which was implemented as a text file that is read by the diary agent. By default, all the diary entries existing in the user's diary are considered as possessing the highest precedence (interruption level IL1). The future version of the diary agent would address this limitation and might enable the user to associate priority and urgency levels with the diary entries. It is also intended to enhance the diary agent implementation in order to make it able to communicate with the user's preferred diary application. This may be achieved for example by using the functionality provided by the vCalendar[18] standard.

Printer agent

The printer agent is an application that monitors the printer queues corresponding to the local or network printers available for access from a user's computer. The printer agent determines which documents belong to a user by comparing the username entered at login with the username that appears in the document descriptions contained in the printer queue.

---

[18] vCalendar defines a platform-independent transport format for exchanging diary and scheduling information concerning events and to-dos (Internet Mail Consortium, 1996).

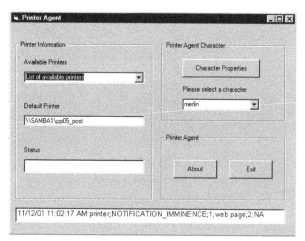

Figure 20. The Printer Agent configuration window

Figure 20 illustrates the printer agent configuration window, highlighting the network printer that the agent is currently monitoring. As before, the text box at the bottom of the configuration window illustrates the context elements the printer agent has extracted concerning a World Wide Web page recently printed by the user.

Given that the username of the current user is *nribeiro*, Figure 21 illustrates the printer queue status at the instant the document was sent to the printer, and shows that the document was waiting to be printed in the third position. Accordingly, the printer agent built a notification alerting the user that the user's document would have to wait behind two other documents, which were already in the printer queue.

In the current implementation, the printer agent is capable of detecting all installed printers, but it only monitors the printer queue the operating system indicates is the default. This is an obvious limitation since users may choose to print their documents on a printer other than the default, and these documents will obviously not be monitored. This issue might be addressed in a future implementation of the printer agent.

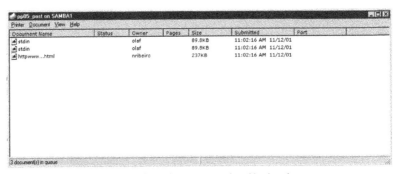

Figure 21. Status of the printer queue monitored by the printer agent

5.6.3.   Communication protocol

The implementation of the communication protocol followed the design of the message formats and contents presented in section 5.4. However, the method of interconnection was not specified in the design, because any asynchronous communication method is suitable to transport the messages exchanged between the agents used in the experimental environment.

In the current implementation, the method of interconnection elected to transport the messages between the agents was the Dynamic Data Exchange[19] (DDE) mechanism. This method was chosen because of its simplicity, and because it provided sufficient functionality to support the communication of messages between the agents. However, other message transport protocols (e.g. TCP[20]) could be employed.

The Dynamic Data Exchange protocol allows applications defined as *DDE Servers* (source of information) to send messages to other applications defined as *DDE Clients* (destination of information) through a *DDE Link*. However, the protocol also allows the reverse communication; that is, *DDE Clients* are allowed to send messages to *DDE Servers*. As far as the inter-agent

---

[19] Dynamic Data Exchange (DDE) is an asynchronous communication protocol based on shared memory, for transferring data between Windows applications. Additional information about the DDE protocol may be found in the MSDN Library (Microsoft, 2001b).

[20] TCP is the Transmission Control Protocol for the Internet suite. It is responsible for providing end-to-end reliable communication by ensuring that packets are received in the order they are sent, and that lost packets are re-transmitted (Stevens, 1995).

communication method is concerned, in the current implementation of the prototype the specialised agents act as *DDE Servers*, while the speaking agent acts as a *DDE Client*. The specialised agents use the *DDE Link* to send *inform* messages enclosing notifications and reminders to the speaking agent, while the speaking agent uses the *DDE Link* to reply with *acknowledge* messages.

5.6.4.   Speaking agent

The speaking agent was implemented as a client of Microsoft Agent, facilitating access to the text-to-speech (TTS) and to the speech recognition engines, and enabling it to use the character depicted in Figure 17 as its physical representation at the interface. Its implementation followed the architecture designed and presented in Figure 14, including the *dispatcher*, the *aggregator*, the *multimedia engine*, the *multimedia player* and the *executor*. Figure 22 illustrates the speaking agent configuration window, and the specific controls for each of these components. As before, the user interface elements depicted were provided for development purposes, and do not appear at the interface when the experimental environment is being used.

As far as the *dispatcher* is concerned, the *incoming queue* that holds messages communicated by the specialised agents through the Dynamic Data Exchange(DDE) protocol was implemented as a dynamic buffer which holds the messages until they are analysed, sorted and dispatched into the *scheduling queue* (which was also implemented as a dynamic buffer). The dispatcher ensures that no message is allowed to proceed to the language generation component until a previous message finishes processing. The dispatcher also ensures that no message is sent to the language generation component while the user is providing voice input commands.

The three text boxes at the top left corner of Figure 22 illustrate the context elements contained in the content part of the messages sent by the specialised agents. At the time the image was captured, the dispatcher had just received the message sent by the printer agent (which was illustrated in the example provided in Figure 20). Accordingly, since the message had high precedence (interruption level IL1), the speaking agent generated a spoken monitor report using a template from the template-base. This is seen in the text box at the bottom of Figure 22, which exhibits the last message issued by the speaking agent. In this case the message corresponds to a NOTIFICATION_IMMINENCE for the printer domain:

"Your web page is waiting behind 2 other documents".

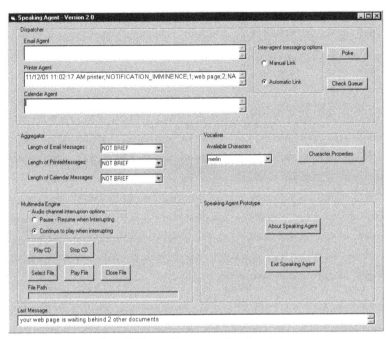

Figure 22. The speaking agent configuration window

The *aggregator* component of the speaking agent implemented a simple language generation process, which relied on the set of templates presented in Appendix A. The template-base was implemented as a separate Windows initialisation text file (INI) in order to give the designer the possibility of editing the templates in the quickest and simplest way, using a text editor.

Figure 22 illustrates that, in this session, the *aggregator* was configured to use the longer style of message, as indicated by the "NOT BRIEF" length configuration value. Additionally, the prototype enables the designer to apply separate message length settings to the different kinds of e-mail, printer and diary monitor reports, or to include them as part of the user profile.

The *vocaliser* component was implemented to take advantage of the Microsoft Agent Speech Output Tags[21], which enable the speech output to be modified through special markers that are

---

[21] The documentation describing the full range of tags supported by Microsoft Agent may be found in the Microsoft Agent World Wide Web site (Microsoft, 2001a).

embedded in the text sent to the text-to-speech engine. In the current implementation of the speaking agent, the following tags were used by the *vocaliser* to include phonetic variation: *Ctx* (determines how symbols and abbreviations are spoken), *Emp* (emphasises words), *Pau* (pauses speech for a number of milliseconds), *Pit* (sets the baseline pitch of the output) and *Spd* (sets the baseline average talking speed of the speech output).

The *multimedia engine* was implemented to control the Windows sound mixer through the *multimedia player*, in order to realise the fading approach to interrupting the audio channel, as explained in section 5.5.5.

However, before interrupting the audio channel, the *multimedia engine* must insert a polite expression at the beginning of the sentence sent by the *vocaliser*. These expressions act as attention-grabbers. Examples of expressions used by the multimedia engine are illustrated in Appendix A, and include: *"Excuse me"*, *"Attention"*, and *"Sorry to interrupt you ... but "*. The attention-grabbing functionality was implemented at the *multimedia engine* level so that the designer would be able to experiment with other kinds of non-linguistic attention-grabbers, such as audio snippets.

In Windows, speech is always output through the mixer's *wave out* channel. The *multimedia engine* is thus faced with two different situations: either (case A1) the user is playing an audio clip that uses the *wave out* channel (e.g. Wave files or MP3 files), or (case A2) the user is playing a CD, which uses the *CD out* mixer channel or a MIDI file, which uses the *MIDI out* channel.

Moreover, there are two approaches to interrupting the audio channel, as described in section 5.5.5: either (case B1) the original audio clip is gradually reduced to a pre-defined volume, but allowed to continue to play in the background while the spoken message is conveyed, and then gradually increased back to its original sound level; or (case B2) the original audio clip is faded-out and stopped, being resumed and faded-in at the end of the speech output. Figure 22 illustrates how these behaviours may be selected by the developer through the controls provided in the *multimedia engine* section of the speaking agent configuration window.

The most problematic situation arises when cases A1 and B1 arise. In this situation, the *wave out* channel must be shared by two audio sources (the original clip and the speech output), and the *multimedia engine* has to control the *multimedia player* in such a way that it *mixes* both sources. This has been implemented through a special *mixing* function. When there are combinations that do not require sharing the same output channel (e.g. cases A1 and B2, cases A2 and B1, and cases A2 and B2) the processing is simpler because there is not the need for mixing. Figure 22 illustrates that at the time the image was captured the *multimedia engine* was configured to allow an audio clip that might be playing to continue to play in the background while the spoken monitor report was being conveyed. It also illustrates that there are a number of controls that enable the *multimedia player* component to play any audio or music files that the user wishes.

After performing the modulation of the audio channel, the *multimedia engine* is able to send the full spoken monitor report to the text-to-speech synthesiser, and thus be conveyed to the user. The current implementation of the experimental environment uses the Lernout & Hauspie (L&H) TruVoice text-to-speech engine for American English.

In order to enhance the interactivity of the experimental environment, a number of voice commands were included in the speaking agent implementation. These commands could also be selected from the Speaking Agent character's context menu as shown in Figure 23.

Figure 23. The voice commands understood by the Speaking Agent

In order to support the voice commands shown in Figure 23, the *executor* component was implemented with a *grammar*, which includes a set of words, or expressions, that the speech recognition engine listens to, and matches with the execution commands. By defining such a grammar the developer is allowed to include optional and alternative words for the same command. For example, the user might wish to invoke the e-mail application by using alternative expressions such as "*let's check the mail*", "*show me the mail*" or "*I wish to see my e-mail*". Whenever the user issued these voice commands, the *executor* would run the default e-mail application (bringing its corresponding window to the front if the application was already running).

As shown in Figure 23, the speaking agent is capable of executing such functions as playing or stopping audio CD-DA (Compact Disc-Digital Audio) discs and launching the user's favourite web browser and word processing applications, as well as being able to show the printer queue and the user's diary.

5.6.5.   Using the prototype and future development

After running the speaking agent executable, the system prototype starts monitoring the e-mail, printer and diary information sources and issues spoken monitor reports as appropriate. Such an experimental environment can thus be used to investigate the acceptability of the various anthropomorphised behaviours included in the system design, which fulfil the objectives of this research.

The experimental environment is flexible in the sense that it may be easily extended to include additional specialised agents, additional service agents, or extended to support more complex categories of spoken information presentation (such as the ones suggested in Table 2). In this way, the prototype may serve as the basis for carrying out experiments focussed on testing users' reactions and opinions regarding the inclusion of additional system anthropomorphic traits, beyond the existing interruption, linguistic variation and politeness behaviours.

For example, in the *specialised agents* category, the experimental environment could be extended to include a *travel agent*. This agent would search for destinations and suitable accommodation, build a list of alternatives to be reviewed by the user, maintain a record of a user's travels and inform the user about the imminence of planned excursions, reminding the user about special requirements and destinations. Another useful agent that could be added to the environment is the *personal finances agent*. This agent would monitor the user's investments and issue notifications and reminders concerning updated news that could affect the user's investments, in addition to the obvious notifications and reminders concerning statements and prices of shares. A *Usenet newsgroups agent* could be actively searching for interesting postings concerning on-going discussions, conferences, products or other topics that the user may be interested in, issuing notifications about new items and reminders concerning existing but unseen items. Another specialised agent might schedule meetings, communicating with the diary agent, issuing notifications about new events that have been automatically entered into the diary, or reminding the user that there are still events that should be manually scheduled by the user. Beyond these examples, there could be specialised agents for helping in managing specific items of personal information such as picture albums, music collections and personal video clips.

In the *service agents* category, a *user profile agent* would help to centralise the user's preferences that are common to all the specialised agents, and could provide the specialised agents with updated information about the user's changing interests. Another useful service agent would be a *user activity monitor agent*, which could provide contextual information about the user's current activity, in order to personalise the spoken messages conveyed by the speaking agent. For example, instead of saying "I'm sorry to interrupt you...", the speaking agent could say "*I'm sorry to interrupt your writing*" or "*I have to interrupt your browsing*". The context information provided by the user monitor agent could also be used to improve the interrupting behaviour of the speaking agent. For example, if the agent is provided with information that clearly indicates that the user is speaking on the telephone and does not wish to be interrupted, the speaking agent might postpone the delivery of a spoken message.

In order to support the more complex spoken information delivery categories, such as the reportages and the interactive guide, the experimental environment could be extended to include an additional interface agent for the presentation of graphical-based material. This would require that a co-ordination component be designed in order to synchronise the presentation of visual material with speech output. The resulting reports would be essentially multimedia presentations, which could provide interactivity at the presentation level.

The system prototype could also be used to conduct experiments concerning other anthropomorphic behaviours such as creating artificial personalities. For this purpose, the researcher might design a set of different voices (by controlling the vocaliser settings) and different linguistic styles (by designing the language generation templates), for example following the characteristics of the different personality types described by Myers (1974). In effect, recent research has suggested that people are more influenced by synthetic voices that mirror their own personality type (Nass and Lee, 2001). For example, extraverted people prefer an "extraverted" computer voice (e.g. faster and varied in pitch). The experimental environment could be used to investigate whether this finding holds in the information awareness arena.

Finally, the prototype could also be used to investigate the effects of obtaining the user's attention with carefully designed audio snippets, or to investigate the social acceptability associated with embodying the system, by taking advantage of the character animation functionality provided by Microsoft Agent.

5.7   Summary

This chapter has described the specification and prototype implementation of an experimental environment (the speaking assistant) that enables the importance of a humanised spoken interface for information awareness to be evaluated.

The work described in this chapter highlighted the main design considerations that should be taken into account when creating an assistant-like system that aims to humanise the interface. It does this by employing speech output, by employing social norms to deliver spoken monitor reports, and it supports information awareness through the provision of contextual cues that notify and remind users about the occurrence of event-triggered information.

The system enables users' perceptions and reactions to anthropomorphised spoken notifications and reminders to be tested. The use of speech to complement existing graphical presentation can be evaluated, and the overall suitability of adopting agent-based techniques for the provision of anthropomorphised systems for information awareness can also be evaluated.

Chapter 6

EVALUATION OF SPEAKING SYSTEMS: AN EMPIRICAL STUDY

6.1 Overview

This chapter presents and discusses the results of an experiment undertaken to test if speech induced anthropomorphism, employed as a complementary interface mechanism for user interruption (with notifications and reminders), as provided by the experimental environment, allows reinforcing the social acceptability of the system, enabling it to be perceived as a humanised work companion. The work companion conveys information that is hidden from view, and does so with politeness and linguistic variation. The experiment also evaluated whether information awareness is a situation in which speech output provides benefits over a purely graphical-based approach.

To this end, the study was designed with a set of specific questions in mind. These questions are tests of functionality and humanisation of the system and include the following:

- How **useful** do users find being interrupted using spoken language at the interface to convey information that is hidden from view?

- Does polite, linguistically varied and urgency- and priority-based interrupting speech reinforce the **social acceptability** of the interface?

- How **humanised** does such a system appear to be?

A quasi-natural experiment was designed to simulate a typical research environment in which users would be searching for specific information to answer a set of questions and write a report, while having to perform other common activities such as printing, managing e-mail and performing other tasks previously entered in their diary. As far as participants are concerned, the experimental situation was not intended to indicate the true motivation of the study.

The overall objectives of the experiment were as follows.

1. To assess the perceived *adequacy* of the various speaking assistant *anthropomorphic characteristics* in relation to the overall goal of providing a humanised work environment. To identify any *differences* in these perceptions according to their inherent preferences for perceiving and processing information. Other personal attributes such as gender and level of expertise were also included in the assessment.

2. To assess the perceived *usefulness* and the *degree of humanisation* of the speaking assistant, and identify any *differences* in these perceptions when compared with ones emanating from previous experience with the MS Office Assistant.

These objectives caused a variety of research issues to be stated. Each issue is stated below in the form of a research question addressing specific items. The following sections present the fourteen research questions that this study aimed to investigate.

6.1.1. Adequacy of anthropomorphic behaviours

In order to assess the perceived adequacy of specific anthropomorphic characteristics, a number of questions were devised in order to examine users' reactions to those system behaviours. The data collected during the experiment allows identifying the extent to which urgency and priority-based interruptions, linguistic variation and polite behaviour contribute to the perception of a humanised work companion. This data was collected through the research questions presented in the following paragraphs.

The speaking assistant employs an interruption mechanism based on urgencies and priorities of notifications and reminders. In this respect, the research question is as follows.

Q1: *How appropriate and useful are the urgency- and priority-based interruptions generated by the speaking assistant?*

The system emphasises the importance of a notification and reminding mechanism that is based on spoken messages delivered in complement to the graphical presentation of personal information, in order to minimise the disruption on the user. Hence, the following question is appropriate.

Q2: *Are the spoken interruptions generated by the speaking assistant to notify and remind users viewed as non-disruptive alerts that complement the graphical presentation of information?*

The speaking assistant uses a single voice to convey notifications and reminders about different kinds of personal information.

Q3: *Does the single voice used by the speaking assistant to convey notifications and reminders promote the perception of homogeneity? How appropriate and non-confusing is it perceived to be?*

Whenever a spoken interruption must be generated, the system fades out the current audio presentation in order to convey the message, then brings up the original audio to its previous sound level.

Q4: *Is fading out an existing audio presentation, without stopping it, so as to provide a spoken message, a natural way of modulating the audio channel? Does it minimise the interference between the on-going audio presentation and the spoken message to be conveyed?*

The speaking assistant uses a speech-based attention-getting mechanism whenever the system is to notify or remind the user.

Q5: *Is getting the user's attention through spoken utterances a natural way to interrupt? How useful and annoying is it perceived to be?*

The system also makes assumptions on the context cues that provide the semantics conveyed in the spoken message.

Q6: *Do the semantics conveyed through the context cues embedded in the spoken notifications and reminders enhance the user's awareness of the information that is hidden from view? How easy are such messages to understand? Do these context elements provide sufficient detail to help users appreciate the meaning of event-triggered information?*

The system delivers polite utterances in order to grab the user's attention when it is to interrupt.

Q7: *Does employing polite utterances to obtain the user's attention promote the perception of a humanised interface? Is this perceived as both an appropriate and non-irritating way of interrupting?*

Another design characteristic of the speaking assistant's spoken messages is the linguistic variation of the utterances. These messages repeat over time as similar events occur. Thus, from time to time there is the need to convey a similar notification or reminder corresponding to repeating events. If messages were presented as only graphical outputs, variation would not be an issue, or it would even be an unwanted characteristic since it could cause confusion. However, this situation changes when spoken information is considered. In fact, listening to a repetitive utterance over time can be a significant source of irritation. There is the need to investigate whether linguistically varied messages are or are not equally irritating.

Q8: *Is the linguistic variation of the words used by the speaking assistant when saying the same thing in different ways at different times, a non-irritating way to convey similar messages?*

In addition to the above questions concerning the specific anthropomorphic characteristics, there is also an interest in finding out opinions regarding the quality of the assistance provided by the system, which is promoted by using speech to enhance information awareness. More specifically, the interest is in uncovering the degree of assistance the system is perceived to provide regarding tasks that require being aware of information that is hidden from view.

Q9: *Does the speaking assistant facilitate tasks that require awareness of information that is hidden from view? Is it perceived as providing valuable assistance?*

It is also interesting to find out the degree to which people would continue to use the system. This provides an additional indicator of the adequacy of the anthropomorphic speech-based approach.

Q10: *Would participants continue to use the speaking assistant if given the opportunity to do so?*

There is also the need to investigate the suitability of using such a system for a wider range of functions associated with personal information management (for example checking for specific e-mail messages from certain people or organisations, looking for meeting requests, issuing birthday reminders with gift suggestions, monitoring shares, issuing low-balance warnings or watching Usenet newsgroups for updated postings).

Q11: *Would participants like to have the speaking assistant perform a wider range of functions associated with personal information management?*

It is also tempting to investigate the degree to which users find the implemented system characteristics sufficient in order to provide for an automated guide, especially when participants are actively searching for information.

Q12: *Would participants like the speaking assistant to guide them while searching for information?*

6.1.2.   Usefulness and humanisation of the assistant

The design of the speaking assistant stressed the importance of providing a work environment that is both humanised and useful. Therefore, there is an interest in studying to what extent the implemented system characteristics promote the perception of a humanised interface that simultaneously provides useful assistance. In order to assess these dimensions, they were first defined through a number of individual characteristics, such as helpfulness and pleasantness, which allow users to express their opinions and perceptions about using the speaking assistant. A factor analysis conducted on the experimental results gave the following distribution of characteristics for the usefulness and humanisation dimensions.

- The *usefulness* dimension is defined as the degree of helpfulness, convenience, and comfort.

- The *humanisation* dimension is defined as the degree of pleasantness, unobtrusiveness, satisfaction, reliability, efficiency and likeability.

The research question that relates to these dimensions is now stated.

Q13: *To what extent is the speaking assistant perceived to be both useful and humanised?*

However, of equal importance is to compare participants' perceptions of the speaking assistant with their perceptions of a purely graphical-based assistant, again along both dimensions. This comparison determines whether users feel that the speaking assistant's characteristics, which rely on employing speech output, provide a more useful and humanised work environment as far as notifications and reminders are concerned. The system chosen for the comparison was the MS Office Assistant since it is widely available as part of a very popular productivity software package, and it also fulfils the criteria of being a graphical-based approach to personal assistance. The research question associated with this comparison is stated in the following manner.

Q14: *Is the speaking assistant perceived as a more humanised and useful assistant than the MS Office Assistant?*

6.1.3.   Differences in user perceptions by personal characteristics

Given that the system is providing users with notifications and reminders about personal information that is hidden from view, it is important to find out whether it is providing this information in a suitable way. The main objective of the system is to provide sufficient information about an event associated with personal information so as to allow the user to infer the meaning of that event. Thus, from an *information acquisition* point of view, the aim is to provide speech-based messages which provide overviews of events that allow a person to *appreciate the significance* of an event; that is, the meaning behind the facts. In this way, the system enhances a person's awareness of event-triggered information. This corresponds to a psychological heuristic approach to information acquisition. In summary, the main purpose of the system is to support the heuristic component of human information acquisition. In contrast, the analytical component of human information acquisition is centred on depth rather than breadth, and tends to focus on the particular details of an event in a systematic and organised way. This preference is likely to be better supported through the graphical-based presentation of event related information.

In order to investigate whether the designed system characteristics support the heuristic approach for human information acquisition, this experiment draws on the comparison of people's perceptions of the system characteristics grouped by their psychological preferences for acquiring (and processing) information according to the Myers-Briggs Type Indicator (MBTI) personality inventory.

The MBTI personality inventory (Myers, 1974) is a well-tested model of human behaviour and decision-making that categorises people according to their tendencies in each of four pairs of personality traits: Extraversion (E) / Introversion (I), Intuition (N) / Sensing (S), Feeling (F) / Thinking (T) and Judgement (J) / Perception (P). These psychological categories have often been used in studies of behavioural decision-making (Fritz, 1995).

The E/I dimension differentiates people according to where they prefer to focus their attention in order to understand the environment (Myers, 1993). **Extraverts** (E) prefer to understand the environment through externalising and reacting, and focus on the external world of people and events, receiving energy from external events, experiences and interactions. On the other hand, **Introverts** (I) understand the environment through careful consideration, and focus on their own inner world of experiences and ideas, receiving energy from their internal thoughts, feelings and reflections.

According to Myers (1993), **Intuitives** (N) tend to acquire information through relationships with people, patterns and intuition, by seeing the "big picture" and focusing on the relationship and connections between facts. On the other hand, **Sensors** (S) prefer to determine information through careful consideration, through their eyes, ears and other senses to find out about events. Intuitives tend to be more heuristic in their approach to information gathering, whereas Sensors tend to be more analytical information gatherers.

The F/T dimension categorises people according to how they prefer to process perceived information; that is, how they make decisions or form judgments. **Feelers** (F) tend to consider what is important to them and to other people, basing their decisions on person-centred values, while **Thinkers** (T) tend to be logical and deliberate in their decision making, relying on provable facts, examining events objectively and analysing cause and effect.

Finally, the J/P characteristic differentiates people on the basis of how they tend to orientate towards the outer world, that is, how people prefer to deal with change and uncertainty. People who have a **Judging** (J) preference are more comfortable with organised and manageable lives that they can control through careful planning and scheduling, whereas people with a **Perceiving** (P) preference tend to live in a flexible, spontaneous way, avoiding deadlines and seeking to experience and understand life rather than control it.

In summary, types E, N, F, and P can be thought as giving a measure of different aspects associated with a heuristic approach, while types I, S, T, and J refer to different aspects of an analytical approach (Mallach, 1994).

It should be emphasised that the Myers-Briggs Type Indicator is a self-report questionnaire designed to reflect "normal" behaviour provided that the person answers honestly to the questions. Accordingly, the experiment reported here attempts to simulate a "normal" situation in which there is relative calm. However, different circumstances may force a person to behave in certain ways that do not necessarily reflect their true selves. For example, if a person has a demanding job that requires being always on time, meeting deadlines and making critical decisions, this situation requires that the person acts as if possessing a Judging (J) preference. Nevertheless, the true psychological preference for this person may be that of Perceiving (P); that is, in more peaceful circumstances the person would prefer to live in a more flexible and spontaneous way.

One of the main objectives of this study is the identification of observable and significant differences in people's perceptions about the speaking assistant traits, when compared across the pairs of the MBTI personality traits, so as to investigate whether the assistance being provided by the system supports a heuristic approach to information gathering. For each system characteristic introduced through the research questions presented in sections 6.1.1 and 6.1.2, participants' perceptions were systematically compared along the four pairs of psychological traits. The orthogonal question applied to each and every research question stated in those two sections is as follows: *are there any differences in people's perceptions of the speaking assistant characteristics when compared across the MBTI personality dimensions? What do these differences indicate in terms of the support the system provides for information acquisition?*

Since data was being gathered at the time of the experiment, it was also possible to obtain information about differences in peoples' perceptions of the system that might arise from their gender, their level of experience with the operating system and their degree of familiarity with speech synthesisers. An additional orthogonal question concerning these personal characteristics can be stated as follows: *are there any differences in people's perceptions of the speaking assistant characteristics when compared across gender, level of experience with the operating system and level of familiarity with speech synthesisers? What do these differences indicate in terms of the support the system provides for different personal characteristics?*

6.2   Experimental method

6.2.1.   Rationale

There is a wide variety of evaluation methods described in the HCI literature (e.g. see (Dix et al., 1998; Preece et al., 1994)). Of these, some are more appropriate for evaluating the system design, while other methods are more appropriate for evaluating the system implementation or its prototype (see for example (Fritz, 1995) for a good overview of evaluation methods most suited to each category). In this study, the main interest was *not* the evaluation of the system design, but the use of the experimental environment prototype as a way to investigate whether a number of anthropomorphic characteristics it *implemented* adequately contributed to the perception of a humanised work environment, as well as to assess their relative importance. Also of interest was to uncover the situations where speech may be used to advantage as a complement to a graphical user interface. In this context, the range of methods to choose from lied in the second category – methods to evaluate a system prototype.

The possible approaches in evaluating a system prototype range from field tests, also known as natural experiments, to controlled experiments. In between there are the quasi-natural experiments, also known as mixed experiments. Details and advice about using these types of test can be found in the literature (Elmes et al., 1989; Robson, 1993).

Originally, this study was designed as a field test, since the main interest was to observe users in real work conditions, so as to assess the importance of the system characteristics in a natural setting, with users performing tasks in realistic conditions. This would have been the best option to test the social acceptability of the system caused by its anthropomorphic characteristics, as well as its usefulness, over an extended period of time. However, there are practical disadvantages of this approach which impede its successful application. For example, it is very difficult to find an organisation willing to spare the time and effort of its employees in experiments with prototypical software. Moreover, field tests involve careful observation of the test participants, frequent interactions with the test monitor, and additional time spent filling-in questionnaires.

For these reasons, it was decided to conduct a quasi-natural experiment. Quasi-experimental research (Elmes et al., 1989) involves using independent variables that are selected rather than manipulated by the researcher (also called subject variables) such as gender or age, and attempts to design laboratory tests that simulate as far as possible a naturalistic situation. This means designing representative tasks in an environment that simulates closely a user's typical work environment. It also means arranging a sample of participants that is representative of real users for the tasks devised for the experiment. However, this approach is not without problems, especially control and interpretive problems, which arise because the independent variables are not directly manipulated (Elmes et al., 1989). Nevertheless, the interpretation limitations associated with the quasi-natural approach did not adversely affect the objectives of this study.

6.2.2.   Experimental design and procedure

In order to conduct the experiment, participants were recruited from the Computer Science department population. Effort was spent in the preparation of the scripts and the questionnaires, a realistic environment was prepared for the experiment, and a suitable task scenario was devised as illustrated in Figure 24.

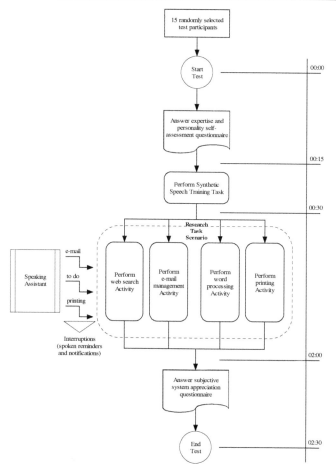

Figure 24. Experimental design and procedure

Participants were told that this experiment was being conducted to investigate how easy it is for people to use an interactive system to find information in an environment where there is some interruption. They were instructed that the experiment required them to use the World Wide Web to find answers to forty-eight questions.

Furthermore, it was stressed that knowing the answer to each question would not be sufficient, and that the participant should find evidence to support the answer and paste it into a word-processor document along with its Uniform Resource Locator (URL). Once participants had finished each group of questions they were told to print off their word processor document, and open a new one for the next group of questions. The diagram in Figure 24 illustrates the experimental design.

The research scenario depicted in Figure 24 consisted of performing a research task involving the following typical activities: to use a web browser to search the World Wide Web for answers to a set of given questions, to use an e-mail client to read and reply to e-mail messages, to use a word processor to write down answers and to paste source information in support of them, and finally to use the printer to obtain paper-based versions of word processor documents and important e-mail messages.

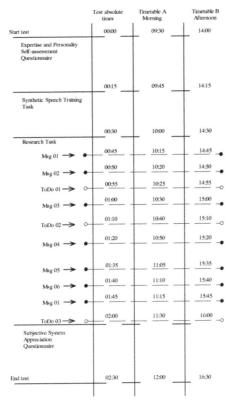

Figure 25. Diagram of timed interruptions for the experiment slots A and B

Fifteen randomly selected participants performed the experiment. Each participant had to complete an expertise and personality self-assessment questionnaire. Then each had a fifteen-minute training session with the particular speech synthesiser used in the experiment. All participants were actually familiar with speech synthesis. Each participant took two and a half hours to complete the exercise, allowing for two participants to take part per day. The daily schedule is shown in Figure 25. As can be seen, the time for each interrupting event was precisely timed. Just before the end of the session, participants were asked to fill in a subjective system appreciation questionnaire designed to measure their opinions and attitudes concerning their interaction with the speaking assistant.

All the activities included in the experiment could be completed without using the prototype, but with the prototype running, the participants were made aware of information that was not in view. The environment simulated a realistic research situation, involving representative tasks and representative data, in a "normal" environment, which was representative of the participant's typical work environment.

The experiment was based on this quasi-natural model, and there was no control group. The inclusion of a control group would have allowed the testing of several hypotheses in order to examine the difference in performance between the system prototype and a normal environment (the control), but this was not the objective of the empirical study reported here.

6.2.3.   Measurement of variables

To collect data, two questionnaires were used. The first questionnaire was completed by participants before they started the task. The second questionnaire was completed after the task was finished. The design of these questionnaires took into account guidelines and advice presented in the literature (Alreck and Settle, 1994; Bouchard, 1976; Chin et al., 1988; Saunders et al., 2000). The independent variables (IV) in this experiment, collected through the first questionnaire, were those that describe the participants: gender, age range, level of operating system proficiency, degree of familiarity with speech synthesis, and the participant's personality type as given by the self-test (Tieger and Tieger, 1995) that determines the Myers-Briggs Type Indicator (MBTI) which categorises people according to their dominant psychological preferences in each of four pairs of personality traits. The dependent variables (DV) were the measures taken in the second questionnaire. In this study, only subjective measures consisting of users' opinions, feelings or attitudes about the system characteristics were taken. These measures were obtained by having participants rate their perception (either opinion, feeling or attitude) about specific system characteristics on 5-point and 7-point scales.

Assessment of the adequacy of anthropomorphic characteristics

For assessing the adequacy of the anthropomorphic characteristics in relation to the overall goal of providing a humanised work environment, users were asked to rate their perception of the suitability of given adjectives to describe certain system features on 7-point numeric scales ("1" = "Not at all", "7" = "Very much so"). Each adjective corresponds to one dependent variable. For each anthropomorphic characteristic the variables are shown in Table 8.

Anthropomorphic characteristics	Dependent variables (adjectives)
Interruptions	Appropriate Useful Disruptive
Single voice	Confusing Uniform Appropriate
Music interruption	Natural Interfering
Attention-getters	Useful Annoying Natural
Spoken message semantics	Easy to recognise words Easy to understand meaning Helpful Appropriate
Politeness	Degree Appropriate Irritating
Linguistic variation	Irritating Appropriate

Table 8. Dependent variables for assessing anthropomorphic characteristics

Assessment of the speech-based assistance quality

In order to assess the perceived overall quality of the assistance provided by the system, participants were asked to use 5-point Likert scales (Alreck and Settle, 1994) to rate their level of agreement with given statements about the system ("1" = "Strongly Disagree", "2" = "Disagree", "3" = "Neither Disagree nor Agree", "4" = "Agree", "5" = "Strongly Agree"). Each statement corresponds to one dependent variable. For each evaluation topic the variables are shown in Table 9.

Characteristics	Dependent variables (statements)
Task assistance	The speaking assistant made the task easier to perform. The system was assisting me. I would continue to use the system.
Assistant evolution	I would like the system to perform more PIM functions. I would like the system to guide me while searching for information.
Task complexity	Finding information to answer the research questions was easy.

Table 9. Dependent variables for assessing the speech-based assistance quality

Dependent variables	Values (semantic differential)	
scale	1	7
Assistant pleasantness	Unpleasant	Pleasant
Assistant helpfulness	Unhelpful	Helpful
Assistant convenience	Inconvenient	Convenient
Assistant reliability	Unreliable	Reliable
Assistant comfort	Uncomfortable	Comfortable
Assistant efficiency	Inefficient	Efficient
Assistant satisfaction	Frustrating	Satisfying
Assistant intrusiveness	Unobtrusive	Intrusive
Assistant likeability	Horrible	Lovely

Table 10. Dependent variables for assessing usefulness and humanisation

Assessment of the usefulness and humanisation of the assistant

In order to assess the perceived usefulness and humanisation of the speaking assistant, participants were asked to use a 7-point semantic differential scale (Osgood et al., 1967), and to rate their overall feelings about the system for nine different dimensions. Each pair corresponded to a dependent variable as shown in Table 10.

6.2.4.　Materials and apparatus

6.2.4.1.　Setting up the prototype

As the prototype played such an important role in the outcome of this experiment, care was taken that the software was fully functional and error-free in regard to the tasks it was intended to support. If any problem occurred as a consequence of poor implementation, then that fact alone would negatively influence the outcome of the experiment, and introduce distortions that would impede a proper analysis and discussion of the research questions. The prototype used during the experiment provided speech-based messages to enhance information awareness for three source domains of personal information as follows.

- E-mail awareness: notification of new e-mail messages, reminding of unread messages.

- Printing awareness: notification of the actual position in the printer queue of printed documents, reminding the user of just printed documents.

- Diary awareness: notification of upcoming scheduled events and to-do's, reminding the user of events just started and missed to-do's.

The settings of specific functions in the prototype were adjusted as follows.

The speaking assistant prototype allowed for selecting between three different modes for the length of the spoken message, as described in section 5.5.3. Each mode conveyed an increasing number of context cues, providing for more detailed and semantically richer notifications and reminders. By default, the most detailed level was chosen for every experimental session.

The system prototype allowed for linguistically varied English language sentences for notifications and reminders that are sent to the text-to-speech (TTS) engine. By default, this was accomplished by randomly selecting an appropriate template from a template-base, as described in section 5.5.3. The full template-base used during the experiment can be found in Appendix A.

The prototype allowed for the generation of English language utterances that were used as polite attention-getters. By default, this was accomplished using the list of polite expressions presented in Appendix A.

The prototype used the Lernout & Hauspie (L&H) TruVoice text-to-speech (TTS) engine (version 6.0.0), provided as part of the MS Agent software package. The following default settings were kept constant for all participants:

a) Language: American English.

b) Speaking rate of synthesised voice: 150 words per minute.

c) Gender of synthesised voice: adult male.

The Assistant prototype allowed for a fading-based modulation of the audio channel when other multimedia clips were already playing. It also allowed playing and stopping audio clips from within the system. The system was set up to play a music Compact Disc (Smooth Jazz) especially prepared for the experiment, at a fixed volume level that was considered comfortable by all participants. The "CD Play" function was set up to restart from the beginning of the Compact Disc, so that the music did not stop for the whole duration of the research task. The system was set up to fade out the music whenever a spoken message was to be conveyed.

Finally, the system prototype allowed for a limited input grammar for commands issued through a speech-recognition engine. By default, this option was de-activated for all participants. This meant that no speech input tests were conducted.

6.2.4.2. Scripts and questionnaires

Five handouts were created: the task script, the synthetic speech training task script, the research task questions and the pre- and post-experiment questionnaires.

The task script described the tasks to be performed and included the instructions participants should observe in performing those tasks. The synthetic speech training task script contained a list of proverbs, some of which were spoken by the system; the task here was to tick off just those that were heard so that the user could gain familiarity with the voice. The research task question list[22] contained forty-eight questions which participants were required to answer by means of searching the World Wide Web. These questions were further sub-divided into eight sections, each section containing three main topics, and each topic including two questions. These materials can be found in Appendix B.

Questionnaire A was a self-assessment questionnaire administered prior to the research task. This was designed to gather expertise and personality data about each participant. Questionnaire B was administered after the completion of the research task and was designed to gather the opinions and attitudes of participants towards the system. This questionnaire had three sections. The first section gathered subjective quantitative data in the form of opinions about the anthropomorphic characteristics. The second section gathered subjective quantitative data concerning attitudes

---

[22] The author is grateful to Dr. Bill Freeman, Department of Computer Science of the University of York, who kindly provided the questions for the World Wide Web search activity.

towards the assistance provided by the system, and the third section included a number of open-ended questions to gather subjective qualitative data about the participants' experience with the system. The questionnaires are included in Appendix C.

6.2.4.3.   The test site

The test location in which the experiment was performed was designed so that participants could enjoy a peaceful environment. The test site included the following hardware materials:

- a Personal Computer running the MS Windows NT workstation 4.0 operating system,

- a 10x CD-ROM player, a soundcard and a pair of speakers,

- a standard keyboard and a standard three-button mouse,

- a 17-inch colour monitor,

- a fast connection to the local network.

The test site included the following software:

- Internet Explorer, version 5.5, and Netscape Navigator, version 4.5 Web browsers,

- MS Word 97 word processor,

- MS Outlook Express e-mail client,

- the Proverbs Application used for the Speech Training task, employing a list of pre-defined proverbs, as illustrated in Table 28 presented in Appendix D,

- the Speaking Assistant prototype, using a text file to simulate each participant's diary including appointments and to-dos, as shown in Table 31 presented in Appendix D.

An additional workstation was used for monitoring purposes and to run an automated e-mail sending application that accepted the precise starting time of the research task and automatically sent the e-mail messages at the appropriate times indicated in Figure 25. The e-mail messages sent to participants during the experiment are shown in Table 29 and Table 30, which may be found in Appendix D.

Finally, a pilot experiment was conducted before the main experiment in order to fine tune a number of experimental parameters such as the task descriptions, the questionnaires, and other details such as the physical location of the network printer, and the e-mail and login accounts used by the participants during the experiment. The activities to be performed by the test monitor before and during the experiment were also included as part of an additional script (see Appendix D) to ensure that all participants would perform under the same conditions.

6.2.5.   Profile of participants

A sample of fifteen participants was used in the experiment. All participants were recruited from the Computer Science department population, and were selected by being the first ones to demonstrate interest in participating by responding to a message broadcast throughout the department. The sample consisted of nine undergraduate students, five postgraduate students and one staff member. Four were females and eleven were males; their ages ranged between 18 and 45 years old. Participants were provided with a financial reward (£10). All participants had adequate domain knowledge of the task suggested, and were medium or high proficiency users of the MS Windows NT operating system (as illustrated in Figure 26). All had either heard speech synthesis a few times or many times before the experiment (as illustrated in Figure 27). The original data can be found in Table 32, which may be found in Appendix E.

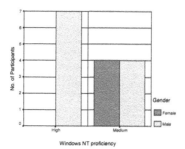

Figure 26. Distribution by MS Windows NT Experience (self-evaluation)

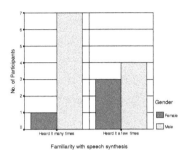

Figure 27. Distribution by Familiarity with Speech Synthesis (self-evaluation)

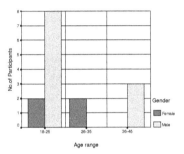

Figure 28. Distribution by Age Range

The range of participants' personality traits is illustrated in Figure 29 through to Figure 32. These charts summarise the Myers-Briggs psychological characteristics of the participants. Note that these psychological traits are a subjective measure and can only be treated as indicators of the participants' dominant psychological preferences; that is, how they are most likely to respond to a "normal" situation.

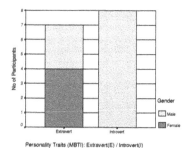

Figure 29. Distribution by Extraversion/Introversion (self-evaluation)

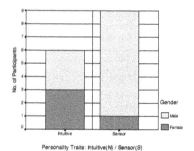

Figure 30. Distribution by Intuition/Sensing (self-evaluation)

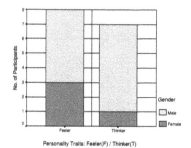

Figure 31. Distribution by Feeling/Thinking (self-evaluation)

It may be observed that all the female participants were extraverts – this may have happened by chance since they were fewer in number compared with males. It will also be observed that female participants seem to be more heuristically oriented than males (types E, N, F and P).

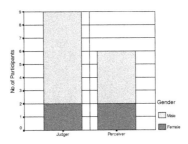

Figure 32. Distribution by Judgement/Perception (self-evaluation)

Table 11 below presents the correlation coefficients between the participants' characteristics. The table shows that there are no strong correlations. Of course there was some correlation between gender and E/I, precisely because in this sample all the female participants happened to be extraverts. A significant degree of correlation was also found between gender and Windows NT proficiency. It so happened that in this sample all the female participants self-evaluated as having medium Windows NT proficiency (as may also be noted from Figure 26 above).

		Windows NT proficiency	Familiarity with speech synthesis	Age range	Gender	Extravert(E) / Introvert(I)	Intuitive(N) / Sensor(S)	Feeler(F) / Thinker(T)	Judger(J) / Perceiver(P)
Windows NT proficiency	Correlation Coefficient	1	0.339	0.334	-0.564 *	-0.339	-0.218	-0.464	-0.055
	Significance (2-tailed)	.	0.216	0.224	0.029	0.216	0.435	0.081	0.847
Familiarity with speech synthesis	Correlation Coefficient		1	-0.111	-0.342	-0.196	0.218	0.196	0.327
	Significance (2-tailed)		.	0.693	0.211	0.483	0.435	0.483	0.234
Age range	Correlation Coefficient			1	-0.084	-0.111	0.113	-0.111	-0.34
	Significance (2-tailed)			.	0.767	0.693	0.688	0.693	0.215
Gender	Correlation Coefficient				1	0.645 **	0.431	0.262	-0.123
	Significance (2-tailed)				.	0.009	0.109	0.346	0.662
Extravert(E) / Introvert(I)	Correlation Coefficient					1	0.055	0.071	-0.327
	Significance (2-tailed)					.	0.847	0.8	0.234
Intuitive(N) / Sensor(S)	Correlation Coefficient						1	0.218	-0.167
	Significance (2-tailed)						.	0.435	0.553
Feeler(F) / Thinker(T)	Correlation Coefficient							1	0.055
	Significance (2-tailed)							.	0.847
Judger(J) / Perceiver(P)	Correlation Coefficient								1
	Significance (2-tailed)								.

* Correlation is significant at the .05 level (2-tailed).
** Correlation is significant at the .01 level (2-tailed).

Table 11. Correlation coefficients for participant characteristics

6.3   Experimental results and discussion

This section presents and discusses the results in the context of the fourteen research questions introduced for each of the two evaluation objectives stated in section 6.1. The tables containing the data that supported the statistics presented throughout this section can be found in Appendix E. Appendix F contains the tables that supported the comparisons presented in this section. These were performed by employing t-tests (where M denotes the mean).

6.3.1.   Adequacy of anthropomorphic behaviours

The results presented in this section were collected by having participants rate their perception of each anthropomorphic characteristic on a 7-point numeric scale, 7 being the highest rating. The number of responses always equals the number of participants (N = 15), except in the cases where it is explicitly noted. Participants were asked to consider a set of statements about each type of anthropomorphic behaviour exhibited by the assistant, and then answered by indicating their level of agreement ("1" = "Not at all", "7" = "Very much so"). Ratings were then compared across personal characteristics to see whether there were any differences.

Research Question 1

The first research question (Q1) related to the users' perceptions of appropriateness and usefulness of the interruptions produced by the speaking assistant. The focus was in finding out the relevance of the interruptions. Participants rated their opinion on the following statements:

*"I think that the interruptions were **appropriate**".*

*"I think that the interruptions were **useful**".*

The users' mean ratings of these two characteristics are presented in Table 12, indicating that users moderately agreed that the interruptions were perceived as both appropriate and useful.

	Mean	Median	Mode	Std. Deviation
Interruptions: appropriateness	5.67	6.00	6	1.05
Interruptions: usefulness	5.87	6.00	6	.92

Table 12. Average ratings for interruptions

In order to investigate the quality of the interruptions an index of *relevance* was created by aggregating both items (Cronbach alpha = .87). The mean rating obtained was 5.76 out of a possible 7, with a standard deviation of .92. This indicates that on average users felt the interruptions to be relevant. Moreover, no differences were found among the user's personality characteristics. Here it is worth considering the comments made by users regarding positive features of the system (see Table 52 in Appendix G). As far as interruptions are concerned three users pointed out that the system only delivered relevant (necessary) information, and four users liked being interrupted with spoken notifications (alerts to upcoming and just occurred events), which they classified as timely.

Research Question 2

The second research question (Q2) involved an investigation of the perceived disruptiveness caused by spoken interruptions. Participants were asked to consider the following statement:

*"I think that the interruptions were **disruptive**".*

This variable was recoded during analysis in order to obtain an index of non-disruptiveness associated with the interruptions. The result presented in Table 13 indicates that on average users slightly agree that the interruptions did not disrupt them, while the majority agreed that interruptions were not disruptive. If the result had indicated a perception of disruptiveness then the suitability of speech as an alternative to graphical-based interruptions would be questionable. However, this result suggests that speech has a role to play as a complementary mechanism to graphical-based presentation of information when the main concern is to minimise the disruption associated with information awareness.

	Mean	Median	Mode	Std. Deviation
Interruptions: not disruptive (recoded)	5.00	5.00	6	1.65

Table 13. Average ratings for interruptions non-disruptiveness

This finding is also supported by five positive opinions about the unobtrusive nature of spoken notifications and reminders (see Table 52 in Appendix G). The comments these users provided were that the messages did not demand immediate action. This means that, depending on the importance of the alert, the verification of the items of information mentioned in the message can be postponed until the user's current task is finished, or until the user's attention can be diverted from the current task. In either case, the user is able to decide when to deal with the interruption without having to perform any other overt action.

Research Question 3

Research question Q3 is concerned with the perception of consistency that is promoted by using a single voice to convey different types of notification and reminders, without compromising the clarity of the message. One design decision that could be made might have been to use a different voice for each type of information. For example, using one voice for notifications and reminders concerning e-mail, and a different voice for messages about printing. But how many voices are acceptable? As the system grows to cover more and more personal information domains, so the number of different voices grows. Therefore, an alternative possibility, which was chosen during the design, involves using a single voice to convey every message. In exploring this alternative, the aim is to investigate the degree of confusion that may be caused by having a single voice convey a range of different types of information. Participants were asked to consider the voice used by the system to issue different kinds of message (e.g. about e-mail, printing and other to-do's), and rated their opinion on the following statements:

> *"I think that having the same voice provided **uniformity**".*

> *"I think that having the same voice was **appropriate**".*

> *"I think that having the same voice was **confusing**".*

	Mean	Median	Mode	Std. Deviation
Same voice: uniformity	5.67	6.00	6	.98
Same voice: appropriateness	5.33	6.00	6	1.68
Same voice: not confusing (recoded)	5.93	7.00	7	1.49

Table 14. Average ratings for employing a single voice

Table 14 presents users' average ratings for these statements. These results indicate that users slightly agreed that the same voice provided uniformity and that it was appropriate. Moreover, they definitely agreed that having one voice to convey disparate notifications is not confusing (this variable was recoded from "confusing" to "not confusing"). While this provides enough evidence to consider the route of integration, where a centralised entity speaks for a number of other entities that deal with specific domains of personal information management, the results do not provide sufficient evidence to rule out the possibility of using multiple voices. What these results suggest is that a single voice promotes the perception of consistency. This finding is further supported by the index of *consistency*, which was created by aggregating the uniformity and appropriateness variables (Cronbach alpha = .65). The mean rating obtained was 5.5 out of a possible 7, with a standard deviation of 1.18.

Research Question 4

The fourth research question (Q4) concerned the way the system dealt with the audio channel when it is already in use for other audio presentations. The main concern is in maximising the naturalness of the interruption while minimising the interference between the spoken message and the existing audio presentation. In order to test the suitability of the fading approach, music was continuously playing in the background (at a suitable volume that was kept constant during the experiment). Participants first considered the way the music was interrupted by the system whenever a spoken message was conveyed, and then were asked to rate the following statements:

*"I think the way the music was interrupted by the system voice was **natural**".*

*"I think that the music **interfered** with the spoken message".*

Users' average ratings for these statements can be found in Table 15. As noted, these are very positive results regarding the fading technique for the audio channel modulation, with users definitely agreeing on the naturalness of the modulation and on the low level of interference. No significant differences were found across the user's personality characteristics under analysis.

	Mean	Median	Mode	Std. Deviation
Music interruption: naturalness	6.20	6.00	6	.68
Music interruption: music did not interfere with spoken message (recoded)	6.07	6.00	7	1.33

Table 15. Average ratings for music interruption

To investigate further the *quality* of the modulation, both variables were aggregated (Cronbach alpha = .61) during analysis. Consistently, the mean rating obtained was 6.1 out of a possible 7, with a standard deviation of .89. Since the fading technique is widely used in radio broadcast to insert spoken comments over ongoing music, it is understandable that users would perceive it as a natural, or at least a familiar means of modulating the audio channel. However, there was always the risk that the spoken message would be misunderstood because of the music, or that the music would be interrupted by the spoken message in an irritating way. Results demonstrated that these risks were largely attenuated in the system prototype. However, the experiment was limited in that it only tested interruptions of music. Thus, further research is needed to investigate the appropriateness of this technique to interrupt other multimedia presentations, such as video clips and narratives.

Research Question 5

The fifth research question (Q5) is an investigation of the quality of the attention-getting using speech. The main emphasis is in assessing the perceptions of naturalness, usefulness and annoyance raised by obtaining the user's attention using short spoken expressions. In order to obtain users' perceptions along these dimensions, participants were asked to consider the way the system got their attention, by saying for example "Excuse me". Then, they were asked to rate their views on the following statements about the attention-getters:

*"I think they were **useful** at getting my attention".*

*"I think they were **annoying**".*

*"I think they were **natural**".*

Table 16 illustrates users' average ratings for these statements. These results indicate that users slightly agree on the usefulness, naturalness and non-annoying nature of the expressions used by the system to obtain their attention. However, there is a considerable variation in the results. This may be indicating that more research is needed in order to achieve higher quality and more humanised ways of getting a user's attention. In fact, the index of the *quality* of attention-getting, obtained through the aggregation of all three variables (Cronbach alpha = .72) supports this conclusion: the mean rating obtained was 4.93 out of a possible 7, with a standard deviation of 1.18.

	Mean	Median	Mode	Std. Deviation
Attention-getters: usefulness	4.87	6.00	6	1.68
Attention-getters: not annoying (recoded)	5.00	5.00	6	1.56
Attention-getters: naturalness	4.93	5.00	5	1.16

Table 16. Average ratings for spoken attention-getters

In order to clarify these results, it is useful to consider the comments users provided concerning the characteristics of the attention-getting mechanism (see Table 52 in Appendix G). While three users mentioned that the attention-getters promoted reliable interruptions by preventing them from missing important information, another user mentioned that attention-getting was pleasant because it prevented the occurrence of sudden interruptions, which could lead to them missing part of the information conveyed in the message.

The negative comments also provide interesting suggestions: one user commented on the annoyance caused by the low level of linguistic variation in the short utterances that the system used to obtain their attention (see Table 53 in Appendix G). Another three users were annoyed because there was not enough intonation in the speech-based attention-getters (see Table 54 in Appendix G). While this provides an indication of the annoyance caused by repetitive utterances, the design of variable attention-getters is necessarily a limited process in that there are only a few expressions that can be used to get a person's attention. However, varying the intonation with which these expressions are spoken might alter the way they sound and, thus, solve both problems.

Two interesting differences among user groups were found concerning the average ratings of attention-getters. First, as Figure 33 illustrates, users who were less familiar with text-to-speech (TTS) synthesis tended to find attention-getters more useful (M = 5.86) than those with more familiarity (M = 4.00), t(13) = -2.497, p = .027. It may be the case that the spoken attention-getters are really performing a useful function for the first group of users by drawing their attention before the actual message is spoken and helping them momentarily focus their attention to improve the understanding of the synthesised speech. For the second group, this result indicates a neutral opinion. This constitutes further evidence of the comments made above regarding the need to improve the linguistic variation and the intonation of spoken attention-getters.

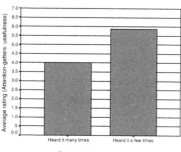

Figure 33. Average ratings for the usefulness of attention-getters by familiarity with TTS

The other difference, depicted in Figure 34, concerns the annoyance of spoken attention-getters: Introvert users tended to find them less annoying (M = 5.75) than Extravert participants (M = 4.14), t(13) = 2.269, p = .041.

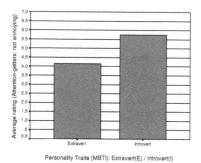

Figure 34. Average ratings for the annoyance caused by attention-getters by E/I

Since Introverts are more committed to their inner world, and receive energy from the inside, it may be that the annoying characteristics of the attention-getters, such as the lack of variation and intonation, are less important and less noticeable than for people who are attuned to the external environment, and pay more attention to the sociable characteristics of interaction. Thus, people in the second group would naturally feel more annoyed by unnatural attention-getters than people in the first group. This reveals that further research is needed in order to design a more humanised attention-getting mechanism.

Research Question 6

Research question Q6 covered the investigation as to whether there was an adequate level of semantics in spoken notifications and reminders. The main requirement was to enhance the user's awareness of information that is hidden from view through the contents of the spoken messages. To measure perception of the quality of information awareness, users were first invited to consider the meaning of the spoken messages they were presented with during the experiment. Then, they were asked to rate their opinion on the following statements:

> *"I **easily** recognised the words spoken by the speaking assistant".*

> *"I **easily** understood the meaning of the spoken messages".*

> *"I think the spoken messages **helped** me understand what was happening".*

> *"I think the amount of detail provided in the spoken messages was **appropriate**".*

The average ratings for these statements can be found in Table 17. As shown, on average participants agreed on the understandability of the message contents, and on the awareness of events that they provided. These are positive indicators concerning the context cues selected by design to be conveyed in notifications and reminders. But to validate further this conclusion, an index of *semantic quality* was derived by the aggregation of three variables: words easy to recognise, meaning easy to recognise and messages helped to understand event (Cronbach alpha = .63). The mean rating obtained was 5.84 out of possible 7, with a standard deviation of .86.

	Mean	Median	Mode	Std. Deviation
Semantics: words easy to recognise	5.60	6.00	6	1.45
Semantics: meaning easy to understand	6.00	6.00	7	1.07
Semantics: messages helped to understand event	5.93	6.00	6	.80
Semantics: messages detail appropriateness	5.40	6.00	6	1.64

Table 17. Average ratings for the semantics of spoken messages

However, some variation in opinions is still apparent in the results. In order to investigate the origins of this variation, further analysis was conducted to examine the differences across user groups according to their personality characteristics. Significant differences were found in average ratings of all these variables. Figure 35 illustrates the differences along the Intuition / Sensing personality dimension (N/S).

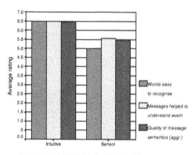

Figure 35. Average ratings for message semantics by N/S

As shown in Figure 35, Intuitive participants rated significantly higher (M = 6.50) the facility in recognising words when compared with Sensor participants (M = 5.00), t(13) = 2.213, p = .045. Intuitive oriented people also rated significantly higher the help provided by the spoken messages (M = 6.50) when compared with the Sensor participants (M = 5.56), t(13) = 2.701, p = .018.

These differences can be regarded as positive indicators. Given that messages work as surrogates to the actual event-triggered information (by providing an overview of what happened), people will acquire that information without having to interrupt their current activity (that is, without having to look for the graphical locations of the new information and then go back to their original task). This corresponds to the way people with an Intuition preference like to take in information: they prefer to see the "big picture", focusing on the meaning behind facts. Sensors prefer to focus on the practical details of facts and rely on the combination of their senses (primarily eyes and ears) to find out about events. Since the main objective of spoken monitor reports is to provide sufficient cues, the combination of which enhances the awareness of information, and not to substitute the graphical presentation of information, these results seem to support this objective.

The third difference shown in Figure 35 relates to the *semantic quality* index and it consistently supports this finding: Intuition-oriented people rated the quality of the message semantics significantly higher (M = 6.45) than Sensors (M = 5.45), t(13) = 2.621, p = .021.

Other interesting differences were found by making comparisons of the message semantics ratings across other personality characteristics. For example, regarding the facility to recognise the meaning of the spoken messages, Figure 36 illustrates that people with a Perceiving (P) preference found that the meaning of the spoken message was easier to understand (M = 6.83) than people with a Judging (J) preference (M = 5.44), t(11.296) = -3.686, p = .003.

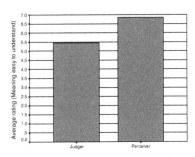

Personality Traits (MBTI): Judger(J) / Perceiver(P)

Figure 36. Average ratings for the facility in recognising message meaning by J/P

Given that the psychological dimension of Judging / Perceiving is seen as a reference to a personal preference for either acquiring information (Perception function) or processing information (Judging function), and given that Perception oriented people found it easier to recognise the meaning of the spoken messages, this result suggests that the message contents facilitate the acquisition of the meaning of information; that is, the messages facilitate the awareness of information.

It is also worth considering the positive comments made by participants regarding the spoken messages. First, six users mentioned that the notifications of e-mail messages, which include information about the subject and the sender of new messages, helped them decide whether to look at them or to ignore newly arrived messages (see Table 52 in Appendix G). Furthermore, ten participants mentioned the usefulness of notifications about the printer queue as helping them carry on with their work until they were sure the documents were printed (see Table 52 in Appendix G).

These results suggest that the messages enhanced the awareness of information that is hidden from view because they allowed people to appreciate the significance of event-triggered information.

Additionally, significant differences were found when comparing the average ratings of the appropriateness of the detail conveyed in the messages across participants' characteristics. Figure 37 illustrates that users less familiar with speech synthesis (TTS) rated the appropriateness of the message detail significantly higher (M = 6.29) than users who have more familiarity with speech synthesis (M = 4.63), t(9.53) = -2.330, p = .043. It may well be that people less familiar with text-to-speech (TTS) synthesis have difficulties in understanding short messages and thus need longer messages to appreciate properly the meaning of the event. Conversely, people more familiar with text-to-speech (TTS) synthesis are likely to feel more comfortable with shorter messages, as long as they convey sufficient cues. However, further research is required to investigate the adequate amount of detail according to different levels of familiarity with synthetic text-to-speech (TTS).

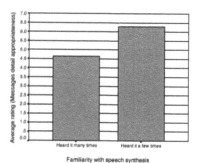

Figure 37. Average ratings for appropriateness of messages detail by familiarity with TTS

Finally, a significant difference was found across gender as far as appropriateness is concerned. Figure 38 illustrates that, while both female and male users are in agreement that the detail is appropriate, female users felt more comfortable (M = 6.50) with the amount of detail provided than male users (M = 5.00), t(13) = 2.514, p = .026. Further research should investigate what level should the amount of detail be for females and males, or whether male users need different types of cue when compared with female users.

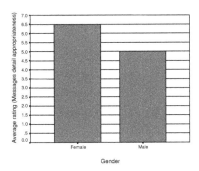

Figure 38. Average ratings for the appropriateness of spoken message detail by gender

Research Question 7

The seventh research question (Q7) sought to clarify what is an appropriate level of politeness that would make the system appear to be a humanised work companion. In this experiment, the main thrust was to uncover whether politeness in general is perceived to be an adequate aspect of spoken interaction from the perspective of reinforcing the social acceptability of the computer (by reducing its rudeness). The concept of politeness was investigated in a generic way: the experiment focussed on the most basic aspects of politeness, leaving more elaborate aspects to future experiments given that the results presented here justify such investigation.

In order to collect the user's opinions about the appropriateness of politeness, the system prototype provided simple polite utterances whenever obtaining the user's attention to an imminent notification or reminder. Participants were first asked to indicate whether they noticed the system politeness; all of them did. Then, they were asked to consider a set of statements and to rate their opinion on how well each statement described their feelings about the spoken messages:

"I think that the messages were **polite**".

"I think that the politeness was **appropriate**".

"I think that the politeness was **irritating**".

	Mean	Median	Mode	Std. Deviation
Level of politeness	6.07	6.00	6	.70
Appropriateness of polite messages	5.20	6.00	6	1.37
Polite messages do not irritate (recoded)	4.60	4.00	7	1.92

Table 18. Average ratings for the perception of the system politeness

The average ratings for these statements can be found in Table 18. On average, participants agreed that the messages were polite and that the polite messages were appropriate. However, the result is not so positive regarding the irritation caused by the polite attention-getters: some participants felt quite irritated while others did not feel irritated at all.

Since there is a considerable level of variation in this result, it is helpful to consider the comments made by participants about this topic. Users mentioned as particularly annoying the way in which the system kept repeating *"Excuse me"*. They also felt annoyed with naïve attention-grabbing utterances such as *"If you're not too busy"*.

These results indicate that careful choices must be made regarding the polite expressions, but it also indicates that the system should not be overly polite all the time. In fact, although people like politeness, the typical human behaviour is not to be overly polite all the time. Sometimes, a neutral, or even a more serious tone is the appropriate human behaviour for the situation.

On the positive side, three users welcomed the "courteous" nature of the system. It was also apparent that a completely unrelated feature of the system, the modulation of the audio channel through fading, was also perceived as polite behaviour because it avoided sudden transitions in the music. This reinforces the importance of designing systems that take into account social aspects which avoid a rude behaviour.

Also noteworthy are the differences found in users' ratings when compared across gender and operating system proficiency. First, a significant difference was found in average ratings of the perception of the degree of politeness: female participants found the system expressions significantly more polite (M = 6.75) than male participants (M = 5.82), t(13) = 2.747, p = .017. This is illustrated in Figure 39.

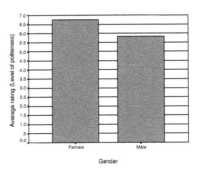

Figure 39. Average ratings for degree of politeness of system utterances by gender

As far as the appropriateness of polite messages is concerned, Figure 40 illustrates that participants with less operating system (O.S.) proficiency found the polite messages more appropriate (M = 5.88) than more experienced participants (M = 4.43), t(13) = -2.337, p = .036. These results seem to indicate that as users gain more experience with the computing environment, polite behaviour can sometimes be regarded as superfluous, even though it is welcome.

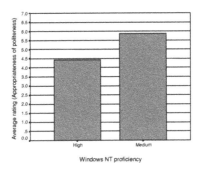

Figure 40. Average ratings for appropriateness of politeness by O.S. proficiency

These results highlight that while politeness reinforces the social presence of the computer, it will only enhance social acceptability if there is a careful design when including linguistic style. More specifically, there must be a careful choice of polite expressions and of the situations in which it is appropriate for the system to express more politeness through more indirect linguistic style strategies. There should also be an appropriate balance of indirect and direct behaviour over time in order to avoid irritation. Further research on this topic may uncover, for example, the relationship between the user's personality and the preferred linguistic style or styles.

Research Question 8

The research question Q8 was concerned with minimising user irritation, when listening to spoken notifications and reminders, by including another typical anthropomorphic behaviour: linguistic variation. Initially, participants were asked to consider the way the system said the same thing in different ways at different times. Then participants were invited to indicate whether they had noticed this system behaviour. Only eleven participants answered positively. Subsequently, these participants were asked to indicate their feelings about the linguistic variation, by rating the following statement:

*"I think that the variation was **irritating**".*

Table 19 illustrates the average ratings (N = 11) for this statement. It can be seen that participants did not feel irritated at all with linguistic variation (this variable was recoded during analysis). This is a positive result since the system was designed precisely to reduce irritation by varying otherwise repetitive messages. Furthermore, no significant differences were found.

	Mean	Median	Mode	Std. Deviation
Varied messages do not irritate (recoded)	6.09	6.00	7	1.04

Table 19. Average ratings for non-irritating varied spoken messages

Interestingly, four participants did not notice the linguistic variation even though it was a salient system feature. This is a further positive indicator that implies a high degree of naturalness: those features, which go unnoticed, behave in a natural way. Thus, it is safe to assume that non-repetitive spoken messages do *not* have a negative impact on user's irritation. Given this evidence, there is still the need to identify more precisely the amount of linguistic variation that makes the system cross the frontier between a non-irritating and an irritating assistant.

6.3.2.   Assessing speech-based assistance quality

In addition to the evaluation of specific anthropomorphic characteristics, there is also the need to investigate opinions concerning the quality of the assistance provided by the system, which is promoted by using speech to enhance information awareness. The set of results presented in this section was collected by asking participants to rate their views on a 5-point Likert scale - 5 being the highest rating. Participants were to consider a statement about the system, and then to answer by indicating their level of agreement ("1" = "Strongly Disagree", "3" = "Neither disagree nor agree", "5" = "Strongly agree"). The resulting ratings were subsequently compared across personal characteristics to uncover significant differences.

Research Question 9

Research question Q9 attempted to reveal the degree of assistance the system was perceived to provide in supporting the awareness of information that is hidden from view. Participants were asked to consider the influence of the system in all the activities they had to perform in order to conduct successfully the research task (e.g. they were required to check for particular e-mail messages, they had to print specific documents, and they were asked to perform certain searches on the World Wide Web (WWW), as described in section 6.2.2). Then, participants were invited to rate their opinion on the following statements:

"The assistant made the research task activities, like printing, managing things to do, checking e-mail and searching for answers, easier to perform".

"I felt the system was assisting me".

The average ratings for these statements can be found in Table 20. On average, participants definitely agreed that the system provided assistance for the tasks they had to perform that required them to be aware of dynamic information that was hidden from view. An index for *assistance quality* was obtained through the aggregation of both variables (Cronbach alpha = .97). Its value confirms that the system was perceived as providing good assistance for information awareness. The mean rating obtained was 4.10 out of a possible 5, with a standard deviation of .80.

	Mean	Median	Mode	Std. Deviation
The speaking assistant made the task easier to perform	4.07	4.00	4	.80
The system was assisting me	4.13	4.00	4	.83

Table 20. Average ratings for system assistance (on a 1 to 5 scale)

Significant differences concerning users' ratings of these variables were only found along the Intuition/Sensing dimension, as Figure 41 illustrates. Intuitive participants rated significantly higher ($M = 4.67$) the facility in performing the research task activities (that required them to be aware of hidden information) with the system assistance than Sensor participants ($M = 3.67$), $t(13) = 2.962$, p

= .011. Intuitive users also found that the system was assisting them to a higher extent (M = 4.67) than Sensor users (M = 3.78), t(13) = 2.317, p = .037.

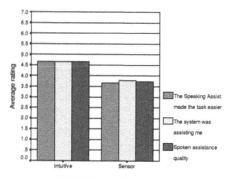

Personality Traits (MBTI): Intuitive(N) / Sensor(S)

Figure 41. Average ratings for system assistance by N/S personality traits

As before, these results seem to reveal that the system supports a heuristic style of information acquisition, which is based on providing a summary of an event related to personal information, leaving the concrete details for the most suitable graphical-based presentation. By enhancing the awareness of the meaning behind events, the system can be seen to facilitate the process of acquiring information that is graphically hidden from view.

The third difference shown in Figure 41 is related to the *assistance quality* index derived above. It consistently confirms this conclusion: Intuition-oriented people rated the quality of the assistance significantly higher (M = 4.67) than sensor participants (M = 3.72), t(13) = 2.662, p = .020. Given these results, it may be assumed that the context cues conveyed through speech-based messages help users to appreciate the meaning of information that is hidden from view.

Research Question 10

The next research question (Q10) was concerned with the acceptability of the system: the extent to which participants would continue to use the system prototype. Participants were asked to indicate their opinion by rating the following statement:

*"I would **continue** to use this system".*

Table 21 illustrates the user's average ratings on this statement. While on average participants agreed that they would continue to use the system, the result is not as high as the results shown in Table 20 for the system assistance. Since no significant difference among users' personality characteristics was found, it is helpful to consider the negative aspects participants expressed through their comments, which indicate their reservations about continuing to use the system.

	Mean	Median	Mode	Std. Deviation
I Would Continue to Use the system	3.87	4.00	4	.52

Table 21. Average ratings for continued system usage (on a 1 to 5 scale)

During content analysis, participants' comments were grouped into two main categories: those related to the anthropomorphic characteristics, and those related to the functional characteristics. Each of these categories was further subdivided to reveal the specific characteristics that require further research. Tables detailing the aspects presented below can be found in Appendix G.

In the **anthropomorphic characteristics** category the following aspects were generalised based on the users' comments (which are indicated below each item).

1. There is the need for better *linguistic naturalness*.

    • "There was insufficient variation in utterances and attention-getters".

    • "There was a lack of awareness of prior messages, so the system did not combine similar messages spoken in succession".

2. There is the need for better *speaking naturalness*.

    • "There was a low speaking rate".

    • "There was a low level of intonation both in utterances and attention-getters".

    • "Some attention-getters were overly polite and others were seen as inappropriate".

3. There is the need for *spontaneous behaviour*.

    • "The system had no sense of humour (e.g. did not tell any jokes)".

4. There must be a *balance* in the presentation of information.

   - "Messages were over-informative about printing starting status".

5. There is the need for higher-quality speech synthesis (and it may be interesting to explore the alternative possibility of using pre-recorded speech).

   - "Sometimes it was difficult to understand the voice, and that was annoying".

   - "The voice had a foreign accent".

In the **functional characteristics** category the following aspects were identified based on the analysis of the specific users' comments indicated below.

1. The graphical character was too intrusive.

   - "The character takes screen real estate", and sometimes it was mentioned as an "unnecessary presence".

   - "The character obfuscates graphically presented information and graphical controls".

2. There was a lack of context awareness.

   - "There was a lack of awareness of the user activity" (sometimes the system provided notifications and reminders about activities already completed or about information already seen).

The analysis presented above suggests a number of research issues that should be addressed both to reinforce the social acceptability of a speaking computer, and to enhance the functionality provided by a speech-based system for information awareness. Such improvements may result in an overall more humanised system.

Research Question 11

Another set of comments provided by the participants helped to obtain some evidence concerning research question Q11. Participants expressed their interest in having the system provide support for other personal information management domains, which disclose information that users wish to be aware of. Their comments are consistent with the results obtained concerning the ratings of the following statement:

"I would like the system to perform more spoken functions that were important to me".

Table 22 illustrates the average ratings for this statement on a 1 to 5 scale. As shown, users agree that they would like the system to make them aware of information related to other domains of personal information management (PIM). No differences were found between user characteristics. As before, the motivation for using the system is likely to increase if the anthropomorphic and functional aspects mentioned during the analysis of research question Q10 are taken into consideration.

	Mean	Median	Mode	Std. Deviation
I would like the system to perform more PIM functions	3.87	4.00	4	.74

Table 22. Average ratings for extending the domains monitored by the system

Research Question 12

Research question Q12 intended to collect the participants' opinions about making the system operate as an automated personal guide that would be actively providing spoken hints and directions while people were searching for information. Table 23 illustrates the average ratings for the following statement:

"I would like this system to also guide me while searching for information".

As can be seen, the results indicate that most participants disagree with the view that the experimental environment would provide a suitable guide. For example, it may be possible that some participants did not *trust* the system to an extent that would make them believe it was sufficiently competent to allow it to guide them. Furthermore, the system was designed to address specific information awareness problems. But guidance involves more than just helping people to stay aware of hidden information. While a guide should provide cues that allow a person to appreciate the information that is hidden behind a set of search results, it should also establish a dialogue with the user, accepting questions and clarifying statements. This implies that further research is needed concerning the specific requirements associated with humanised guidance, but the experimental environment that has been designed for this study may serve as a basis to investigate the issues involved in the provision of a humanised guide.

	Mean	Median	Mode	Std. Deviation
I would like the system to guide me while searching for information	2.67	2.00	2	1.23

Table 23. Average ratings for the interest in making the system operate as a guide

6.3.3.   Assessing humanisation and usefulness

This section presents the results found in studying the extent to which the anthropomorphic characteristics implemented in the prototype promote the perception of both a humanised and useful assistant (research question Q13).

	Mean	Median	Mode	Std. Deviation
Speaking assistant: pleasantness	4.73	4.00	4	1.10
Speaking assistant: helpfulness	5.80	6.00	5	.86
Speaking assistant: convenience	5.33	5.00	5	.90
Speaking assistant: reliability	5.60	6.00	7	1.55
Speaking assistant: comfort	5.47	6.00	6	1.13
Speaking assistant: efficiency	4.87	5.00	5	1.36
Speaking assistant: satisfaction	5.07	5.00	6	.88
Speaking assistant: unobtrusiveness (recoded)	4.73	5.00	6	1.94
Speaking assistant: likeability	5.00	5.00	5	1.00

Table 24. Average ratings for perceptions about system's humanisation and usefulness

The data was collected by asking participants (N=15) to rate their feelings using 7-point semantic differential scales (as illustrated in Table 10). Participants were asked to think in terms of their overall reactions to using the assistant, and then to rate their views on a set of nine variables, which were introduced in section 6.1.2. The intrusiveness variable was recoded during analysis into a measure of unobtrusiveness. Table 24 shows participant's average ratings for those variables.

On average all users' perceptions of the system are positive (the collected data may be found in Table 35 in Appendix E). These results indicate that users found the spoken assistance helpful and reliable. After performing factor analysis, two indices were derived through the aggregation of the variables. The index for system *usefulness* was obtained by the aggregation of the helpfulness, convenience and comfort variables (Cronbach alpha = .85). The index for *humanisation* was obtained by aggregating the remaining six variables (Cronbach alpha=.74). Table 25 shows that the system was considered both useful and humanised.

	Mean	Std. Deviation
Speaking assistant: usefulness (aggregated)	5.53	.85
Speaking assistant: humanization (aggregated)	5.00	.90

Table 25. Average ratings for system usefulness and humanisation

However, some of the results presented in Table 24 show that some variation exists among users' perceptions. As before, it is useful to investigate the differences in perceptions by establishing comparisons among users' personal characteristics. Some interesting differences were found.

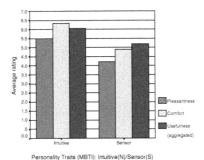

Figure 42. Average ratings for system pleasantness, comfort and usefulness by N/S

First, three significant differences were found along the Intuition/Sensing dimension. As Figure 42 illustrates, Intuitives tended to find the system more pleasant (M = 5.50) than Sensors (M = 4.22), t(13) = 2.629, p = .021. Similarly, Intuitives also found the system significantly more comfortable (M = 6.33) than Sensors (M = 4.89), t(13) = 3.091, p = .009.

There was also a difference in terms of the system usefulness (aggregation of helpfulness, convenience and comfort): Intuitives found the system more useful (M = 6.05) than Sensors (M = 5.18), t(13) = 2.181, p = .048. These results are consistent with the results found during the analysis of the specific system characteristics: the speaking assistant seems to be effectively supporting a heuristic approach to information acquisition. Furthermore, as far as the process of information acquisition is concerned, it seems that the prominent system feature is one of functionality: the usefulness afforded by the provision of contextual cues that enable people to appreciate the meaning behind events.

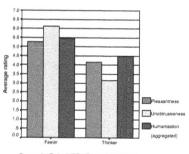

Personality Traits (MBTI): Feeler(F)/Thinker(T)

Figure 43. Average ratings for pleasantness, unobtrusiveness and humanisation by F/T

Significant differences were also found along the Feeling/Thinking dimension. These differences are illustrated in Figure 43. Feelers found the system more pleasant (M = 5.25) than Thinkers (M = 4.14), t(11.569) = 2.271, p = .043. Similarly, Feelers found the system far less intrusive (M = 6.13) than Thinkers (M = 3.14), t(13) = 4.677, p = .000. This is the most significant difference found during the study. It may be suggesting that such behaviours as interrupting just to convey relevant information, varying otherwise repetitive messages, and drawing attention in a polite way make the system appear as if it based its decision of interrupting on person-centred values. That is, participants may have perceived the system to be evaluating the impact of its interruptions, and trying to behave in a way so as to preserve harmony. This is precisely the kind of behaviour that would be noticed by Feelers, because it is their distinctive mode of making decisions. This may explain why Feelers found the system less intrusive, more pleasant, and globally more humanised (M = 5.45) than Thinkers (M = 4.47), t(13) = 2.470, p = .028.

Significant differences were also found along the Judging/Perceiving dimension. Figure 44 illustrates that Perceiving-oriented people found the system more helpful (M = 6.33) than those who are Judging-oriented (M = 5.44), t(13) = -2.212, p = .045. Perceivers also found the system more convenient to use (M = 6.00) than Judgers (M = 4.89), t(13) = -2.896, p = .013. Similarly, Perceiving-oriented participants found the system more useful (M = 6.05) than Judging-oriented participants (M = 5.18), t(13) = -2.181, p = .048.

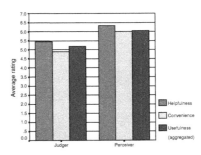

Figure 44. Average ratings for system helpfulness, convenience and usefulness by J/P

Before drawing conclusions from these results, it is worth making two observations. First, helpfulness and convenience are both aspects of the system's usefulness. Second, as stated before, the psychological dimension of Judging/Perceiving can be seen as a reference to a personal preference for either a Judging function (Thinking or Feeling) or a Perception function (Intuition or Sensing). Since the results concerning the ratings of the system usefulness were higher for Perception-oriented people than for Judging-oriented people, this indicates that the system emphasises its support for the information acquisition process (the Perception function). So, these results are consistent with those already presented for the Intuition/Sensing dimension: their emphasis was also found to be on the system usefulness. In summary, these results appear to indicate that the system provides useful support for information awareness (which corresponds to the heuristic approach to information acquisition).

The last research question this study was designed to investigate (Q14) concerns the comparison of users' perceptions of the Speaking Assistant with those of the MS Office Assistant (the original data may be found in Table 51 in Appendix F). Figure 45 illustrates the differences in users' average ratings for the nine dimensions introduced above. The number of responses used for the comparison (N = 13) is less than the number of participants in the experiment because two users did not provide any answers concerning their perceptions of the MS Office Assistant; they did not have previous experience with the assistant.

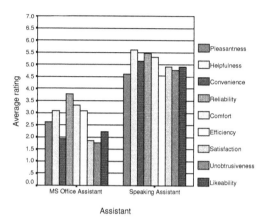

Figure 45. Differences in ratings for the MS Office Assistant and the prototype

It must be noted however that only participants' perceptions of the assistance provided by both systems are being compared. In fact, because both systems offer assistance in different domains, it is not possible to compare the functionality they offer. But since both interrupt the user to provide information that might be useful, one system emphasising a graphical approach (MS Office Assistant), and the other a speech-based approach (Speaking Assistant prototype), it is possible to compare users' reactions to the way each system delivers information.

On average the speech-based approach to interrupting (as implemented in the Speaking Assistant prototype) was rated significantly higher than the graphical approach employed by the MS Office Assistant in all dimensions under analysis. Interestingly, the major differences were found for average ratings of helpfulness and convenience (dimensions related to the system usefulness), and average ratings of satisfaction and unobtrusiveness (dimensions related to the system's humanisation). Moreover, all the differences shown in Figure 45 are statistically significant as the results of the comparison test in Table 26 illustrate.

Paired Samples t - Test

		Paired Differences						df	Sig. (2-tailed)
		Mean	Std. Deviation	Std. Error Mean	95% Confidence Interval of the Difference		t		
					Lower	Upper			
Pair 1	MS Office assistant: pleasantness – Speaking Assistant: pleasantness	-2.00	2.00	.55	-3.21	-.79	-3.606	12	.004
Pair 2	MS Office assistant: helpfulness - Speaking Assistant: helpfulness	-2.54	1.45	.40	-3.41	-1.66	-6.312	12	.000
Pair 3	MS Office assistant: convenience - Speaking Assistant: convenience	-3.23	1.17	.32	-3.94	-2.53	-9.992	12	.000
Pair 4	MS Office assistant: reliability - Speaking Assistant: reliability	-1.69	2.14	.59	-2.98	-.40	-2.856	12	.014
Pair 5	MS Office assistant: comfort - Speaking Assistant: comfort	-2.00	1.29	.36	-2.78	-1.22	-5.586	12	.000
Pair 6	MS Office assistant: efficiency - Speaking Assistant: efficiency	-1.46	2.15	.60	-2.76	-.17	-2.456	12	.030
Pair 7	MS Office assistant: satisfaction - Speaking Assistant: satisfaction	-3.08	1.26	.35	-3.84	-2.32	-8.835	12	.000
Pair 8	MS Office assistant: unobtrusiveness (recoded) - Speaking Assistant: unobtrusiveness (recoded)	-3.00	2.12	.59	-4.28	-1.72	-5.099	12	.000
Pair 9	MS Office assistant: likeability - Speaking Assistant: likeability	-2.69	1.70	.47	-3.72	-1.66	-5.703	12	.000

Table 26. Differences between the MS Office Assistant and the Speaking Assistant

However, it is important to note that while users had previous experience with the MS Office Assistant, this was their first experience ever with the Speaking Assistant. Thus, it is not possible to draw any general conclusions from the differences presented above. However, it is possible to take those differences as an indication that speech induced anthropomorphism, used as a mechanism for enhancing the awareness of dynamic information that is hidden from view, is a potentially interesting alternative over an approach that is purely based on the graphical delivery of information.

6.4   Further discussion and design implications

The experiment described in the previous sections aimed at being an initial, but thorough, study of the effects caused by speech-induced anthropomorphism, when used at the interface to enhance the awareness of information that is hidden from view.

This experiment allowed tight control of the tasks that the participants performed using the experimental environment prototype, while simulating a computer-based work environment that reproduced a familiar research environment. This made it possible to obtain observations of the participant's perceptions which could be compared in a consistent way. Given the reduced dimension of the experimental group and the lack of a control group with which to compare the results, the subjective measures analysed only serve as useful indications for the design of speech-based interfaces for information awareness. These measures may be verified through more controlled experiments.

The empirical study reported here has provided a number of findings related to the objectives of this research. These findings provide partial answers to the three main questions posed in section 6.1. The first question was the following:

"How useful do users find it to be interrupted using spoken language at the interface to convey information that is hidden from view?"

The study demonstrated that the participants in the experiment found it useful to be interrupted using speech to convey information that is hidden from view, as an unobtrusive complement to the graphical presentation of information. The prototype was perceived as supporting the awareness of visually hidden information, since it appears that the exploitation of speech-based alerts was considered useful by those with a distinct preference for a heuristic style of information acquisition. This means that speech-based notifications and reminders allowed the participants to appreciate the relationship and connections between the facts presented through the speech-based alerts. Since heuristic information gatherers also prefer to acquire information through relationships with people, this finding also suggests, and reinforces the idea, that using speech to convey information may cause the person to establish an unconscious social relationship with the computer.

The way speech was exploited to support information awareness was to summarise information that would otherwise be visually obtrusive. These alerted the participants to the imminence or occurrence of personal information related events. The alerts offered a number of context cues (called *forward cues*), which were designed to allow the participant to appreciate an item (or a number of items) of information in a non-disruptive way; that is, without having to look at it (or at them). The study demonstrated that this is a *valid* approach to exploit speech as a complementary medium for information presentation. Participants indicated that the context cues provide the right semantics of events and thus helped them to understand the meaning of event-triggered information, and thus helped them to stay aware of information that is hidden from view. Participants also indicated that speech-based interruptions were not disruptive, and that they allowed them to decide when to deal with the visually hidden information.

The second question presented in section 6.1 was as follows.

"Does polite, linguistically varied and urgency- and priority-based interrupting speech reinforce the social acceptability of the interface?"

The study demonstrated that all three anthropomorphic characteristics are *important* and *adequate* to reinforce the social acceptability of a speech-based interface, and surprisingly the system was indeed *well accepted* by those who participated in the experiment. This means that proper interrupting behaviour, linguistic variation and politeness combine to avoid socially incorrect manners such as, respectively unnecessary interruptions, irritating repetitions and rudeness. In fact, the urgency- and priority-based interruptions were perceived as relevant (indicating that the system appeared to know "when to interrupt"). Additionally, the way the spoken alerts obtained the user's attention and interrupted the audio channel was also perceived as a natural means of interrupting (indicating that the assistant prototype made the right decision about "how to interrupt").

These findings suggest that an appropriate filtering mechanism for interruptions, the prevention of sudden interruptions through attention-getting, and a correct modulation of the audio channel are all major aspects to take into account when designing speech-based interruptions, in order to promote the perception of the computer as a well-behaved social companion.

But in order to reinforce the social acceptability of a speech-based interface, the spoken messages must also employ linguistic variation. The study demonstrated that when spoken messages were varied that did not irritate the participants in the experiment. Moreover, the varied messages were perceived as being so natural, that some participants did not even notice that the messages were being varied. Conversely, when linguistic variation was insufficient it caused irritation amongst participants, who mentioned the annoying repetitive tone of some messages.

This finding suggests that linguistic variation is also a major factor to be taken into account when designing speech-based interfaces for information delivery.

The last anthropomorphic characteristic studied was politeness (or linguistic style). It was exploited in a simple way by making the system adopt a limited range of linguistic expressions that obtained the participant's attention through indirect linguistic styles. So instead of just interrupting and conveying a message straight away, participants were first cued with polite expressions that served as introductions to the actual content to be conveyed. However, the results arising from the politeness studies are not as clear as those obtained for the other anthropomorphic behaviours. While the study demonstrated that the "behaviour" of the system was perceived as polite, and that this polite behaviour was sometimes appropriate, it caused negative reactions on some participants, who stated they were annoyed with some expressions.

These findings suggest that linguistic style may reinforce the social acceptability of a speech-based interface, but they also suggest that politeness may reinforce social rejection of the same interface. Thus, an overly polite behaviour is likely to be seen as inappropriate and irritating. It is important for a speech-based interface to avoid rudeness and express courtesy, but what is clear is that this implies that there must be a careful design of polite expressions, and that there must be a match between the linguistic style adopted and the type of message being conveyed. Furthermore, linguistic style is often used by people to cue others as to their personality. In the case of this study, it was not clear to participants the kind of "personality" the system was trying to exhibit. This suggests that once a linguistic strategy is chosen to convey a certain kind of information, it must be consistently applied to subsequent interactions, in order to allow the user to consistently attribute a "personality" to the computer as it is implied through the polite expressions. For example, a more serious and direct tone might be used for urgent information, while more indirect strategies could be employed for less urgent information that still requires the user to perform some action, and this choice of styles should be applied consistently by the system.

The last question presented in section 6.1 was the following.

"How humanised does such a system appear to be?"

The study demonstrated that speech induced anthropomorphism contributes to the enhancement of the perception of a humanised, socially acceptable interface for information awareness in the e-mail, diary and printing domains. The results show that participants were pleased and satisfied with such a system, and that it promoted the perceptions of reliability and efficiency. A humanised system for information awareness should also promote an enjoyable interaction and, above all, it should effectively assist in maintaining awareness of information instead of imposing the actual information. This means that the system should be unobtrusive while drawing the attention to the information. The results show that participants liked the system prototype and that it was perceived as being moderately unobtrusive.

Although the results of this study cannot be generalised, the findings discussed above suggest some important implications for the design of speech-based systems for personal information management, and in particular for information awareness.

First, speech appears to be an appropriate and visually unobtrusive means of alerting the user to information that is hidden from view. It can be used in this way to complement the graphical presentation of the information.

Second, speech should be used to convey short summaries about event-triggered information, and this may be achieved by including context cues that characterise the events. This facilitates the heuristic acquisition of information in that it enables people to appreciate the meaning of event-triggered information.

Third, since using speech invokes an unconscious social response from the user, it should be conveyed using typical social norms such as importance-sensitive and well-structured interruptions, and linguistic variation. Using these anthropomorphic characteristics reinforces the social acceptability of the speech-based system and enhances the perception of a humanised assistant.

Fourth, using speech is likely to give the system a personality. The choice of linguistic style may reinforce the social acceptability of the speech-based system, but it also may irritate users if it is not used in a way that is consistent with the personality that was expected. *Spontaneity* seems to be the key aspect that users would welcome in future speech-based systems for personal information management. This should promote the perception of an interrupting behaviour that arises naturally rather than resulting from an inflexible personality. For example, the design of spontaneity might be coupled with urgency or importance of the message. A spontaneous system may have a positive impact, rather than causing irritation, on a user's disposition when working with a computer. Spontaneity may therefore increase the social acceptability of a speaking system by making it appear to possess a native tendency to assist and please the user, without imposing the obligation of making precipitated decisions.

6.5   Summary

This chapter has described an empirical study undertaken to assess whether speech induced anthropomorphism, employed as an unobtrusive mechanism for user alerting, enhances information awareness and reinforces the social acceptability of the computer, enabling it to be perceived as a humanised work companion. The experiment used a working prototype, an experimental environment that was designed to exhibit a range of anthropomorphic characteristics, such as knowing when and how to interrupt, linguistic variation and politeness, when conveying notifications and reminders. These alerts included context cues extracted from e-mail messages, printed documents and diary entries.

It should be emphasised that the study was designed using a quasi-experimental set up, which attempted to simulate as close as possible a typical research environment. It used research students and research staff who are not typical of other work environments such as corporate environments. Fifteen participants were selected to perform a search task which involved being aware of information that was hidden from view. They gave their opinions and perceptions about the various characteristics implemented in the prototype. Participants were all familiar with the computer-based environment, with text-to-speech (TTS) synthesis, and with the tasks they were asked to perform.

The research determined that the participants perceived the system to be both useful and humanised. The speech-based notifications and reminders have been shown to be an effective way of enhancing information awareness through "forward cues". These reduced the participants' activity because the spoken messages allowed them to keep looking at the screen while being able simultaneously to listen to urgent and high-priority alerts. Participants kept on working but they were made aware of upcoming or new events, and aware of information that still needed their attention.

Because it makes the interaction more social, speech induced anthropomorphism may significantly increase the productivity of a person working with a computer because it increases the acceptability of interruptions and reduces the rudeness and irritation inherent in interruptions.

Although the results of this study cannot be generalised, the findings reported and discussed in this chapter suggest some important implications for the design of future speech-based systems for information delivery, which may be verified through more controlled experiments.

Chapter 7

CONCLUSIONS: DESIGN GUIDELINES AND CONTRIBUTIONS

7.1 Overview

This research work was motivated by the belief that speech output should be used to complement current graphical interfaces for personal information management, in order to reduce the disruptive effect that graphical interfaces have on the tasks being performed. For example, finding information that is hidden from view is distracting and cognitively costly. User alerting interruptions, often unimportant, cause a loss of concentration and reduce productivity. Alerts designed to notify and remind users either do not convey sufficient semantic information about the interrupting event, or they are conveyed in such a way that they require users to perform some action before they can resume their current activity. Moreover, these interruptions are raised in a non-integrated way that poses an additional burden on the user's memory through inconsistency in the user interaction.

Whether they realise it or not, people react socially to computers (Reeves and Nass, 1996) and this reaction is amplified when speech output is used. This justifies the need to humanise the speech so that the computer's behaviour is perceived to be like that of a human. By reinforcing the anthropomorphic perception of a speaking computer it is possible to reinforce its social acceptability and provide a more enjoyable and less irritating system for information awareness. This research has addressed a number of key anthropomorphic behaviours that relate to speech output: well-structured interruptions, linguistic variation and politeness.

This chapter reviews the achievements and limitations of the research work, and presents the findings in relation to other research efforts. The chapter concludes with a summary of the research contributions and a number of directions for future work.

7.2 Achievements of this research

The literature review explored the anthropomorphic characteristics that reinforce the social acceptability of a speech-based system, and the psychological aspects that can be used to guide the design of an enhanced interface for information awareness using speech output. The research necessitated the design of an extensible experimental environment that was based on the assistant metaphor, as applied to the e-mail, diary and printing domains. An empirical study was undertaken to investigate the usefulness of speech, and to investigate the adequacy of anthropomorphic behaviours in promoting the perception of a humanised system that enhances information awareness.

7.2.1.   How and why to reinforce the social acceptability?

In investigating how to reinforce the social acceptability of a speech output system, this research has proposed the inclusion of important anthropomorphic aspects in the design; these include: well-behaved interrupting behaviour, linguistic variation and politeness.

Deciding when and how to interrupt

Sawhney and Schmandt (2000) addressed the problem of managing interruptions delivered by a wearable device and suggested an interruption model that enables the system to decide "when to interrupt" based on three pieces of contextual evidence: the priority of messages, the usage level of the wearable device and the environmental context. The model proposed in this book differs from Sawhney and Schamndt's in that (1) it addresses a desktop-based work environment, and (2) it bases the decision of "when to interrupt" on the distinct notions of urgency (immediate relevance) and priority (long-term relevance). Unlike Sawhney and Schmandt's (2000) approach, the model proposed here relies on storing urgency and priority information associated with pieces of personal information in a user profile, which is then consulted by the system to decide when to interrupt the user.

Horvitz et al. (1999) also suggest a context-based approach, but they use Bayesian models to infer the user's focus of attention under uncertainty. The model proposed in this book differs in that it does not attempt to predict the user's level of engagement in an activity, but it associates a precedence level to interrupting messages, which depends on their calculated urgency and priority values. So the high-precedence interrupting messages will always be conveyed regardless of the user's level of attention.

The problem of deciding how to interrupt has also been addressed by Sawhney and Schmandt (2000), who propose a method relying on structuring and assembling increasingly intrusive aural messages that employ both ambient sound and speech output. The model proposed in this book differs in that it is based on a simple two-phase process that uses short speech-based expressions to obtain the user's attention, and then conveys the actual content. However, while Sawhney and Schmandt (2000) rely on conveying parts of the actual contents of an information item being monitored (e.g. parts of the contents of an e-mail message), the approach taken in this research work differs in that it relies on extracting contextual cues from information items and assembling language expressions which convey a summary of information rather than their actual contents. Additionally, the method proposed in this book also modulates the audio channel to cater for the cases when it is already being used by other audio-based presentations. The importance of an appropriate interruption to the audio channel is also stressed by Papp and Blattner (1996) who highlight the need for a centralised audio presentation system that addresses "the problems that occur when multiple programs running simultaneously attempt to use the audio output of a computer system" (Papp and Blattner, 1996). The work described in this book also recognises the perceptual problems that arise from overlapping audio output from a number of applications and provides a mechanism that co-ordinates audio presentations through a modulation technique based on fading.

However, the approaches taken in this research to decide when and how to interrupt are still limited. The decision as to "when to interrupt" is based on just two basic (low and high) values for the urgency and priority parameters. Expanding the number of values would refine the granularity of choice. Furthermore only music is interrupted. Future work should accommodate the interruption of the visual channel so as to cater for the cases where a video presentation must be interrupted. Finally, the system should be enhanced to include situations where the user is engaged in a spoken dialogue with the system.

Linguistic variation

The need for variation in speech output has been stressed by Witten (1982), who proposes varying the prosody of speech output, and Reiter and Dale (1995), who propose varying the words used to express a concept, in order to minimise the irritation caused by listening to repetitive spoken messages.

This research work has analysed a hierarchy of linguistic layers, proposed by Schmandt (1994), which highlight the processes that humans employ to communicate verbally. Based on this framework, this research has identified the types of linguistic variation in a more systematic way so that variation does not interfere with the underlying meaning of a message. Linguistic variation may be achieved through phonetic, lexical, and syntactical variations. This book proposed a model for linguistic variation that *integrates* these three types of variation in the global process of generating speech output. The model involves using a template-based approach for including lexical and syntactical variation, and an approach based on controlling the prosody of utterances by annotating their text representations prior to sending them to the text-to-speech (TTS) engine.

This method is limited in that it requires the system designer to expend a great amount of effort on creating a template-base that is appropriate for the personal information domains in which the system operates. However, this method may be regarded as an advantage rather than a limitation if it is considered that it allows the naturalness of the resulting expressions to be enhanced when compared with the results produced by more automatic methods of natural language generation, such as the ones described by Hovy (1996). Ball et al. (1997) also employ a template-based approach including some variation in the responses generated by an assistant which allows the user to select and play music from a collection of audio Compact Discs. While their approach addresses a different application domain, it provides further evidence that the template-based approach might be a suitable method for enabling a tight control of the naturalness of the resulting varied speech expressions.

The linguistic variation generation method proposed in this book is also limited in that the inclusion of phonetic variation is achieved after the language generation is completed. However, the process can be made even more integrated by annotating the language-generation templates with prosody markers rather than annotating just the resulting language expressions. This would allow the designer to exert even more control over "how varied and natural" the resulting speech messages sound.

Politeness

The phenomenon of politeness, or linguistic style, has been addressed by previous research, which attempted to influence the way in which listeners of interactive story and dialogue systems infer the personality and the character of a speaking computer, so as to make computer-based life-like characters appear to be more believable (Walker et al., 1997a). Other research has attempted to study and explain the linguistic phenomena that allow assigning character to a speaking computer, as the work described for example by Ardissono et al. (1999).

In contrast, the research work described in this book has investigated this phenomenon as a way of reducing the irritation inherent in interruptions while still maintaining a measure of harmony with the user. This research has investigated the relationship between indirect speech acts (Searle, 1975), the notion of *face* (Brown and Levinson, 1987) and the linguistic styles that might be adopted to reduce the irritation associated with interruptions. A number of polite expressions, which express varying degrees of indirectness in the attention-getters are used to cue the user for an upcoming spoken message. The aim was to investigate how users reacted to politeness, in order to establish its importance as a contributing factor to reinforcing the social acceptability of a speaking system.

The approach taken in this research is nevertheless limited in that the politeness phenomenon was included in a non-systematic way both on the attention-grabbing mechanism and on the spoken messages themselves. Thus, this research did not attempt to simulate a consistent personality by manipulating the politeness strategies that might be associated with different types of message. These limitations might be addressed by (1) integrating the politeness strategies in the construction language-generation templates in a systematic way, and (2) by associating different types of message with consistent politeness strategies (e.g. a more serious tone for messages that must interrupt immediately, and more indirect tones for messages that require the user to perform some action).

7.2.2.   How to enhance information awareness?

Speech output was used to convey alerting messages (notifications and reminders) that allow users to be aware of personal information related events (e.g. new items, items still needing attention, items to be used as part of a task) without them having to look at the graphical presentation of the actual information. It took into account the characteristics of human memory by including context elements in the design of the alerting messages. These context elements semantically cue the user to the underlying event, and were dubbed *forward cues* because they allow the person to appreciate the meaning of the information items, and provide a clear indication of what is going to be found, allowing users to decide when to interrupt what they are doing so as to look for the actual information.

Previous research in personal information management also recognised the importance of context as an aid to human memory, but those solutions mainly addressed information organisation problems rather than the problem of information awareness. For example, the *Memoirs* system (Lansdale and Edmonds, 1992) placed an emphasis on the exploitation of the human memory's episodic nature and tried to assess the effectiveness of an event-driven approach to information storage and retrieval. Other research efforts that used context elements as a means of facilitating information storage and retrieval include *Forget-Me-Not* (Lamming and Flynn, 1994), a wearable device which recorded interactions with people and devices, and stored this contextual information in a database for later query; the *Remembrance Agent* (Rhodes and Starner, 1996; Rhodes, 1997), which stored context elements along with text notes, and provided textual information relevant to a user's context (for example it would provide class notes when the user was entering a specific classroom); and other systems such as *Lifestreams* (Freeman and Gelernter, 1996), the *Hive Event Browser* (Bovey, 1996), and *Moneypenny* (Williamson, 1998). The research work described in this book differs in that it extracts and exploits context to enhance information awareness rather than information storage and retrieval.

Other research efforts in context-awareness applications for handheld and ubiquitous computing, rely on recognising the user's context in order to tailor the presentation of information that might be appropriate in that context. For example, information services may present different information depending on the user's location, the people around the user or even the objects that surround the user (see, for example (Brown et al., 1997); (Dey et al., 1999))(Pascoe, 1998; Schilit and Theimer, 1994). The work described in this book differs in that context is used to characterise the semantics of information items rather than the user's surroundings, so as to allow the user to commit event-related information to memory in a way that is more compatible with the cues that are used in subsequent retrieval of that information from memory.

Silverman (1997) states that the most common organising metaphor in computing, the desktop metaphor, both *enables* and *constrains* reminder opportunities. It enables reminding because it allows for example folders to be left visible, e-mail messages to remain unfilled or application windows to be left open, all acting as reminding cues of pending actions. However, this visual approach clearly favours location-based reminding and breaks down as the number of items grows, and clutters the screen.

Visual reminding alone is not sufficient and the research described in this book has suggested that it should be complemented with aural utterances for event-triggered notifications and reminders, in order to enhance the awareness of personal information. A number of issues have been explored including: (1) how to structure speech-based alerts; (2) deciding on what content to convey in alerts, which would benefit the future recognition of information; and (3) studying the effects of conveying simultaneous alerts as part of a single speech-based message.

In addressing these issues, this research achieved the following. First, it proposed a hierarchy consisting of four main types of structure for speech-based information presentation. Second, it specified the design of speech-based alerts (called monitor reports) as notifications (alerts to the imminence or to the occurrence of events) and reminders (alerts to events that have already occurred, but which still need the user's attention or action). Third, it specified a set of contextual cues (called *forward cues*) to be used in assembling the content part of monitor reports.

Finally, an experimental environment was developed which facilitated the study of the beneficial effects of conveying simultaneous alerts concerning several information items generated by the same source, as part of a combined monitor report (e.g. notifying the user about a number of newly arrived e-mail messages through a single spoken message, reminding the user of a number of upcoming to-do items, or notifying the user about the status of a number of printed documents). Future research would investigate how to combine items produced by different sources.

7.2.3.   Design and implementation of the speaking assistant

The design of the experimental environment highlighted a number of issues that are related to the adoption of agent-based techniques to create an assistant-like system which humanises information awareness. The design described in this book illustrated how to split the environment's functionality into a number of independent software agents, including *service* and *specialised agents*, and an *interface agent*. It illustrated an effective global software architecture comprising those software agents, and showed how to realise the internal architecture of each software agent so that it senses and communicates contextual information. The architecture enabled the agents to communicate with each other so as to decentralise the control. The system was able to transform collected information into appropriate speech-based messages designed to alert the user, and combine spoken information with a number of anthropomorphic traits so as to reinforce the social acceptability of the speech-based system.

The overall objectives of the experimental environment, which were fulfilled through its design and prototype implementation were as follows. First, it enabled the realisation of an empirical study of users' subjective perceptions and reactions to anthropomorphised spoken notifications and reminders, as well as to test the extent to which exploiting speech as a complementary mechanism for information awareness provides advantages over pure location-based approaches for user alerting (as are afforded by graphical user interfaces). Second, the experimental environment verified the suitability of agent-based techniques for designing and implementing speech induced anthropomorphic systems in support of information awareness.

There has been a growing body of related research either directed towards the application of agent-based technology to address personal information management problems, or focussed on the investigation of the effects of endowing computers with anthropomorphic qualities (also referred in the literature as believable or life-like characteristics). For example, Maes (1994) describes learning interface agents that reduce information overload by automatically handling e-mail messages, scheduling meetings, filtering Usenet newsgroups messages, and recommending entertainment sources. The agent-based experimental environment described in this book addresses similar personal information domains, but differs in that it complements Maes's (1994) approaches by automating the awareness of information that is hidden from view, rather than automating its organisation.

Mitchell et al. (1994) describe an interface agent that assists users in managing meetings entered in the user's diary by automatically learning that user's scheduling preferences through machine learning techniques. The experimental environment described in this book also employs a diary agent that relies on a set of user's preferences, but it differs from Mitchell's agent in that it is designed to help users stay aware of their meetings and other appointments through the generation of appropriate notifications and reminders, rather than attempting to automate the entry of events in users' diaries according to their preferences.

A personal assistant for helping users in repetitive personal information management tasks (Cesta and D'Aloisi, 1996) has been proposed by previous research. This was composed of a society of specialised agents (e.g. a mail agent and a meeting agent) that are co-ordinated by an interface agent, and which also communicates with the user. While the experimental environment described in this book is based on a similar decomposition of tasks among a number of specialised software agents, it differs in the nature of the tasks performed by these specialised agents. The monitoring and context extraction tasks performed by the specialised agents require different internal architectures and different communication capabilities, such as the ones described in sections 5.3 and 5.4 respectively.

Ball et al. (1997) describe a life-like conversational interface agent that employs speech input to select and play music from a collection of audio Compact Discs. It produces verbal responses to provide feedback to the user, along with animated gestures. Ball et al.'s (1997) aim was to investigate how to achieve a level of conversational competence and visual reactivity that would enable a user to "suspend disbelief" and interact with the system "in a natural fashion". The experimental environment developed in this book had a similar aim: to investigate the level of social competence that would enable users to perceive the speech-based assistant for information awareness as an anthropomorphised work companion. While interruptions and linguistic variation are common concerns addressed both by Ball et al. (1997) and by the research work described in this book, the target domains are clearly different. Ball et al. (1997) were more concerned with allowing the user to establish a "natural" dialogue with a computer-based assistant in order to carry out a very specific interactive task, while the research described in this book is more concerned with ways of enhancing the social acceptability of the speech produced by the assistant that draws the user's attention to information that is hidden from view.

Van Mulken et al. (1998) were interested in finding out what were the effects of anthropomorphising interface agents that support learning experiences, in terms of objective measures such as comprehension and recall. They describe a life-like interface agent that presents multimedia material to the user generated automatically or retrieved from the World Wide Web. It used a "repertoire of presentation gestures" (Van Mulken et al., 1998) that were designed to express emotions, communicative intentions and referential acts. In a similar vein, the research work described in this book investigated the effects of anthropomorphising an interface agent, but instead of relying on the analysis of objective measures, it studied subjective perceptions and reactions to the presentation of speech-based information that was conveyed to enhance the awareness of e-mail, printing and diary items. After all, objective measures are often not sufficient to evaluate the overall system quality as observed from the point of view of the user (Grosz et al., 1996).

Nevertheless, the experimental environment developed as part of this research work suffers from a number of limitations. First, it only enhanced the awareness of visually hidden information in the e-mail, printing and diary domains. This choice of domains is clearly biased towards a "research environment". This has limited the generality of the conclusions that could be drawn from the empirical study. Thus, there is the need to augment the range of personal information source domains supported in the system with additional specialised agents. Section 5.2.2.2 presents a range of examples of other domains that would benefit from enhanced information awareness. This requires an extension to the language generation template library. By enhancing the experimental environment in this way, it could be taken out of the research laboratory and used in a real-world situation.

Another limitation of the experimental environment has to do with the method of detecting the presence of the user. The *user monitor agent* is very limited in that it relies on testing the activation of the screen saver to detect whether the user is present at a given instant. An approach that is based on infrared detection would provide more reliable information concerning the user's whereabouts.

While four categories for the delivery of spoken information were proposed, the design of the experimental environment only included attention-getters and monitor reports. The inclusion of reportages and of the interactive guide requires extending the design with at least a co-ordination mechanism to synchronise the presentation of speech and graphical information. A mechanism for controlling a full dialogue with the user would be another enhancement.

A further limitation of the experimental environment includes the lack of additional *service agents* such as a *user profile agent* and a *user activity monitor*, which would further enhance the perception of a real work-companion, as described in section 5.6.5.

7.2.4.   Evaluating speaking systems: an empirical study

The experimental phase of the research evaluated the main hypothesis: that the incorporation of speech, conveyed using human discourse characteristics, reinforces the perception of a work companion, enhances information awareness, and therefore contributes to the humanisation of the computerised work environment.

The study was designed following a quasi-experimental model and simulated as close as possible a typical research environment. Fifteen participants were selected to perform a research task which involved being aware of information that was hidden from view. They provided their opinions and perceptions about the various anthropomorphic characteristics implemented in the prototype.

Participants were all familiar with the computer-based environment, including the text-to-speech (TTS) synthesis and the tasks they were asked to perform.

The experiment allowed collecting subjective measures that determined the following four key results.

First, it was determined that the participants perceived speech-based assistance for information awareness to be both useful and humanised.

Second, the study indicated that the speech-based monitor reports constitute an effective way of enhancing information awareness through *forward cues*, and facilitate the appreciation of the meaning behind events.

Third, the results indicate that speech induced anthropomorphism may increase the social acceptability of interruptions when they are relevant and sensitive to the user's work environment; in this way the irritation and rudeness inherent in interruptions may be more acceptable.

Finally, the study evaluated the adequacy of a number of specific anthropomorphic behaviours, and the results suggest that relevant and well-structured interruptions and linguistic variation contribute to the reinforcement of social acceptability. The investigation of polite behaviour suggests that it may lead to being rejected if the perception of a consistent personality is not reinforced using consistent indirect linguistic strategies.

It is this author's opinion that more controlled experiments should be carried out to validate the four suggestions given above.

In the study reported here, participants merely listened to messages, while in a full "personal assistant" scenario they would need to interact with it using speech input (e.g. to ask the assistant to present graphical information related to the speech-based alerts). As Lai et al. (2001) point out, this would require users both to remember the correct commands or expressions that the system understands, as well as to keep the context of the interaction in mind, which would further tax the person's cognitive resources (Lai et al., 2001). While this study did not address this problem, the experimental environment was designed in a way that allows future work to investigate the impact of establishing a full spoken dialogue on a user's cognitive resources.

An interesting remark emerged from the aspects participants did not like about the system (see Table 52 in Appendix G). One user indicated that the system had a foreign accent, and because of that the voice did not sound as expected. In fact, the language used during the experiment was American English. This may be suggesting that people would prefer listening to a voice that mimicked the voice of their own country. For example, perhaps Welsh people would like to listen to a Welsh accent. Further research would investigate whether this aspect contributes to enhance the perception of a work companion.

7.2.5.   Practical results: the design guidelines for speaking systems

Speech is an appropriate and visually unobtrusive medium that can be exploited to convey event-triggered alerts concerning information that is hidden from view.

Speech-based messages should be used to convey short summaries comprised of contextual cues in order to facilitate the user's acquisition of the meaning underlying event-related personal information.

Because speech invokes an unconscious social response in users, it should be conveyed following typical social norms. In particular, relevant and well-structured interruptions and linguistic variation should be adopted in order to reinforce the social acceptability of the system.

Finally, using speech is likely to encourage users to believe that they are in the presence of a personality. Thus, the choice of linguistic style (or polite expressions) must be made in a way that reinforces the consistency of that personality, or else should be avoided.

7.3   Contributions of this book

7.3.1.   Enhancing information awareness

The first key contribution of this book is in exploring speech output in desktop-based environments as a visually unobtrusive way of enhancing the support offered to human cognition as far as the awareness of dynamic and timely information is concerned, allowing a person to maintain the focus on the primary activity.

In fact, relatively few techniques have been explored for desktop-based environments that enable users to maintain awareness of the contents of personal information sources which produce dynamic information that is updated at frequent intervals, or which disclose information that should be conveyed to users in a timely fashion. Existing research efforts addressing information awareness in desktop-based environments have explored exclusively visual techniques, such as "constant and cyclic animations" (McCrickard, 2000), or "adjusting windows" (Bailey et al., 2000) to communicate information in the periphery and allow a person to focus on the primary task; or background audio techniques to assist in awareness, such as in the "Audio Aura" system (Mynatt et al., 1998).

In investigating how to exploit speech output as a complementary medium to a graphical user-interface so as to enhance the awareness of personal information that is hidden from view, this book contributes in addressing a number of under-investigated issues which are "still blocking further advances in the reminding arena" (Silverman, 1997).

First, this book contributes in identifying information awareness as a feature where speech output plays an important role as a complementary medium to the visual display of information - a need which has been pointed out by Cohen and Oviatt (1995). This book also identifies *forward cues* as valid contents of speech-based alerts that are compatible with human memory processes - a need which has been stressed by Silverman (1997). This book has also contributed to the understanding of the beneficial effects that systems have on users when many simultaneous alerts disclosed by a common source of information are spoken as a single message - a need that was pointed out by Silverman (1997).

In summary, this research has demonstrated that for a narrow experimental group the exploitation of speech to convey *forward cues* facilitates information awareness because it enables people to appreciate the meaning behind event-triggered personal information.

7.3.2.   Anthropomorphic-based information awareness

The second key contribution of this book lies on the design of a computer-based system which is, as far as the author is aware from the reported literature, the first to integrate the speech-induced anthropomorphic characteristics of knowing when and how to interrupt, linguistic variation and politeness into a single speaking assistant, which served as an experimental environment for investigating their usefulness in the information awareness arena.

There was no reason to believe that such anthropomorphic characteristics would be well accepted, but the research demonstrated that a careful design including those traits effectively reinforced the acceptability of the system, and in consequence the system was perceived as being less rude and less disrupting compared with conventional graphical-based methods.

In addition, while linguistic variation has been addressed in previous research from the point of view of making speech recognition systems more robust to varied voice input (Oviatt, 1996), no attempts have been made until now to systematically characterise, incorporate in the design, and evaluate its importance from the point of view of generating spoken output. As far as politeness is concerned, the empirical study indicated that linguistic style might have a negative impact on some user's disposition. So it should be incorporated with care in the design of speech-based systems in general.

In synthesis, this research has identified that well-behaved interruptions, linguistic variation and politeness are important design factors that contribute to humanising a speech-based environment for information delivery because they avoid rudeness. It is this author's opinion that the social competence of a speaking computer is a critical factor for promoting the perception of a satisfying and enjoyable work companion.

7.3.3.   An extensible speaking assistant

While this work does not contribute in the understanding of agent technologies, the speaking assistant designed in this book contributes to understand the appropriateness of agent-based techniques to the development of anthropomorphic-based solutions to information awareness.

The speaking assistant contributes to the research community in that it provides an extensible agent-based software architecture that can be used in the future to incorporate and experiment with other typical speech induced anthropomorphic characteristics, such as the gender of the voice, back-channel expressions, personality and emotion, and to conduct more controlled experiments with larger and more varied types of user.

7.3.4.   Additional subjective measures to evaluate speaking systems

This work makes another contribution to understand how to evaluate users' perceptions of anthropomorphic systems that employ speech output. The empirical study has focussed on evaluating users' *subjective* opinions and reactions to a number of anthropomorphic characteristics included in a speech-based experimental environment for information awareness.

Grosz et al. (1996) argue that objective measures are as important as subjective ones when evaluating the output of a speech-based system. But previous research on the evaluation of speech output has emphasised objective metrics related to the success of the dialogue, such as the total time of an utterance, the number of user/computer dialogue turns, the rate of correction / repair turns, the response delay and the rate of appropriate/inappropriate utterances (Grosz et al., 1996; Oviatt and Adams, 2000; Sanders and Scholtz, 2000; Walker et al., 1997b; Walker et al., 1998; Litman and Pan, 1999).

However, in a previous study aiming at measuring the impact of synthetic and pre-recorded speech on users' performance, perception and attitude it is suggested that subjective measures are useful to evaluate a speech-based system, the voice used by the system and the user's experience (Gong and Lai, 2001). These researchers suggest collecting subjective measures to evaluate the system's ease of use, the clarity and the liking of the voice and the user's effort.

In a similar vein, this book suggests applying questionnaires to gather subjective measures, but it concentrates on the measurement of the adequacy of speech-induced anthropomorphic behaviour, and it extends Gong and Lai's (2001) measures with the evaluation of the following perceptions.

- The appropriateness, usefulness and disruptiveness associated with speech-based interruptions.

- The uniformity, appropriateness and confusion caused by having a single voice.

- The naturalness and interference associated with the technique used to interrupt the audio channel.

- The usefulness, annoyance and naturalness related to speech-based attention-getting.

- The facility of recognising the meaning conveyed through the contents of speech-based messages.

- The appropriateness and irritation related to polite utterances.

- The irritation and appropriateness associated with linguistically varied speech.

This work also suggests evaluating the perceptions of usefulness and humanisation promoted by the combination of speech-induced anthropomorphic traits through the following measures.

- The usefulness may be measured through the perceptions of helpfulness, convenience and comfort.

- The humanisation may be measured through the perceptions of pleasantness, unobtrusiveness, satisfaction, reliability, efficiency and likeability.

Finally, the book suggests evaluating the quality associated with speech-based assistance through the following perceptions.

- The facility in performing tasks which require the delivery of speech-based information.

- The degree of assistance provided by speech-based messages.

- The extent to which speech-based assistance would be used in future tasks.

7.4   Extensions and Future Work

7.4.1.   Addressing current problems and limitations

The empirical study collected participants' comments that provided invaluable indications about what they really *need* and *expect* from a humanised speech-based system for information awareness, as noted in section 6.3.3. For example, there is a need to improve the *user profiles* used by the specialised agents in order to make the system filter out unnecessary information and avoid interrupting the user with needless notifications and reminders. It is also necessary to extend the *template-base* to support the provision of more effective linguistic variation both at the sentence generation level and especially at the speech-based attention-getters generation level.

Given current limitations in the naturalness of text-to-speech (TTS) synthesis technologies, it would be worth replacing the text-to-speech (TTS) engine with pre-recorded speech and then performing a comparative study in order to verify whether using pre-recorded speech reinforces the social acceptability of the system beyond the level provided by mechanical speech synthesis. However, improving the speaking rate and the intonation produced by the text-to-speech (TTS) engine may be sufficient to increase the social acceptability of the synthetic speech approach.

There is also the need to extend the range of information the system senses from the surrounding environment. For example, including an additional *service agent* to *monitor the user's activity* may prevent the system from conveying alerts concerning activities already completed by the user, or alerts concerning information the user has already processed. Monitoring the user's activity may provide additional benefits. A recent initial study on the effects of instant visual messaging interruptions on computing tasks suggests that (1) interruptions which are relevant to the user's current task are less disruptive than those that are irrelevant; and (2) alerts delivered while the user is typing or processing chunks of other information may be problematic (Cutrell et al., 2000). The incorporation of a user monitor agent in the software architecture of the experimental environment proposed in this work would help to determine whether the message content is relevant to a user's current task prior to interrupting, and could provide updated information about the user's activity in order to avoid interrupting while the user is processing other chunks of information. Of course, this leads to an additional research issue, which needs further investigation: do users want to be constantly monitored? Do they dislike or feel uncomfortable with that?

As stated earlier, four categories for the delivery of spoken information were proposed in this book, but the design of the experimental environment only explored the purely aural attention-getters and monitor reports. This necessarily limits the information awareness support that could be offered by the system. The inclusion of *reportages* and of the *interactive guide* has the potential to create and deliver more engaging, but longer, presentations of information that are hidden from view. Such types of information delivery will require the creation of a co-ordination mechanism that enables the synchronisation of speech output with graphical material. The specialised agents need to be able to gather graphical content and deliver it together with the spoken messages. Early results (presented in this work) suggest that users are a little wary of a system that speaks to them in order to guide them to information.

The empirical study results have indicated that participants considered the graphical character to be visually intrusive and an unnecessary presence because it took up screen space and obfuscated other visual information being accessed as part of an ongoing task. This points to the need to perform further comparative studies in order to investigate whether the absence of a visual presence at the interface leads users to feel confused and uncertain whether the assistant is still running.

A problem that may be raised by a speech-based system for information awareness is related to the user's physical workplace. What happens when users work in an open space and are likely to listen to other speaking computers? Of course, in open plan offices there is always a murmur, so if the volume is kept low this problem may be reduced. Another way to address this problem is through the use of wearable devices (Billinghurst and Starner, 1999) that deliver aural information in a private manner. But will users be willing to wear such devices?

7.4.2.   Extending information awareness to other domains

As stated earlier, this research has investigated information awareness in a limited set of personal information management domains (those of e-mail, diary and printing). It has been demonstrated that for these domains speech induced anthropomorphism facilitates the acquisition of information that describes the meaning of dynamic and timely information in an unobtrusive way. However, further research is needed to extend information awareness support to other domains of personal information where such availability would contribute to a more productive work environment. This book has provided a number of suggestions for target domains that would disclose information useful to a user. The suggestions provided in section 5.2.2.2 include Usenet Newsgroups messages, birthday alerts, general announcements, auction alerts, personal finance warnings, investment opportunities and generic World Wide Web searches.

In order to extend information awareness to such domains future research may draw on the existing experimental environment features described in this book, and extend it incrementally to enable the realisation of further experiments aimed at investigating their suitability and acceptability.

Extending information awareness to other domains might enable the validation of the conclusions presented in this work with different groups of users. For example, corporate users may be more interested in the additional domains of Usenet newsgroups, general announcements, investments and generic World Wide Web searches, while home users might be more interested in birthdays, auctions and personal finance alerts.

This book has proposed a set of *forward cues* that can be used to create spoken messages with varying degrees of detail. By extending information awareness to other domains, such as the ones suggested above, it will be necessary to investigate which *forward cues* are appropriate for the generation of alerts and how much they may be varied.

7.4.3.   Extending the range of anthropomorphic traits

As mentioned earlier, this work has proposed and implemented a limited set of speech induced anthropomorphic traits: interruptions, linguistic variation and politeness. However, the experimental environment was designed in a way that it may be used as a basis for including and testing the importance of a number of other traits.

For example, previous research has determined that the gender of a pre-recorded voice used by a computer tutor cued stereotypical responses from users: the male-voiced computer tutor was rated significantly more informative than the female-voiced computer when providing exactly the same information (Nass and Gong, 2000). Two research issues follow from this finding. First, does this finding hold for synthetic speech? Second, what other demographic characteristics would invoke similar stereotypical responses from users? To address these issues, the experimental environment could easily be modified to generate male and female voices (perhaps from varying parts of the world). It could also be extended to promote the perception of other more complex demographic characteristics such as age, personality, emotion and expertise, through the manipulation of such parameters as the fundamental frequency, frequency range, amplitude and speech rate (Nass and Lee, 2001), combined with a careful choice of linguistic styles, such as the ones described in section 2.4.2.

Nass and Gong (2000) suggest further research issues related to the anthropomorphic characteristics of voice that could be incorporated in the experimental environment to enable the realisation of additional experiments:

- Should a particular synthesised voice be assigned to a specific user, or should the user be able to select the voice from a range of options?

- What are the consequences of computer-based speaking systems that refer to themselves as "I", the "Cartesian claim of personhood"? (Nass and Gong, 2000)

7.4.4.   Creating an automated personal assistant

An automated personal assistant can be seen as an artefact that collects fragments of personal information, stores them in a personal digital library and organises the presentation of this material using a combination of visual and audio mechanisms, according to the needs of the user. In essence this will be a high-level interface object that acts much like a *memory prosthesis* (Lamming et al., 1994) which exploits the human's memory capabilities of remembering the location and pathway to stored information.

The main objectives of such an assistant include the following.

- To facilitate the storage of personal information, supporting and automating the organisation, categorisation and classification processes.

- To facilitate the retrieval of personal information, supporting effective browsing and searching of the personal repository, and making relevant suggestions to the user during those activities, taking advantage of context and semantic meta-information.

- To facilitate information awareness; that is, the notification and reminding of dynamic and timely information, as well as of tasks to be done.

- To be aware of the user's presence and of the user's activities at the interface.

- To report back to the user in a conversational way, using speech output with or without visual material, and accepting speech input combined with other input modalities.

As shown in Figure 46, the automated personal assistant has a software architecture comprising four high-level functional modules, each of which can be regarded as separate assistants that communicate with each other: the Semantic Assistant (SA), the Context Assistant (CtxA), the Visual Assistant (VA) and the Conversational Assistant (CA). The research work presented in this work has concentrated on the speaking part of the humanised conversational assistant. Future research may investigate the specific requirements associated with the other three assistants, and investigate how to implement the high-level architecture proposed in Figure 46.

However, such a system poses additional interesting research issues. For example, with the advent of calculators, our performance to do mental arithmetic was reduced due to the lack of practice. If we had a *memory prosthesis*, a perfect memory assistant, would a similar effect happen to our memory? How do we avoid the equivalent negative aspects of the calculator? How can the system *enhance* the user's memory rather than make it stale? For example, this work has suggested that a possible enhancement would be to present users with their information in order to keep it fresh in their memory. The most important thing should be to ensure that the user remembers the location of information. But it is possible that the *memory prosthesis* will document a person's life. What happens then if this personal information falls into the wrong hands? (Bos, 1995; Norman, 1993).

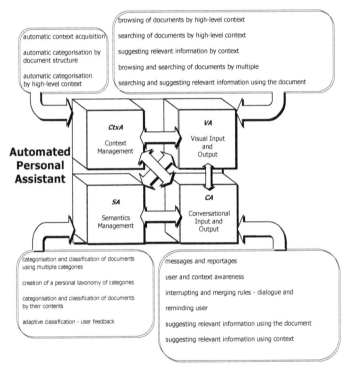

Figure 46. Automated personal assistant high-level software architecture.

7.4.5.   Other application areas

7.4.5.1.   Assistive Technologies for blind users

The term *assistive technologies* is used to refer to computer-based systems designed to help people with disabilities access computer-based information, and use computers to perform their work (Brown, 1992). For example, blind users gain access to computer-based information by enabling the computer to display information in an auditory mode (Brown, 1992; Raman, 1997). Since the approach to information awareness proposed in this book relies on exploiting speech to convey alerting messages, it would be interesting to investigate whether the experimental environment described here could be used as a useful complement to existing auditory solutions for blind users such as the "auditory desktop" (Raman, 1997; Raman, 1998).

7.4.5.2.   E-learning systems

E-learning is nowadays an alternative to traditional classroom-based education, and is founded on distributing and delivering courses and classroom lectures through the World Wide Web (Dorai et al., 2001). This mode of on-line learning is also popular as a means of employee training and education among business enterprises (Dorai et al., 2001).

In order to achieve an effective computer-based learning environment, a useful lecture browsing system, such as the Book Emulator (Benest, 1997) would enable access to all the materials pertaining to a course (e.g. slides, white-board contents and lecture notes) in an integrated manner. An On-Line Lecture attempts to mimic a live lecture, and includes an audio narrative which is synchronised with slide changes, revelation of information, animation and narrated construction of diagrams (Benest, 2000). Besides being available 24 hours a day, and being repeatable as often as required (Benest, 1997), this has the potential to facilitate searching (Benest, 2001) for a topic, a slide or a specific lecture note.

In this context, further research could investigate how to complement an On-Line Lecture with the speech-based mechanism for information awareness proposed in this work. This could be used for example to alert the student to relevant material that is related to the topic being consulted, and it would enable the student to be aware of a larger corpus of information without deviating the attention from the main visual presentation. Furthermore, the anthropomorphic aspects explored in this book may be applied to structure and create more engaging and less tedious presentations of material to be learnt (for example by delivering *reportages* to summarise a topic explored in a set of slides, or making available an *interactive guide* that could be summoned by students whenever there was the need to browse a large collection of slides).

7.4.5.3.   Digital Libraries

Digital libraries have proliferated in recent years and an increasing number of documents are currently being accessed via the World Wide Web. As more and more content is provided through digital libraries, an important research question is how to ensure that users are aware of new content added to the library, which matches their interests.

Because such repositories of digital documents have rather "poor usability from a reminding perspective"[23] (Silverman, 1997), current approaches rely on sending automated and personalised e-mail messages notifying users about new additions that match their interests. However, this approach only contributes to the problem of information overload.

A possible alternative would be to exploit the speech-based approach for information awareness described in this work. In order to investigate the suitability of this approach, the experimental environment could be extended with a specialised agent that would be responsible for monitoring the digital libraries subscribed to by a particular user, and look for new additions that match the topics of interest (which could be stored in a user profile and updated regularly). This agent could then issue notifications as soon as new content is added, as well as reminders concerning previously seen items that might have been forgotten. Whenever the user is looking for a specific topic, further extensions to the specialised agent functionality would enable the agent to be asked to generate a *reportage* summarising new additions or summarising a collection of documents of interest. The agent could gather the material required to guide the user to the specific locations of the required documents in a more interactive way.

7.4.5.4.   Workflow management

Silverman (1997) states that computer-based alerts play a critical role in software that connects people across space and time to help them co-operate, converse and exchange documents; all

---

[23] Digital libraries can be browsed to explore for new contents or to remind users of previously consulted material, but they provide access to such a huge number of documents that they cannot be effective in this "reactive fashion" (Silverman, 1997).

important aspects of workflow management. Workflow can be described as the movement of documents and tasks through a business process, while workflow management systems enable organisations to define and control the activities associated with a business process (DiCaterino et al., 1997). One important feature of workflow management systems is the "event notification" functionality which should enable staff and managers to be notified when milestones occur, workload increases, or new tasks are assigned, and reminded of overdue items and the personnel assigned to handle those items (DiCaterino et al., 1997). Silverman (1997) suggests that workflow reminders should make people more productive. Alerting messages comprising not only reminders but also notification messages of the kinds suggested above should help in making the overall workflow more co-ordinated and efficient.

In this context, complementing workflow management systems with the incorporation of the speech-based approach for information awareness suggested in this work could provide additional benefits in that it would support the provision of visually unobtrusive alerts, helping people to maintain awareness of critical workflow-related information, while maintaining their focus on their current task. Anecdotal evidence collected by the author (of this book) indicates that much time is spent looking for workflow-related alerts, normally conveyed through e-mail messages, which adversely affects users' concentration and diminishes their productivity.

7.5   Final Remarks

Overall, this research has contributed to the understanding of the nature of the information awareness problem, and has concluded that speech induced anthropomorphism offers a valid and visually unobtrusive alternative to graphical-based methods to assist in maintaining awareness of the significance of event-related information. This book provides a framework for future research on the exploitation of speech-based interaction employed to enhance information awareness, as well as for future investigations of the anthropomorphic properties of truly enjoyable and socially acceptable personal assistants for personal information management. This work has uncovered and addressed a number of design issues which the author expects may serve as useful guidance for the creation of more humanised systems. The author's perception of the importance of using speech induced anthropomorphic behaviours in reinforcing the social acceptability of a system designed to enhance information awareness has been confirmed at a level beyond that expected. Further empirical studies should be used to validate this conclusion in a more general way.

Appendices

Appendix A: Prototype implementation materials

Appendix B: Accompanying handouts for the experiment

Appendix C: Questionnaires used in the experiment

Appendix D: Experiment implementation materials

Appendix E: Supporting tables of experimental results

Appendix F: Tables of statistical tests

Appendix G: Data from participants' comments

Appendix A

PROTOTYPE IMPLEMENTATION MATERIALS

Template-base

[EMAIL_NOTIFICATION]
00="mail1s0#you've got one new e-mail message"
01="mail1s1#there is one new message in your inbox"
02="mail1s2#there's one new message in your inbox"
03="mail1s3#you've got a new message"
04="mail1p0#you've got [quantity] new messages"
05="mail1p1#there are [quantity] new messages in your inbox"
06="mail1p2#there's [quantity] new e-mail messages"
07="mail2s0#you've got one new e-mail message from [people]"
08="mail2s1#there is one new message from [people]"
09="mail2s2#there's one new e-mail message from [people]"
10="mail2s3#you've got a new message from [people]"
11="mail2p0#you've got [quantity] new messages, including ones from [people]"
12="mail2p1#there are [quantity] new messages from [people]"
13="mail2p2#there's [quantity] new e-mail messages from [people]"
14="mail3s0#you've got one new e-mail message from [people]. This message is about [description]"
15="mail3s1#there is one new message from [people]. The subject line is [description]"
16="mail3s2#there's one new e-mail message from [people]. The message is about [description]"
17="mail3s3#you've got a new message from [people]. This message is about [description]"
18="mail3p0#you've got [quantity] new messages, including ones from [people]. Description of these messages include: [description]"
19="mail3p1#there are [quantity] new messages. These came from [people]. The description include: [description]"
20="mail3p2#there's [quantity] new e-mail messages. They were sent by [people]. The messages cover: [description]"
21="mail1n0#you've got no new messages"
22="mail2n0#there's no new messages in your inbox"
23="mail3n0#sorry! no new e-mail yet"

[EMAIL_REMINDER]
00="mail1s0#don't forget there's an unread email message in your inbox"
01="mail1s1#please remember that there's still one email message to be read"
02="mail1s2#there is one old email message for you to read"
03="mail1s3#did you remember to read your unread email?"

04="mail1p0#you've still got [quantity] unread messages"

05="mail1p1#don't forget you have [quantity] unread messages in your inbox"

06="mail1p2#please remember the [quantity] e-mail messages that you didn't read yet"

07="mail1p3#did you remember the [quantity] e-mail messages left in your inbox?"

08="mail2s0#you've still got one unread e-mail message from [people]"

09="mail2s1#don't forget there's one unread message from [people] in your inbox"

10="mail2s2#please remember that there's still one email message from [people] to be read"

11="mail2s3#there is one old email message from [people] for you to read"

12="mail2p0#you've still got [quantity] unread messages, including ones from [people]"

13="mail2p1#don't forget you have [quantity] unread messages in your inbox. The messages came from [people]"

14="mail2p2#please remember the [quantity] e-mail messages that you didn't read yet. These messages were sent by: [people]"

15="mail3s0#you've still got one unread e-mail message from [people]. This message is about [description]"

16="mail3s1#there's still one unread message from [people]. The subject line is [description]"

17="mail3s2#don't forget there's one unread e-mail message from [people]. The message is about [description]"

18="mail3s3#did you remember the message from [people] left in your inbox? He was talking about [description]"

19="mail3p0#you've still got [quantity] unread messages, including ones from [people]. Description of these messages include: [description]"

20="mail3p1#don't forget there are [quantity] unread messages in your inbox. These messages came from [people]. The description include: [description]"

21="mail3p2#did you remember to check the [quantity] e-mail messages you left unread? They were sent by [people]. The messages cover: [description]"

22="mail1n0#you've got no unread messages"

23="mail2n0#there's no unread messages in your inbox"

24="mail3n0#sorry! you already checked all your email"

[PRINTER_NOTIFICATION_IMMINENCE]

00="printer1s0#your document is in the printer queue"

01="printer1s1#document waiting to be printed"

02="printer1s2#printer is quite busy at the moment"

03="printer1s3#waiting to be printed"

04="printer1p0#your documents are in the printer queue"

05="printer1p1#documents waiting to be printed"

06="printer1p2#printer is quite busy at the moment"

07="printer2s0#your [nature] is waiting in the printer queue"

08="printer2s1#the [nature] you printed is waiting to be printed"

09="printer2s2#document consisting of a [nature] is waiting to print"

10="printer2s3#your [nature] is in the printer queue"

11="printer2p0#your [nature] are waiting in the printer queue"

12="printer2p1#the [nature] you printed are waiting to be printed"

13="printer2p2#documents, including a [nature] are waiting to be printed"

14="printer3s0#your [nature] is waiting behind [description] other"

15="printer3s1#there's a lot of traffic in the printer today. Your [nature] is waiting for other [description]"

16="printer3s2#before your [nature] is printed, there's still [description] in front"

17="printer3s3#unfortunately, your [nature] will have to wait for other [description] "

18="printer3p0#your [nature] are waiting behind [description] other"

19="printer3p1#there's a lot of traffic in the printer today. Your [nature] are waiting for other [description]"

20="printer3p2#before your documents are printed, there's still [description] in front"

21="printer1n0#there aren't any new messages"

22="printer2n0#there are no new messages"

23="printer3n0#there's no new mail in your inbox"

24="printer3n1#i am sorry but there's no new mail yet"

25="printer3n2#sorry! no new e-mail yet"

[PRINTER_NOTIFICATION]

00="printer1s0#your document is printing right now!"

01="printer1s1#right! Your document started printing!"

02="printer1s2#excuse me! Just to let you know that your document is now printing"

03="printer1s3#great news! Your document is finally printing"

04="printer1s4#your document will be printed soon"

05="printer1s5#printing shortly"

06="printer1s6#your document is about to be printed"

07="printer1s7#the document you sent to the printer is about to be printed"

08="printer1p0#your documents are printing right now!"

09="printer1p1#right! Your documents just started printing!"

10="printer1p2#just to let you know that your documents are now printing"

11="printer1p3#great news! Your documents are finally printing"

12="printer1p4#your documents will be printed soon"

13="printer1p5#printing shortly"

14="printer1p6#your documents are about to be printed"

15="printer1p7#the documents you sent to the printer are about to be printed"

16="printer2s0#your [nature] is printing right now!"

17="printer2s1#right! Your [nature] started printing!"

18="printer2s2#just to let you know that your [nature] is now printing"

19="printer2s3#great news! Your [nature] is finally printing"

20="printer2s4#your [nature] will be printed soon"

21="printer2s5#[nature] about to be printed"

22="printer2s6#your [nature] is about to be printed"

23="printer2s7#the [nature] you sent to the printer is about to be printed"

24="printer2p0#your [nature] are printing right now!"

25="printer2p1#right! Your [nature] just started printing!"

26="printer2p2#just to let you know that your [nature] are now printing"
27="printer2p3#great news! Your [nature] are finally printing"
28="printer2p4#your [nature] will be printed soon"
29="printer2p5#printing shortly"
30="printer2p6#your [nature] are about to be printed"
31="printer2p7#the [nature] you sent to the printer are about to be printed"
32="printer3s0#your [nature] is printing right now!"
33="printer3s1#right! Your [nature] started printing!"
34="printer3s2#just to let you know that your [nature] is now printing"
35="printer3s3#great news! Your [nature] is finally printing"
36="printer3s4#your [nature] will be printed soon"
37="printer3s5#[nature] about to be printed"
38="printer3s6#your [nature] is about to be printed"
39="printer3s7#the [nature] you sent to the printer is about to be printed"
40="printer3p0#your [nature] are printing right now!"
41="printer3p1#right! Your [nature] just started printing!"
42="printer3p2#just to let you know that your [nature] are now printing"
43="printer3p3#great news! Your [nature] are finally printing"
44="printer3p4#your [nature] will be printed soon"
45="printer3p5#printing shortly"
46="printer3p6#your [nature] are about to be printed"
47="printer3p7#the [nature] you sent to the printer are about to be printed"
48="printer1n0#there aren't any documents printing right now"
49="printer2n0#you don't have any documents printing"
50="printer3n0#there seems to be no document printing right now"

[PRINTER_REMINDER]
00="printer1s0#your document is waiting for you in the printer tray"
01="printer1s1#right! Your document just finished printing!"
02="printer1s2#just to let you know that your document is now printed"
03="printer1s3#great news! Your document is finally printed"
04="printer1s4#i think you would like to know that your document just finished printing!"
05="printer1s5#If you're not too busy, you can go to the printer and pick your document"
06="printer1s6#your printed document is ready"
07="printer1s7#the document you sent to the printer has now finished printing"
08="printer1p0#your documents are waiting for you in the printer tray"
09="printer1p1#right! Your documents just finished printing!"
10="printer1p2#just to let you know that your documents are now printed"
11="printer1p3#great news! Your documents are finally printed"
12="printer1p4#i think you would like to know that your documents just finished printing!"
13="printer1p5#If you're not too busy, you can go to the printer and pick your documents"
14="printer1p6#your printed documents are ready"
15="printer1p7#the documents you sent to the printer have now finished printing"

16="printer2s0#your [nature] is waiting for you in the printer tray"
17="printer2s1#right! Your [nature] just finished printing!"
18="printer2s2#just to let you know that your [nature] is now printed"
19="printer2s3#great news! Your [nature] is finally printed"
20="printer2s4#i think you would like to know that your [nature] just finished printing!"
21="printer2s5#If you're not too busy, you can go to the printer and pick your [nature]"
22="printer2s6#your printed [nature] is ready"
23="printer2s7#the [nature] you sent to the printer has now finished printing"
24="printer2p0#your [nature] are waiting for you in the printer tray"
25="printer2p1#right! Your [nature] just finished printing!"
26="printer2p2#just to let you know that your [nature] are now printed"
27="printer2p3#great news! Your [nature] are finally printed"
28="printer2p4#i think you would like to know that your [nature] just finished printing!"
29="printer2p5#If you're not too busy, you can go to the printer and pick your [nature]"
30="printer2p6#your printed [nature] are ready"
31="printer2p7#the [nature] you sent to the printer have all now finished printing"
32="printer3s0#your [nature] is waiting for you in the printer tray"
33="printer3s1#right! Your [nature] just finished printing!"
34="printer3s2#just to let you know that your [nature] is now printed"
35="printer3s3#great news! Your [nature] is finally printed"
36="printer3s4#i think you would like to know that your [nature] just finished printing!"
37="printer3s5#If you're not too busy, you can go to the printer and pick your [nature]"
38="printer3s6#your printed [nature] is ready"
39="printer3s7#the [nature] you sent to the printer has now finished printing"
40="printer3p0#your [nature] are waiting for you in the printer tray"
41="printer3p1#right! Your [nature] just finished printing!"
42="printer3p2#just to let you know that your [nature] are now printed"
43="printer3p3#great news! Your [nature] are finally printed"
44="printer3p4#i think you would like to know that your [nature] just finished printing!"
45="printer3p5#If you're not too busy, you can go to the printer and pick your [nature]"
46="printer3p6#your printed [nature] are ready"
47="printer3p7#the [nature] you sent to the printer have all now finished printing"

[CALENDAR_NOTIFICATION_IMMINENCE]
00="calendar1s0#your [nature] starts in less than 5 minutes"
01="calendar1s1#you have a [nature] starting in less of 5 minutes"
02="calendar1s2#[nature] is due to start in less than five minutes"
03="calendar1s3#[nature] starts in less than 5 minutes"
04="calendar2s0#your [nature] starts in less than 5 minutes in [place]"
05="calendar2s1#you have a [nature] starting in less of 5 minutes in [place]"
06="calendar2s2#[nature] is due to start in [place] in less than five minutes"
07="calendar2s3#[nature] starts in less than 5 minutes. It is scheduled for [place]"

08="calendar3s0#your [nature] starts in less than 5 minutes in [place]. It will deal with [description]"

09="calendar3s1#you have a [nature] starting in less of 5 minutes in [place]. This is about [description]"

10="calendar3s2#[nature] is due to start in [place] in less than five minutes. Don't forget it is about [description]"

11="calendar3s3#[nature] starts in less than 5 minutes. It is scheduled for [place], and the subject is: [description]"

[CALENDAR_NOTIFICATION]

00="calendar1s0#your [nature] is now starting"

01="calendar1s1#you have a [nature] starting right now"

02="calendar1s2#[nature] is due to start at this moment"

03="calendar1s3#[nature] is about to start"

04="calendar2s0#your [nature] is now starting in [place]"

05="calendar2s1#you have a [nature] starting right now in [place]"

06="calendar2s2#[nature] is due to start at this moment in [place]"

07="calendar2s3#[nature] is about to start. It is scheduled for [place]"

08="calendar3s0#your [nature] is now starting in [place]. It will deal with [description]"

09="calendar3s1#you have a [nature] starting right now in [place]. This is about [description]"

10="calendar3s2#[nature] is due to start at this moment in [place]. Don't forget it is about [description]"

11="calendar3s3#[nature] is about to start. It is scheduled for [place], and the subject is: [description]"

[CALENDAR_REMINDER]

00="calendar1s0#your [nature] has already started"

01="calendar1s1#did you remember your [nature] that started a few moments ago?"

02="calendar1s2#don't forget your [nature] started a few minutes ago"

03="calendar1s3#did you remember your [nature]?"

04="calendar2s0#your [nature] has already started in [place]"

05="calendar2s1#did you remember your [nature] that started a few moments ago in [place]?"

06="calendar2s2#don't forget your [nature] started a few minutes ago in [place]"

07="calendar2s3#did you remember your [nature] ?. It is now happening in [place]"

08="calendar3s0#your [nature] has already started in [place]. It is dealing with [description]"

09="calendar3s1#did you remember your [nature] that started a few moments ago in [place]? It is about [description]"

10="calendar3s2#don't forget your [nature] started a few minutes ago in [place]. It is about [description]"

11="calendar3s3#did you remember your [nature]? It is now happening in [place], and the subject is: [description]"

Expressions for attention-getting

00 = "Excuse me ... "

01 = "Sorry to interrupt you ... but "

02 = "aah! ... "

03 = "Sorry to butt in ... but "

04 = "I think you might like to know that ... "

05 = "Sorry to disturb you ... but "

06 = "If you're not too busy there is ... "

Appendix B

ACCOMPANYING HANDOUTS FOR THE EXPERIMENT

This Appendix contains the materials that were handed out to the participants of the experiment described in **Erro! A origem da referência não foi encontrada.**: the task script, the synthetic speech training task script and the research task questions list.

Task script

Below is the task script for those who completed the experiment in the morning. The task script for the afternoon's slot is identical, except for the timings already noted in **Erro! A origem da referência não foi encontrada.**, section 6.2.2.

Task script

Research using the World Wide Web

Please start by reading this task script <u>all the way through to the end</u> (3 pages) to get a glimpse of the tasks you are expected to perform during this experiment. Please <u>don't</u> perform any task while you are reading it for the first time. When you finish reading it, go back to <u>point 1</u> in the <u>tasks list</u> and then start performing the tasks indicated.

Introduction

We are conducting this experiment to investigate how easy it is for people to use an interactive system to find information in an environment where there is some interruption. The experiment requires you to use the World Wide Web to find answers to 48 questions – 8 groups each of 6 questions. Knowing the answer to each question is not sufficient though. You must find evidence to support the answer and paste it into a word-processor document along with its URL. Keep to the questionnaire as best as you can. Once you have completed a group of questions you must print off your word processor document, and open a new one for the next group of questions.

Summary of tasks

Initially we ask you to fill-in Questionnaire A. This is to gather factual information about you that will be used later to perform statistical analysis of the results.

After that you are asked to perform a short task involving a speech synthesiser to get you accustomed to the kind of spoken information that will interrupt the experiment.

After that comes your main research task. In performing this task, you should use your favourite browser and whichever search engines you prefer. Your objective is to answer the maximum number of questions, so you should make the most out of your time. It is also your objective to deal appropriately with e-mail messages, printing and other to-do's. In order to make your work more enjoyable, you will find some background music playing while you perform your tasks. You will also find a cartoon like character at the interface, which will interrupt you occasionally. Please don't try to dismiss it, as it is part of the information finding environment being tested. Please note that you must find <u>as many answers as you can</u> to the questions until your research deadline: **11:30 AM**.

Just before the end of the session, you will be asked to fill in Questionnaire B. This is to gather information about your opinion concerning some aspects of the task you have been doing.

All the applications you need to perform this experiment are represented by icons in your WindowsNT desktop. Please <u>do not</u> attempt to use any other application.

List of tasks

1. **Task 1** - answer **Questionnaire A**.

   The test monitor will give you this questionnaire when you are ready. When you have finished filling in the questionnaire please hand it to the test monitor.

2. **Task 2** - perform the **synthetic speech training task**.

   In this task, you will listen to ten proverbs spoken by a character through a speech synthesiser. For each proverb you hear, you have to tick it off the **Proverbs list** provided by the test monitor. When you are ready, please run the application titled *Proverbs* and pick up the list of proverbs. When you are ready to go please press the button in the application to start listening to the proverbs. When you finish the task please hand your list to the test monitor.

3. **Task 3** - perform the **research task.**

While you read the research task questions list provided by the test monitor, he will setup the Windows NT environment for your task before you start performing it. As part of your research task you must perform <u>three</u> different <u>activities</u> in parallel, A, B and C as follows:

A] Search activity

Perform your search activity using the **research task questions** list provided by the test monitor. This list is divided into eight sections. For each section of questions here is what you <u>must</u> do:

a)   Open the word processor and create a blank document where you will note down your answers to the questions (save this document to the desktop with the name of the section for example: section1.doc, section2.doc, etc);

b)   Open the web browser and find the correct answer to the questions by searching the WWW;

c)   Copy any text and pictures you have found in support of your answer from the web browser and paste them in your word processor document after your answer, copying also the URL where the support material was found;

d)   When you finish each section of questions print the document using the default printer installed in the system (pp05). As soon as your document is printed, you must go to the printer to get it and write down the time you got it. <u>Please note</u> that the printer is <u>often</u> <u>busy</u> with documents from other people. If the printer is <u>busy</u> with other documents <u>you can start a new set of questions before going to the printer</u>;

e)   Repeat from a) for every one of the eight sections of the questionnaire.

B] To-do activity

While conducting your search activity, you will be subjected to some to-do related interruptions with which you must deal in the following way:

<u>To-do</u>: At exactly <u>10:35 AM</u>, and again at <u>11:10 AM</u> you have to check the share prices of Boots (**BOOT**) and Dixons (**DXNS**) on the London Stock market (use the following URL: http://www.etrade.co.uk). Click the **Log On** button on the top of the site's homepage and use the information below to login to the site. Look for the information you need under the **Index FTSE 100**. Write down the values using another blank document of your word processor and also write the time you did it. Print the document only after the <u>second</u> time you check the values. Login to the site using the following information:

•   <u>Username</u>: experiments

- Password: may2001

C] E-mail activity

While conducting your search activity, you will be subject to some e-mail related interruptions with which you must deal in the following way:

E-mail: during your task you will receive some e-mail messages. Please use MS Outlook Express to read and reply to the messages, as it was configured to manage an e-mail account created especially for you to use during the experiment. Here's what you have to do concerning received messages:

a) Read and print each message you receive from Nuno Ribeiro, because these contain useful hints concerning your main task,

b) Read and reply to messages that have "REPLY: Research Task" in the subject line (suppose these messages are part of a discussion thread you are involved in).

c) Disregard any other message you receive, including junk mail.

d) Note: when the available time for your research task is over (at 11:30), please print immediately the last document you were working on and give all your documents to the test monitor.

4. **Task 4** - answer **Questionnaire B**.

    After the end of the research task, the test monitor will give you Questionnaire B. Please answer it carefully.

5. **End of experiment**: the test monitor will provide you the compensation for your help in this experiment.

Synthetic speech training task script

Proverbs List

Participant number_____

Date_____

Please listen carefully to the proverbs that are spoken by the computer, and indicate the ones you listen by ticking the corresponding blank box in the following list. When you are ready to start listening to the proverbs, start the proverbs program by double-clicking its icon and then pressing the "Start Proverbs Task" button. The computer will speak a proverb every 5 seconds.

Nr.	Proverb	
1	A little knowledge is a dangerous thing.	
2	You can take a horse to water but you can't make him drink.	
3	Too many cooks spoil the broth.	
4	A bird in the hand is worth two in the bush.	
5	Beauty is in the eye of the beholder.	
6	He who laughs last laughs longest.	
7	Absence makes the heart grow fonder.	
8	A rolling stone gathers no moss.	
9	Actions speak louder than words.	
10	Every cloud has a silver lining.	

Table 27. Proverbs list for the synthetic speech training task

Research task questions list

Research Task Questions

Section 1

Archaeology

1.1 What was found at Sutton Hoo?

1.2 Who discovered and named the Minoan civilisation?

Architecture

1.3 Which is the largest cathedral in Britain?

1.4 *'Si monumentum requires, circumspice'* - said of whom, where?

Astronomy

1.5 How many satellites has Mars?

1.6 How long does light take to reach Earth from the Sun?

Section 2

Biology

2.1 What is DNA? What is it made of?

2.2 Who discovered the structure of DNA? When? Where?

Chemistry

2.3 What is uranium hexafluoride used for?

2.4 What is the chemical formula for buckminsterfullerene?

Computer communications

2.5 Who invented packet switching?

2.6 Who invented the World Wide Web?

Section 3

Portuguese

3.1 *'Os Lusíadas'* - Who wrote it? What is it about?

3.2 *'Deus quer, o homem sonha, a obra nasce'* - means?

French

3.3 *Il faut cultiver notre jardin* - means?

3.4 *Dans ce meilleur des mondes, tout est au mieux* - means?

Geography

3.5 Which ocean is at the easternmost end of the Panama Canal?

3.6 Edinburgh, Liverpool, Bristol: put in order, west to east.

Section 4

German

4.1 *Die Welt is Alles, was der Fall ist* - means?

4.2 *Wovon man nicht sprechen kann, darüber muß man schweigen* - means?

Electronics

4.3 Who discovered the electron? When? Where?

4.4 Who invented the transistor? When? Where?

Greek

4.5 Who told a story of Achilles and the tortoise?

4.6 Who, it is said, was killed when an eagle dropped a tortoise on his bald head?

Section 5

Geology

5.1 On which island was the first seismograph constructed?

5.2 What lies underneath Yellowstone National Park?

History (British)

5.3 Who was the most recent king to have been succeeded by his grandson?

5.4 Who was the second most recent king to have been succeeded by his brother?

History (International)

5.5 Who were the Amherst, Berkeley and Monash?

5.6 What have they in common? Who is the odd one out?

Section 6

Latin

6.1 *Radix malorum est cupiditas* - means?

6.2 *'Gallia est omnes divisa in partes tres'* - Who said it?

Literature

6.3 Who wrote *Diary of a Nobody*?

6.4 Which novel contains Captain Nemo?

Mathematics

6.5 What is the formula for the curve of a chain hanging between two points?

6.6 What is the value of $\left(-\frac{1}{2}\right)$!

Section 7

Physics

7.1 What are stuck together with gluons?

7.2 What is the mass of the electron, in kilograms?

Politics (British)

7.3 Who was the only British prime minister to have been assassinated?

7.4 Which lecturer in statistics at LSE went on to become prime minister?

Politics (International)

7.5 What was Bangladesh called, before it was called Bangladesh?

7.6 Who was the world's first female prime minister?

Section 8

Science

8.1 *'All science is physics or stamp collecting'* - Who said it?

8.2 *'The Dismal Science'* - What is it?

Physiology

8.3 Where are your hammer, anvil and stirrup?

8.4 Which parts of your body are said to be deciduous?

University of York

8.5 Who was J. B. Morrel?

8.6 Who were the original architects of the University of York?

Appendix C

QUESTIONNAIRES USED IN THE EXPERIMENT

Pre-test Questionnaire

Questionnaire A

Participant number_____

Date_____

Confidentiality

The information you provide in this questionnaire is strictly confidential. Your answers are strictly anonymous and will <u>only</u> be used for statistical purposes. <u>None</u> of the information you provide herein will be directly associated with you or disclosed to third parties.

Section 1

For the following questions, please tick only the appropriate box:

1 - What is your gender?   Male ☐   Female ☐

2- What is your age-range?   18-25   ☐
                                  26-35   ☐
                                  36-45   ☐
                                  46-55   ☐
                                  56 +   ☐

3 – How are you feeling today?   Well (normal health)   ☐
                                  Not well (sick)   ☐

Section 2

For the following questions, please tick only one box:

3 - What is your level of proficiency with the Windows NT Operating System?

High ☐

Medium ☐

Low ☐

4 - Speech synthesisers produce sounds that resemble the human voice and are generated directly from text without using any human voice. How familiar are you with the sound that speech synthesisers make?

I hear it everyday   ☐

I have heard it many times   ☐

I have heard it a few times   ☐

I have never heard it   ☐

5 – If you never had at least one contact with the Microsoft Office Assistant (also known as the "paper clip") please skip to question 6 in section 3 below.

Using the following rating scales, for each pair of terms please circle the number nearest the term that most closely matches your opinion about the Microsoft Office Assistant?

Unpleasant	1	2	3	4	5	6	7	Pleasant
Unhelpful	1	2	3	4	5	6	7	Helpful
Inconvenient	1	2	3	4	5	6	7	Convenient
Unreliable	1	2	3	4	5	6	7	Reliable
Uncomfortable	1	2	3	4	5	6	7	Comfortable
Inefficient	1	2	3	4	5	6	7	Efficient
Frustrating	1	2	3	4	5	6	7	Satisfying
Unobtrusive	1	2	3	4	5	6	7	Intrusive
It is horrible	1	2	3	4	5	6	7	It is lovely

| | Section 3 | |

6 – The way you prefer to process information is of major importance in the analysis of this experiment. This question was designed to let you express your personal preferences.

For the following group of 30 statement pairs, please tick the box in front of the statement that you consider best describes you. Please, only <u>one</u> tick per pair.

	A		**B**	
Pair 1	I trust what is certain and concrete		I trust inspiration and inference	
Pair 2	I like new ideas only if they have practical applications		I like new ideas and concepts for their own sake	
Pair 3	I tend to value realism and common sense		I tend to value imagination and innovation	
Pair 4	I like to use and hone established skills		I like to learn new skills; I get bored easily after mastering skills	
Pair 5	I tend to be specific and literal; I prefer to give detailed descriptions		I tend to be general and figurative; I prefer to use metaphors and analogies	
Pair 6	I prefer to present information in a step-by-step fashion		I prefer to present information through leaps, in a roundabout manner	
Pair 7	I am more oriented to the present		I am more oriented toward the future	
Pair 8	I am energized by being with other people		I am energized by spending time alone	
Pair 9	I like being the centre of attention		I avoid being the centre of attention	
Pair 10	I prefer to act, then think		I prefer to think, then act	
Pair 11	I prefer to think out loud		I prefer to think things through inside my head	
Pair 12	I think that I am easy to "read" and know; I like to share my personal experiences freely		I think that I am more of a private person; I prefer to share my personal experiences with a select few	
Pair 13	I prefer to talk more than listen		I prefer to listen more than talk	
Pair 14	I prefer to communicate with enthusiasm		I prefer to keep my enthusiasm to myself	
Pair 15	I tend to respond quickly; I enjoy a fast pace		I prefer to respond after taking the time to think things through	
Pair 16	I prefer breadth to depth		I prefer depth to breadth	

	A		**B**	
Pair 17	I tend to take a step back and apply impersonal analysis to problems		I tend to take a step forward and consider the effect of any actions on others	
Pair 18	I tend to value logic, justice, and fairness; I tend to apply one standard for all		I tend to value empathy and harmony; I like to see the exception to the rule	
Pair 19	I naturally see flaws and tend to be critical		I naturally like to please others; I tend to show appreciation easily	
Pair 20	I might be seen to be heartless, insensitive and uncaring		I might be seen as overemotional, illogical and weak	
Pair 21	I consider it more important to be truthful than tactful		I consider it important to be tactful as well as truthful	
Pair 22	I believe feelings are valid only if they are logical		I believe any feeling is valid, whether it makes sense or not	
Pair 23	I am more motivated by a desire for achievement and accomplishment		I am more motivated by a desire to be appreciated	
Pair 24	I am happiest after decisions have been made		I am happiest leaving all my options open	
Pair 25	I would prefer to have a "work ethic": work first, play later (if there's time)		I would prefer to have a "play ethic": enjoy now, finish the job later (if there's time)	
Pair 26	I tend to set goals and work toward achieving them on time		I tend to change goals as new information becomes available	
Pair 27	I prefer knowing what I am getting into		I like adapting to new situations	
Pair 28	I am more product oriented (emphasis is on completing the task)		I am more process oriented (emphasis is on how the task is completed)	
Pair 29	I derive satisfaction from finishing projects		I derive satisfaction from starting projects	
Pair 30	I see time as a finite resource and prefer to take deadlines seriously		I see time as a renewable resource and prefer to see deadlines as elastic	

Thank you very much for having completed this questionnaire.

Post-test Questionnaire

Questionnaire B

Participant number_____

Date_____

Section 1

Using the following rating scales, for each pair of terms please circle the number nearest the term that most closely matches your feelings about the speaking assistant that interrupted you while you were working.

1 – Please rate your overall reactions to using the assistant (please comment only on the assistant and not on the task you did):

	1	2	3	4	5	6	7	
Unpleasant	1	2	3	4	5	6	7	Pleasant
Unhelpful	1	2	3	4	5	6	7	Helpful
Inconvenient	1	2	3	4	5	6	7	Convenient
Unreliable	1	2	3	4	5	6	7	Reliable
Uncomfortable	1	2	3	4	5	6	7	Comfortable
Inefficient	1	2	3	4	5	6	7	Efficient
Frustrating	1	2	3	4	5	6	7	Satisfying
Unobtrusive	1	2	3	4	5	6	7	Intrusive
It was horrible	1	2	3	4	5	6	7	It was lovely

Section 2

For the following questions, please use the scales provided and circle the number nearest the term that most closely matches your <u>feelings</u> and <u>opinions</u> about the speaking assistant.

2 – The system interrupted your work. What is your opinion about the interruptions?

		Not at all						Very much so
2.1	I think that the interruptions were **appropriate**	1	2	3	4	5	6	7
2.2	I think that the interruptions were **useful**	1	2	3	4	5	6	7
2.3	I think that the interruptions were **disruptive**	1	2	3	4	5	6	7

3 – The system spoke to you about e-mail, printing and other reminders using the same voice. What is your feeling about using the same voice?

		Not at all						Very much so
3.1	I think that having the same voice was **confusing**	1	2	3	4	5	6	7
3.2	I think that having the same voice provided **uniformity**	1	2	3	4	5	6	7
3.3	I think that having the same voice was **appropriate**	1	2	3	4	5	6	7

4 – There was music playing in the background. What is your feeling about the way the music was interrupted by the system?

		Not at all						Very much so
4.1	I think that the way the music was interrupted by the spoken voice was **natural**	1	2	3	4	5	6	7
4.2	I think the music **interfered** with the spoken message	1	2	3	4	5	6	7
4.3	Before speaking to me, I think that the system should **always stop the music**	1	2	3	4	5	6	7

5 – When the system wanted to get your attention, it interrupted by saying for example "Excuse me!" What is your view of these attention-getters?

	Not at all						Very much so
5.1 I think they were **useful** at getting my attention	1	2	3	4	5	6	7
5.2 I think they were **annoying**	1	2	3	4	5	6	7
5.3 I think that they were **natural**	1	2	3	4	5	6	7

6 – What about the meaning of the spoken messages, what is your opinion about that?

	Not at all						Very much so
6.1 I **easily** recognised the words spoken	1	2	3	4	5	6	7
6.2 I **easily** understood the meaning of the spoken messages	1	2	3	4	5	6	7
6.3 I think the spoken messages **helped** me understand what was happening	1	2	3	4	5	6	7
6.4 I think the amount of detail provided in the spoken messages was **appropriate**	1	2	3	4	5	6	7

For question 6.4 explain **why** _____

7 – It was intended for the system to be polite when it interrupted and spoke to you. Did you notice this behaviour?

NO, politeness was not noticeable ☐

YES, politeness was a noticeable feature ☐

If your answer to question 7 was **NO**, please **skip to question 9.**

8 - In terms of politeness, how well does each of the following statements describe your feelings about the

	Not at all						Very much so
8.1 I think that the messages were **polite**	1	2	3	4	5	6	7
8.2 I think that the politeness was **appropriate**	1	2	3	4	5	6	7
8.3 I think that the politeness was **irritating**	1	2	3	4	5	6	7

spoken messages?

Skip to question 10.

9 – What is your opinion about having a system such as this one speak in a polite way?

	Not at all						**Very much so**
9.1 Politeness would be a **useful** feature	1	2	3	4	5	6	7
9.2 Politeness would be a **pleasant** feature	1	2	3	4	5	6	7
9.3 Politeness would make my work environment **more enjoyable**	1	2	3	4	5	6	7

10 – The system said the same thing in different ways at different times. For example, when it alerted you about an incoming e-mail message it would say *"you've got one new e-mail message from Nuno"*, but for the next message it would say *"there is a new e-mail message from Nuno"*. Did you notice this behaviour?

NO, variation was not noticeable   ☐

YES, variation was a noticeable feature ☐

If your answer to question 10 was **NO**, please **skip to question 12**.

11 - How did you feel about the variation in words used?

	Not at all						**Very much so**
11.1 I think that the variation was **irritating**	1	2	3	4	5	6	7
11.2 I think that the variation was **useful**	1	2	3	4	5	6	7
11.3 I think that the variation was **appropriate**	1	2	3	4	5	6	7

Skip to question 13.

12 - What is your opinion about having a system such as this one speak with variation in words

	Not at all						**Very much so**
12.1 Variation would be **irritating**	1	2	3	4	5	6	7
12.2 Variation would be a **useful** feature	1	2	3	4	5	6	7
12.3 Variation would be **appropriate**	1	2	3	4	5	6	7

used?

Section 3

13 – Please rate the following statements by ticking the column that most closely reflects your opinion of the research task you performed:

Q	Statement	Strongly Disagree	Disagree	Neither Agree nor Disagree	Agree	Strongly Agree
13.1	Finding the required information to answer the questions was easy.					
13.2	It would have been easier to perform the research task activities like printing, managing things to do, checking e-mail and searching for answers without the assistant.					
13.3	I felt the system was assisting me.					

14 – Please rate the following statements by ticking the column that most closely reflects your opinion of the speaking assistant:

Q	Statement	Strongly Disagree	Disagree	Neither Agree nor Disagree	Agree	Strongly Agree
14.1	I would continue to use this system.					
14.2	I would like to have the system perform more spoken functions that were important to me.					
14.3	I would like this system to also guide me while searching for information.					
12.4	I wish it would guess what I am doing so that it would help me with my work.					

Section 4

15 – Please add your comments about the system in the space provided. We would especially appreciate your opinion on the following topics:

15.1 – What things did you like most about the system?

_____

_____

_____

15.2 – What things did you dislike most in the system?

_____

_____

_____

15.3 – We wanted the system to feel natural. What did we miss that would have made it really natural?

_____

_____

_____

15.4 – We wanted the system to feel like a work companion. What did we miss that would have made you perceive it as your work companion?

_____

_____

_____

15.5 – Have you any other comments about your experience or about the system?

_____

_____

_____

Thank you very much for your participation.

Your help is much appreciated.

Appendix D

EXPERIMENT IMPLEMENTATION MATERIALS

This Appendix contains the materials that were used to implement the experiment, and include: the list of proverbs for the synthetic speech training task, the set of e-mail messages sent to participants, the diary settings used during the experiment and the test monitor script.

List of proverbs for the synthetic speech training task

The following list presents the proverbs that were spoken by the speaking assistant during the synthetic speech training task. Only some of the proverbs were found in the list given to participants, as noted on the following table.

Nr.	Proverb to be spoken	In participant's list	Position in participant's list
1	All that glitters is not gold.	-	-
2	A bird in the hand is worth two in the bush.	YES	4
3	Take care of the pence and the pounds will take care of themselves.	-	-
4	You can take a horse to water but you can't make him drink.	YES	2
5	Penny wise and pound foolish.	-	-
6	Look before you leap.	-	-
7	Every cloud has a silver lining.	YES	10
8	Too many cooks spoil the broth.	YES	3
9	Many hands make light work.	-	-
10	A rolling stone gathers no moss.	YES	8

Table 28. Proverbs to be spoken as part of the synthetic speech training task

E-mail messages sent to participants

The following tables describe the e-mail messages that were sent to participants during the experiment:

Message ID	Msg 01	Msg 02	Msg 03	Msg 04
Type	Relevant to test	Junk mail	Relevant to participant	Relevant to test
FROM	Nuno nribeiro@cs.york.ac.uk	atx@hotmail.com	Ian idb@cs.york.ac.uk	Nuno nribeiro@cs.york.ac.uk
TO	test_sa@cs.york.ac.uk	test_sa@cs.york.ac.uk	test_sa@cs.york.ac.uk	test_sa@cs.york.ac.uk
SUBJECT	Question about DNA	Attention Business Owners	REPLY: Research task	Question about a Portuguese book
TIME Timetable A	10:15	10:20	10:30	10:50
TIME Timetable B	14:45	14:50	15:00	15:20
BODY	<URL to answer question where DNA is found>	Business Owners..Let Us Solve Your Debt Problems! Have the ability to concentrate on your business without being distracted by creditors and collection agencies. Our company will handle all of that for you! We will handle your business AND personal debt for you and HELP YOU SAVE MONEY! DO NOT HESITATE! For more information simply reply with your name and telephone number. Also include the name of your business. We will contact you shortly! To be removed from this list please reply with "remove" in the subject.	Hi! Please reply to this message indicating the status of your research task by stating the question you are working with at the moment	<URL to answer question about "Os Lusíadas">

Table 29. E-mail messages sent to participants (messages 1 to 4)

Message ID	Msg 05	Msg 06	Msg 07
Type	Junk mail	Relevant to participant	Relevant to test
FROM	atx@hotmail.com	Ian idb@cs.york.ac.uk	Nuno nribeiro@cs.york.ac.uk
TO	test_sa@cs.york.ac.uk	test_sa@cs.york.ac.uk	test_sa@cs.york.ac.uk
SUBJECT	Invitation to a perfect club	REPLY: Research task	Question about factorials
TIME Timetable A	11:05	10:30	10:15
TIME Timetable B	15:35	15:00	14:45
BODY	Hello! You have been invited by atx to join the Unlisted Yahoo! Club named "The Unofficial Cuban Cigars Club". To become a member of this club, just go to the Web address below: http://edit.clubs.yahoo.com/config?.k=8513ad3 Note: This invitation will expire after 7 days, or after being used.	Hi! Please reply to this message indicating the status of your research task by stating the question you are working with at the moment	<URL to anser question about(-1/2!)>

Table 30. E-mail messages sent to participants (messages 5 to 7)

Diary settings

Each diary entry is simulated by one line in a text file with the following structure:

<date - hour event start>,<date - hour event end>,<type of event>,<location>,,<status>

For example, the following line describes a seminar starting at 04:00 pm on the 2nd of November 2000 in room CS105. The seminar is about intelligent agents:

2000/11/02 16:00;2000/10/24 14:35;Seminar;CS105;intelligent agents;st

The following table presents the diary for the experiment participants.

Nr.	Date start	Date end	Type of event	Location	Abstract
todo1	date 10:25	date 10:26	share checking task	London stockmarket	shares Boots and Dixons
todo2	date 10:40	date 10:41	share checking task	London stockmarket	shares Boots and Dixons
todo3	date 11:30	date 11:31	next task	your test desk	filling in an appreciation questionnaire

Table 31. Diary entries used in the experiment

Test monitor's Script

A] <u>BEFORE</u> TEST

1. Make an appropriate version of the diary for slots (timetables) A or B or C.

2. Check whether the default printer is pp05.

3. Check the printer for paper jams.

4. Fill-in participant's ID and the date in all test materials (5 documents).

5. Insert the CD in CD Player.

6. Set sound loudness to 2, 3, Max.

7. Delete old messages from the Inbox in MS Outlook.

B] ON PARTICIPANT'S <u>ARRIVAL</u>

1. Show the location of printer pp05.

2. Hand script to be read by the participant, and ask the participant to read it once before performing the first task.

C] <u>BEFORE</u> RESEARCH TASK

1. Start MS Outlook.

2. Start Speaking Assistant.

3. Start CD Play from the assistant context menu.

D] <u>IMMEDIATELY AFTER START</u> OF THE RESEARCH TASK

1. Run the E-mailScheduler application

2. Insert current time and hit "Start" button.

Appendix E

Supporting Tables of Experimental Results

This Appendix includes the statistical data from which the graphs describing the participants' profile in chapter 6 have been generated, and a summary of the data from which the descriptive statistics were obtained.

Personality traits:	Female	Male	Total
E - Extravert	4	3	7
I - Introvert	0	8	8
N - Intuitive	3	3	6
S - Sensor	1	8	9
F - Feeler	3	5	8
T - Thinker	1	6	7
J - Judging	2	7	9
P - Perceiving	2	4	6
MS Windows NT experience:			
High	0	7	7
Medium	4	4	8
Familiarity with speech synthesis:			
Heard it many times	1	7	8
Heard it a few times	3	4	7
Age range:			
18 - 25 years	2	8	10
26 - 35	2	0	2
36 - 45	0	3	3

Table 32. Summary of participants' characteristics

Variable	Number of responses							
scale	1 Not at all	2	3	4	5	6	7 Very much so	Total
Interruptions: appropriateness			1		5	6	3	15
Interruptions: usefulness				1	4	6	4	15
Interruptions: not disruptive (recoded)	1		2	1	4	5	2	15
Same voice: uniformity				2	4	6	3	15
Same voice: appropriateness	1		1	2	1	7	3	15
Same voice: not confusing (recoded)			1	3	1	1	9	15
Music interruption: naturalness					2	8	5	15
interfere with spoken message (recoded)	1				2	5	7	15
Attention-getters: usefulness	1		4	1	1	6	2	15
Attention-getters: not annoying (recoded)			4	2	2	4	3	15
Attention-getters: naturalness	1		1		10	2	1	15
Semantics: words easy to recognise	1		1		3	6	4	15
Semantics: meaning easy to understand				2	2	5	6	15
Semantics: messages helped to understand event				1	2	9	3	15
Semantics: messages detail appropriateness	1		1	1	2	7	3	15
Level of politeness					3	8	4	15
Appropriateness of polite messages			3	1	3	6	2	15
Polite messages do not irritate (recoded)		2	4	2	1	2	4	15
Varied messages do not irritate (recoded)				1	2	3	5	11

Table 33. Summary of opinions about anthropomorphic characteristics

Variable	Number of responses					
scale	1 Strongly disagree	2	3	4	5 Strongly agree	Total
The speaking assistant made the task easier to perform		1	1	9	4	15
The system was assisting me		1	1	8	5	15
I would continue to use the system			3	11	1	15
I would like the system to perform more PIM functions		1	2	10	2	15
I would like the system to guide me while searching for information	2	7	1	4	1	15

Table 34. Summary of opinions about speech-based assistance quality

Variable	Number of responses							
scale	1	2	3	4	5	6	7	Total
Speaking assistant: pleasantness			1	7	3	3	1	15
Speaking assistant: helpfulness					7	4	4	15
Speaking assistant: convenience				2	8	3	2	15
Speaking assistant: reliability			3		3	3	6	15
Speaking assistant: comfort				4	3	5	3	15
Speaking assistant: efficiency			3	3	4	3	2	15
Speaking assistant: satisfaction				5	4	6		15
Speaking assistant: unobtrusiveness (recoded)	1	1	3	1	2	4	3	15
Speaking assistant: likeability			1	3	7	3	1	15

Table 35. Summary of opinions about the Speaking Assistant

Variable	Number of responses							
scale	1	2	3	4	5	6	7	Total
MS Office Assistant: pleasantness	2	4	5	1	1			13
MS Office Assistant: helpfulness	1	4	3	3	2			13
MS Office Assistant: convenience	5	5	2	1				13
MS Office Assistant: reliability		3	1	6	2	1		13
MS Office Assistant: comfort		3	4	5	1			13
MS Office Assistant: efficiency	3	2	3	2	2	1		13
MS Office Assistant: satisfaction	6	3	4					13
MS Office Assistant: unobtrusiveness (recoded)	5	7		1				13
MS Office Assistant: likeability	3	6	2	2				13

Table 36. Summary of opinions about the MS Office Assistant

Appendix F

RESULTS OF STATISTICAL TESTS

The tables provided in this Appendix contain all the statistically significant data that resulted from performing several independent samples t-tests, and one paired samples t-test to compare the differences in participants' mean ratings. The data contained in these tables was used to produce the charts presented in section 6.3. Please note that the data is grouped by the participants' personality characteristics, and the other personal characteristics such as gender, level of experience with MS Windows NT, and degree of familiarity with text-to-speech (TTS) synthesis.

Introvert/Extravert

Group Statistics

	Personality Traits	N	Mean	Std. Deviation	Std. Error Mean
Attention-getters: not annoying (recoded)	Introvert	8	5.75	1.28	.45
	Extravert	7	4.14	1.46	.55

Table 37. Significant mean differences by Introvert/Extravert

	t-test for Equality of Means						
By Personality Traits: I / E	t	df	Sig. (2-tailed)	Mean Difference	Std. Error Difference	95% Confidence Interval of the Difference	
						Lower	Upper
Attention-getters: not annoying (recoded)	2.269	13	.041	1.61	.71	7.67E-02	3.14

Table 38. Results of t-tests for the mean differences by Introvert/Extravert

Intuitive/Sensor

Group Statistics					
	Personality Traits	N	Mean	Std. Deviation	Std. Error Mean
Semantics of spoken messages: words easy to recognise	Intuitive	6	6.50	.84	.34
	Sensor	9	5.00	1.50	.50
Semantics of spoken messages: messages helped to understand event	Intuitive	6	6.50	.55	.22
	Sensor	9	5.56	.73	.24
Semantics of spoken messages: quality of messages semantics (aggregated)	Intuitive	6	6.4444	.6206	.2534
	Sensor	9	5.4444	.7817	.2606
Speaking assistant: pleasantness	Intuitive	6	5.50	1.05	.43
	Sensor	9	4.22	.83	.28
Speaking assistant: comfort	Intuitive	6	6.33	.82	.33
	Sensor	9	4.89	.93	.31
Speaking assistant: usefulness (aggregated)	Intuitive	6	6.0556	.9290	.3792
	Sensor	9	5.1852	.6261	.2087
Research task assistance: the speaking assistant made the task easier to perform	Intuitive	6	4.67	.52	.21
	Sensor	9	3.67	.71	.24
Research task assistance: the system was assisting me	Intuitive	6	4.67	.52	.21
	Sensor	9	3.78	.83	.28
Research task assistance: spoken assistance quality (aggregated)	Intuitive	6	4.6667	.5164	.2108
	Sensor	9	3.7222	.7546	.2515

Table 39. Significant mean differences by Intuitive/Sensor

By Personality Traits: N / S	t	df	Sig. (2-tailed)	t-test for Equality of Means		95% Confidence Interval of the Difference	
				Mean Difference	Std. Error Difference	Lower	Upper
Semantics of spoken messages: words easy to recognise	2.213	13	.045	1.50	.68	3.57E-02	2.96
Semantics of spoken messages: messages helped to understand event	2.701	13	.018	.94	.35	.19	1.70
Semantics of spoken messages: quality of messages semantics (aggregated)	2.621	13	.021	1.0000	.3816	.1756	1.8244
Speaking assistant: pleasantness	2.629	13	.021	1.28	.49	.23	2.33
Speaking assistant: comfort	3.091	13	.009	1.44	.47	.43	2.45
Speaking assistant: usefulness (aggregated)	2.181	13	.048	.8704	.3990	8.383E-03	1.7324
Research task assistance: the speaking assistant made the task easier to perform	2.962	13	.011	1.00	.34	.27	1.73
Research task assistance: the system was assisting me	2.317	13	.037	.89	.38	6.00E-02	1.72
Research task assistance: spoken assistance quality (aggregated)	2.662	13	.020	.9444	.3547	.1781	1.7108

Table 40. Results of t-tests for the mean differences by Intuitive/Sensor

Feeler/Thinker

Group Statistics

	Myers-Briggs type: Feeler(F) / Thinker(T)	N	Mean	Std. Deviation	Std. Error Mean
Speaking assistant: pleasantness	Feeler	8	5.25	1.16	.41
	Thinker	7	4.14	.69	.26
Speaking assistant: unobtrusiveness (recoded)	Feeler	8	6.13	.83	.30
	Thinker	7	3.14	1.57	.59
Speaking assistant: human-likeness (aggregated)	Feeler	8	5.4583	.7278	.2573
	Thinker	7	4.4762	.8133	.3074

Table 41. Significant mean differences by Feeler/Thinker

By Personality Traits: F / T	t-test for Equality of Means					95% Confidence Interval of the Difference	
	t	df	Sig. (2-tailed)	Mean Difference	Std. Error Difference	Lower	Upper
Speaking assistant: pleasantness	2.271	11.569	.043	1.11	.49	4.05E-02	2.17
Speaking assistant: unobtrusiveness (recoded)	4.677	13	.000	2.98	.64	1.60	4.36
Speaking assistant: human-likeness (aggregated)	2.470	13	.028	.9821	.3977	.1229	1.8413

Table 42. Results of t-tests for the mean differences by Feeler/Thinker

Judging/Perceiving

Group Statistics

	Myers-Briggs type: Judger(J) / Perceiver(P)	N	Mean	Std. Deviation	Std. Error Mean
Speaking assistant: helpfulness	Judger	9	5.44	.73	.24
	Perceiver	6	6.33	.82	.33
Speaking assistant: convenience	Judger	9	4.89	.60	.20
	Perceiver	6	6.00	.89	.37
Semantics of spoken messages: meaning easy to understand	Judger	9	5.44	1.01	.34
	Perceiver	6	6.83	.41	.17
Speaking assistant: usefulness (aggregated)	Judger	9	5.1852	.6479	.2160
	Perceiver	6	6.0556	.9047	.3694

Table 43. Significant mean differences by Judger/Perceiver

	t-test for Equality of Means						
By Personality Traits : J / P						95% Confidence Interval of the Difference	
	t	df	Sig. (2-tailed)	Mean Difference	Std. Error Difference	Lower	Upper
Speaking assistant: helpfulness	-2.212	13	.045	-.89	.40	-1.76	-2.09E-02
Speaking assistant: convenience	-2.896	13	.013	-1.11	.38	-1.94	-.28
Semantics of spoken messages: meaning easy to understand	-3.686	11.296	.003	-1.39	.38	-2.22	-.56
Speaking assistant: usefulness (aggregated)	-2.181	13	.048	-.8704	.3990	-1.7324	-8.3827E-03

Table 44. Results of t-tests for the mean differences by Judger/Perceiver

MS Windows NT proficiency

Group Statistics					
	Windows NT Proficiency	N	Mean	Std. Deviation	Std. Error Mean
Politeness is noticeable: appropriateness of polite messages	High	7	4.43	1.40	.53
	Medium	8	5.88	.99	.35

Table 45. Significant mean differences by MS Windows NT proficiency

By Windows NT Proficiency	t-test for Equality of Means						
						95% Confidence Interval of the Difference	
	t	df	Sig. (2-tailed)	Mean Difference	Std. Error Difference	Lower	Upper
Politeness is noticeable: appropriateness of polite messages	-2.337	13	.036	-1.45	.62	-2.78	-.11

Table 46. Results of t-tests for the mean differences by MS Windows NT proficiency

Speech synthesis familiarity

Group Statistics					
	Familiarity with speech synthesis	N	Mean	Std. Deviation	Std. Error Mean
Attention-getters: usefulness	Heard it many times	8	4.00	1.51	.53
	Heard it a few times	7	5.86	1.35	.51
Semantics of spoken messages: messages detail appropriateness	Heard it many times	8	4.63	1.85	.65
	Heard it a few times	7	6.29	.76	.29

Table 47. Significant mean differences by speech synthesis familiarity

By Speech Synthesis Familiarity	t-test for Equality of Means						
	t	df	Sig. (2-tailed)	Mean Difference	Std. Error Difference	95% Confidence Interval of the Difference	
						Lower	Upper
Attention-getters: usefulness	-2.497	13	.027	-1.86	.74	-3.46	-.25
Semantics of spoken messages: messages detail appropriateness	-2.330	9.530	.043	-1.66	.71	-3.26	-6.20E-02

Table 48. Results of t-tests for the mean differences by speech synthesis familiarity

Gender

Group Statistics					
	Gender	N	Mean	Std. Deviation	Std. Error Mean
Semantics of spoken messages: messages detail appropriateness	Female	4	6.50	.58	.29
	Male	11	5.00	1.73	.52
Politeness is noticeable: level of politeness	Female	4	6.75	.50	.25
	Male	11	5.82	.60	.18

Table 49. Significant mean differences by gender

By Gender	t-test for Equality of Means						
	t	df	Sig. (2-tailed)	Mean Difference	Std. Error Difference	95% Confidence Interval of the Difference	
						Lower	Upper
Semantics of spoken messages: messages detail appropriateness	2.514	12.999	.026	1.50	.60	.21	2.79
Politeness is noticeable: level of politeness	2.747	13	.017	.93	.34	.20	1.66

Table 50. Results of t-tests for the mean differences by gender

MS Office Assistant versus Speaking Assistant prototype

Paired Samples Statistics

		Mean	N	Std. Deviation	Std. Error Mean
Pair 1	MS Office assistant: pleasantness	2.62	13	1.12	.31
	Speaking assistant: pleasantness	4.62	13	1.12	.31
Pair 2	MS Office assistant: helpfulness	3.08	13	1.26	.35
	Speaking assistant: helpfulness	5.62	13	.77	.21
Pair 3	MS Office assistant: convenience	1.92	13	.95	.26
	Speaking assistant: convenience	5.15	13	.80	.22
Pair 4	MS Office assistant: reliability	3.77	13	1.24	.34
	Speaking assistant: reliability	5.46	13	1.61	.45
Pair 5	MS Office assistant: comfort	3.31	13	.95	.26
	Speaking assistant: comfort	5.31	13	1.11	.31
Pair 6	MS Office assistant: efficiency	3.08	13	1.66	.46
	Speaking assistant: efficiency	4.54	13	1.13	.31
Pair 7	MS Office assistant: satisfaction	1.85	13	.90	.25
	Speaking assistant: satisfaction	4.92	13	.86	.24
Pair 8	MS Office assistant: unobtrusiveness (recoded)	1.77	13	.83	.23
	Speaking assistant: unobtrusiveness (recoded)	4.77	13	2.01	.56
Pair 9	MS Office assistant: loveliness	2.23	13	1.01	.28
	Speaking assistant: loveliness	4.92	13	1.04	.29

Table 51. Significant mean differences for the paired samples t-test

Appendix G

DATA FROM PARTICIPANTS' COMMENTS

This Appendix includes five tables illustrating the results of the content analysis performed on the comments provided by participants to the open-ended questions of questionnaire B.

What things did you like most about the system

Part.	Spoken Notifications and Reminders					Interruptions				Politeness				Linguistic Variation		Part. total
	Notification of Printing: Queueing, Completion useful in decision making	Notification of e-mail: new messages, subjects, senders (help in decision making)	Reminders of to do's (avoid having to worry about remembering)	Unintrusive Notifications and Reminders (to the person's task - do nor demand immediate action)	Total	Only delivered relevant notifications and reminders (to convey needed information)	Timely notifications (before events happen)	Reliable Interruptions through Attention-getting prevent missing information	Total	Pleasant Attention-getting prevent a sudden interruption	Smooth audio interruption through fading	Courteous Attention-getting (through polite utterances)	Total	Non-repetitive utterances	Total	Total
1	1	1			2				0				0		0	2
2				1	1			1	1			1	1		0	3
3					0				0				0		0	0
4	1	1			2				0			1	1		0	3
5	1	1			2				0				0		0	2
6			1	1	2		1		1	1		1	2		0	5
7	1	1	1	1	4	1	1		2				0		0	6
8	1				1				0				0		0	1
9	1	1	1		3				0				0		0	3
10	1			1	2		1		1				0		0	3
11	1				1				0		1		1	1	1	3
12					0	1	1	1	3				0		0	3
13	1				1				0		1		1		0	2
14	1	1	1	1	4	1		1	2			1	1	1	1	8
15					0				0			1	1		0	1
Total	10	6	4	5	25	3	4	3	10	1	2	5	8	2	2	45

Table 52. Participants' comments concerning the aspects they liked

What things did you dislike most about the system

Part.	Low Quality of Voice (Speech Synthesis)				Graphical Intrusiveness of Character			Poor Selection of Information to Convey (specialised agents)			Lack of Context Awareness		Poor Linguistic Naturalness (aggregator)			Poor Speaking Naturalness (vocaliser)		Part. total
	Difficult to understand (is annoying)	Foreign accent	Slows down OS	Total	Takes screen real estate	Gets in the way (obfuscates information and graphical controls)	Total	Over-informative about printing (starting to print when it has been in queue)	Unnecessary information provision about junk mail	Total	Lack of user activity awareness (notifications and reminders about tasks already completed or information already seen)	Total	Insufficient variation in attention-getting	Lack of awareness of prior messages (to combine successive similar messages)	Total	Slow speaking rate	Total	Total
1				0			0			0		0			0		0	0
2	1			1			0			0		0			0		0	1
3	1			1	1		1			0		0			0	1	1	3
4				0			0			0	1	1			0		0	1
5				0		1	1			0	1	1			0		0	2
6				0			0	1		1		0			0		0	1
7				0		1	1	1		1		0			0		0	2
8				0			0			0	1	1			0		0	1
9	1			1			0	1	1	2	1	1			0		0	4
10				0			0	1		1	1	1	1		1		0	3
11				0			0	1		1		0		1	1		0	2
12	1			1	1		1			0		0			0		0	2
13			1	1			0			0		0			0		0	1
14				0		1	1			0		0			0		0	1
15	1	1		2			0			0		0			0		0	2
Total	5	1	1	7	2	3	5	5	1	6	5	5	1	1	2	1	1	26

Table 53. Participants' comments concerning aspects they did not like

We wanted the system to feel natural. What did we miss that would have made it really natural?

Part.	Poor Context Awareness		Low Quality of Voice (TTS)		Graphical Intrusiveness of Character			Poor Selection of Information to Convey (specialised agents)		Poor Linguistic naturalness (aggregator)				Poor Speaking Naturalness (vocaliser)			Part. total
	Poor user activity awareness (should stop talking about information as soon as user processes it)	Total	Lack of a natural sounding voice	Total	Takes screen real estate (unnecessary constant presence)	Gets in the way (obfuscates information and graphical controls)	Total	Over-informative about printing starting	Total	Insufficient variation in utterances	Lack of awareness of prior messages (to coordinate successive similar messages)	Annoying attention-getters (poor expressions and lack of variation)	Total	Not enough intonation (in attention-getting and in utterances to provide variation)	Slow speaking rate	Total	Total
1		0		0			0		0				0			0	0
2	1	1		0			0		0				0			0	1
3		0		0			0		0				0			0	0
4		0	1	1			0		0				0	1		1	2
5		0		0	1		1		0				0			0	1
6		0		0			0		0		1	1	2			0	2
7		0		0			0		0		1		1			0	1
8		0	1	1			0		0				0		1	1	2
9		0	1	1			0		0				0			0	1
10		0		0			0		0			1	1			0	1
11		0	1	1			0	1	1		1		1			0	3
12		0		0			0		0				0	1		1	1
13		0		0			0		0	1			1	1		1	2
14		0		0			0		0				0			0	0
15		0		0		1	1		0				0			0	1
Total	1	1	4	4	1	1	2	1	1	1	3	2	6	3	1	4	18

Table 54. Participants' comments concerning aspects related to naturalness

We wanted the system to feel like a work companion. What did we miss that would have made you perceive it?

Part.	Spontaneity		User Profiling		More help with P.I.M. (integration)			Context awareness		More feedback		Part. total
	Sense of humour (e.g. telling jokes)	Total	Awareness of user priorities (deal with unimportant information automatically - e.g. do not speak about junk mail and delete it, let user specify some preferences)	Total	A diary	Integrate other applications notifications	Total	More context awareness	Total	Confirmation (e.g. Repeat last message if asked)	Total	Total
1		0		0			0		0		0	0
2		0		0			0		0		0	0
3		0		0			0		0		0	0
4		0		0			0		0		0	0
5		0		0		1	1		0		0	1
6	1	1		0			0		0		0	1
7		0	1	1			0		0		0	1
8		0		0		1	1		0		0	1
9		0		0	1		1		0		0	1
10		0		0			0	1	1		0	1
11		0	1	1			0		0		0	1
12	1	1		0			0		0		0	1
13		0		0		1	1		0	1	1	2
14		0		0			0		0		0	0
15	1	1		0			0		0		0	1
Total	3	3	2	2	1	3	4	1	1	1	1	11

Table 55. Participants' comments concerning aspects contributing to a work companion

Have you **Any Other Comments?**											
Part.	Positive					Negative					Part. Total
	Naturalness (overall behaviour was natural)	Usefulness (would continue to use it)	Likeability (enjoyed, liked it, worked well)	Unobtrusiveness (did not keep pestering me, increased awareness without intrusiveness)	Total	Needs more timely interventions (took a while to realise a printout was done)	Needs better linguistic abilities (combine successive messages about a similar topic)	Should perform more functions (e.g. help, find)	Needs a more natural sounding TTS	Total	Total
1					0					0	0
2	1	1			2					0	2
3					0					0	0
4		1	1		2					0	2
5				1	1			1		1	2
6		1		1	2					0	2
7					0	1				1	1
8					0					0	0
9		1	1		2					0	2
10					0					0	0
11			1		1		1			1	2
12					0				1	1	1
13					0					0	0
14					0					0	0
15			1	1	2					0	2
Total	1	4	4	3	12	1	1	1	1	4	16

Table 56. Participants' open-ended comments

REFERENCES

Agre, P. and Chapman, D. (1987), "PENGI: An Implementation of a Theory of Activity", in *Proceedings of AAAI-87, Sixth National Conference on Artificial Intelligence*, Seattle, WA: AAAI Press, 268-272.

Alreck, P. L. and Settle, R. B. (1994), *The Survey Research Handbook: Guidelines and Strategies for Conducting a Survey*, 2nd ed., New York: McGrawHill Professional Publishing.

Anderson, J. R. (1995), *Cognitive Psychology and its Implications*, 4th ed., New York: Freeman.

André, E., Rist, T., Mulken, S., Klesen, M., and Baldes, S. (2000), "The Automated Design of Believable Dialogues for Animated Presentation Teams", in J. Cassel (Ed.), *Embodied Conversational Agents*, Cambridge, MA: MIT Press, 220-255.

Ardissono, L., Boella, G., and Lesmo, L. (1999), "Politeness and Speech Acts", in *Proceedings of the Workshop on Attitude, Personality and Emotions in User-Adapted Interaction at UM'99, 7th International Conference on User Modelling*, Banff, Canada: 41-55.

Arons, B. and Mynatt, E. (1994), "The Future of Speech and Audio in the Interface", *SIGCHI Bulletin*, **26**(4), 44-48.

Austin, J. L. (1962), *How To Do Things With Words*, Cambridge, MA: Harvard University Press.

Baddeley, A. D. (1986), *Working Memory*, Oxford: Oxford University Press.

Baddeley, A. D. and Hitch, G. L. (1974), "Working Memory", in G. Bower (Ed.), *The Psychology of Learning and Motivation*, New York: Academic Press, 47-90.

Badler, N. I., Bindiganavale, R., Allbeck, J., Schuler, W., Zhao, L., and Palmer, M. (2000), "Parameterized Action Representation for Virtual Human Agents", in J. Cassel (Ed.), *Embodied Conversational Agents*, Cambridge, MA: MIT Press, 256-284.

Bailey, B. P., Konstan, J. A., and Carlis, J. V. (2000), "Adjusting Windows: Balancing Information Awareness with Intrusion", in *Proceedings of HFWeb 2000, Sixth Conference on Human Factors and the Web*, Austin, Texas: 120-129.

Ball, G. and Breese, J. (2000), "Emotion and Personality in a Conversational Agent", in J. Cassel (Ed.), *Embodied Conversational Agents*, Cambridge, MA: MIT Press, 189-219.

References

Ball, G., Ling, D., Kurlander, D., Miller, J., Pugh, D., Skelly, T., Stankosky, A., Thiel, D., Van Dantzich, M., and Wax, T. (1997), "Lifelike Computer Characters: the Persona Project at Microsoft Research", in J. M. Bradshaw (Ed.), *Software Agents*, Menlo Park, CA: AAAI Press/MIT Press, 191-222.

Barreau, D. K. (1995), "Context as a Factor in Personal Information Management Systems", *Journal of the American Society for Information Science*, **46**(5), 327-339.

Bell, G. (1997), "The Body Electric", *Communications of the ACM*, **40**(2), 30-32.

Bell, G. (2001), "A Personal Digital Store", *Communications of the ACM*, **44**(1), 86-91.

Benest, I. D. (1997), "The Specification and Presentation of On-Line Lectures", *Innovations in Education and Training International*, **34**(1), 32-43.

Benest, I. D. (2000), "Towards a Seamless Provision of Multimedia Course Material", *Innovations in Education and Training International*, **37**(4), 323-334.

Benest, I. D. (2001), "Automating Lecture Material Delivery", in *Proceedings of the IEE International Symposium on Engineering Education; Innovations in Teaching, Learning and Assessment*, 27-1-27/6.

Benyon, D. and Murray, D. (1993), "Applying User Modelling to Human-Computer Interaction Design", *Artificial Intelligence Review*, **7**(3-4), 199-225.

Bernsen, N. O., Dybkjaer, H., and Dybkjaer, L. (1998), *Designing Interactive Speech Systems: from First Ideas to User Testing*, New York: Springer-Verlag.

Billinghurst, M. and Starner, T. (1999), "Wearable Devices: New Ways to Manage Information", *IEEE Computer*, **32**(1), 57-64.

Blattner, M. M., Sumikawa, D., and Greenberg, R. (1989), "Earcons and Icons: Their Structure and Common Design Principles", *Human Computer Interaction*, **4**(1), 11-44.

Blum-Kulka, J. (1997), "Discourse Pragmatics", in T. A. Dijk (Ed.), *Discourse as Social Interaction*, London: Sage, 38-63.

Bos, E. (1995), "We Can Make Forgetting Impossible, But Should We?", *Interactions*, **2**(3), 11-14.

Bouchard, J. (1976), "Field Research Methods: Interviewing, Questionnaires, Participant Observation, Systematic Observation, Unobtrusive Measures", in M. D. Dunnette (Ed.), *Handbook of Organizational Psychology,* New York: Rand McNally, 363-413.

Bovey, J. (1996), "Event Based Personal Retrieval", *Journal of Information Science*, **22**(5), 357-366.

Boy, G. A. (1997), "Knowledge Elicitation for the Design of Software Agents", in M. Helander, T. K. Landauer, and P. Prabhu (Eds.), *Handbook of Human-Computer Interaction,* North Holland: Elsevier Science, 1203-1234.

Boyce, S. J. (1999), "Spoken Natural Language Dialogue Systems: User Interface Issues for the Future", in D. Gardner-Bonneau (Ed.), *Human Factors and Voice Interactive Systems,* Norwell, MA: Kluwer Academic Publishers, 37-61.

Bradshaw, J. M. (1997), "An Introduction to Software Agents", in J. M. Bradshaw (Ed.), *Software Agents,* Menlo Park, CA: AAAI Press/MIT Press, 3-46.

Breiter, P. and Sadek, M. D. (1996), "A Rational Agent as a Kernel of a Cooperative Dialogue System: Implementing a Logical Theory of Interaction", in *Proceedings of the ECAI Workshop on Agent Theories, Architectures and Languages,* Berlin: Springer-Verlag, 261-276.

Brennan, S. E. (1990), "Conversation as Direct Manipulation: An Iconoclastic View", in B. Laurel (Ed.), *The Art of Human-Computer Interface Design,* New York: Addison-Wesley, 393-404.

Brewster, S. A., Wright, P. C., and Edwards, A. D. N. (1993), "An Evaluation of Earcons for Use in Auditory Human-Computer Interfaces", in S. Ashlund, K. Mullet, A. Henderson (Eds.), *Proceedings of Interchi '93: Human Factors in Computing Systems* (Amsterdam), Boston, MA: ACM Press, Addison-Wesley, 222-227.

Brooks, R. A. (1986), "A Robust Layered Control System for a Mobile Robot", *IEEE Journal of Robotics and Automation*, **2**(1), 14-23.

Brooks, R. A. (1991), "Intelligence Without Representation", *Artificial Intelligence*, **47**(1), 139-159.

Brown, C. (1992), "Assistive Technology Computers and Persons With Disabilities", *Communications of the ACM*, **35**(5), 36-46.

Brown, P. and Levinson, S. (1987), *Politeness: Some Universals in Language Usage*, Cambridge: Cambridge University Press.

Brown, P. J., Bovey, J. D., and Chen, X. (1997), "Context-Aware Applications: From the Laboratory to the Marketplace", *IEEE Personal Communications*, **4**(5), 58-64.

References

Buttazzo, G. (2001), "Artificial Consciousness: Utopia or Real Possibility?", *IEEE Computer*, **34**(7), 24-30.

Cassel, J. (2000), "Nudge Nudge Wink Wink: Elements of Face-to-Face Conversation for Embodied Conversational Agents", in J. Cassel (Ed.), *Embodied Conversational Agents*, Cambridge, MA: MIT Press, 1-27.

Cesta, A. and D'Aloisi, D. (1996), "Building Interfaces as Personal Agents: A Case Study", *SIGCHI Bulletin*, **28**(3), 108-113.

Chin, J. P., Diehl, V. A., and Norman, K. L. (1988), "Development of an Instrument Measuring User Satisfaction of the Human-Computer Interface", in *Proceedings of CHI'88, Conference on Human Factors and Computing Systems*, Washington, DC: ACM Press, 213-218.

Cohen, P. R. (1992), "The Role of Natural Language in a Multimodal Interface", in *Proceedings of the ACM Symposium on User Interface Software and Technology*, Monterey, CA: ACM Press, 143-149.

Cohen, P. R. and Oviatt, S. L. (1995), "The Role of Voice in Human-Machine Communication", in D. B. Roe and J. Wilpon (Eds.), *Voice Communication Between Humans and Machines*, Washington D.C.: National Academy of Sciences, 34-75.

Cole, R., Hirschman, L., Atlas, L., Hermasky, H., Price, P., Beckman, M., Levinsons, S., Silverman, H., Biermann, A., McKeown, K., and Spitz, J. (1995), "The Challenge of Spoken Language Systems: Research Directions for the Nineties", *IEEE Transactions on Speech and Audio Processing*, **3**(1), 1-20.

Cook, N. J. and Benest, I. D. (2001), "The Generation of Speech for a Search Guide", in *Proceedings of Eurospeech, 7th European Conference on Speech Communication and Technology*, Aalborg, Denmark: 1739-1742.

Covey, S. R. (1989), *The Seven Habits of Highly Effective People*, New York: Simon and Schuster, Inc.

Crabtree, I. B., Soltysiak, S. J., and Thint, M. P. (1998), "Adaptive Personal Agents", *Personal Technologies*, **2**(3), 141-151.

Cutrell, E. B., Czerwinski, M., and Horvitz, E. (2000), "Effects of Instant messaging Interruptions on Computing Tasks", in *Proceedings of CHI 2000, International Conference on Human Factors in Computing Systems*, The Hague, The Netherlands: 99-100.

Dahlback, N., Jonsson, A., and Ahrenberg, L. (1992), "Wizard of Oz Studies - Why and How", in D. G. Wayne & M. Dianne (Eds.), *Proceedings of the International Workshop on Intelligent User Interfaces*, New York: ACM Press, 193-200.

Dale, R., Mellish, C., and Zock, M. (1990), *Current Research in Natural Language Generation*, London: Academic Press.

Dey, A. K. and Abowd, G. D. (1999), *Towards a Better Understanding of Context and Context-Awareness*, (Rep. No. GIT-GVU-99-22), College of Computing, Georgia Institute of Technology.

Dey, A. K., Abowd, G. D., and Wood, A. (1999), "CyberDesk: a Framework for Providing Self-Integrating Context-Aware Services", *Knowledge-Based Systems*, **11**(1), 3-13.

DiCaterino, A., Larsen, K., Tang, M., and Wang, W. (1997), *An Introduction to Workflow Management Systems*, (Rep. No. CTG.MFA - 002), Center for Technology in Government, University at Albany / Suny.

Dix, A., Finlay, J., Abowd, G., and Beale, R. (1998), *Human-Computer Interaction*, 2nd ed., Prentice-Hall Europe.

Dix, A., Ramduny, D., and Wilkinson, J. (1995), *Interruptions, Deadlines and Reminders: Investigations into the Flow of Cooperative Work*, (Rep. No. RR9509), Huddersfield: HCI Research Centre, School of Computing and Mathematics, University of Huddersfield, Queensgate.

Dorai, C., Kermani, P., and Stewart, A. (2001), "ELM-N: E-Learning Media Navigator", in *Proceedings of MM '01, the International Conference on Multimedia*, Ottawa, Canada: ACM Press, 634-635.

Dutoit, T. (1997), *An Introduction to Text-to-Speech Synthesis*, Dordrecht: Kluwer Academic Publishers.

Elmes, D. G., Kantowitz, B. H., and Roediger, H. L. (1989), "Quasi-Experimental Research", in D. G. Elmes, B. H. Kantowitz, and H. L. Roediger (Eds.), *Research Methods in Psychology*, 3rd ed., West, 199-215.

Erickson, T. (1997), "Designing Agents as if People Mattered", in J. M. Bradshaw (Ed.), *Software Agents*, Menlo Park, CA: AAAI Press/MIT Press, 79-96.

Finin, T., Labrou, Y., and Mayfield, J. (1997), "KQML as an Agent Communication Language", in J. M. Bradshaw (Ed.), *Software Agents*, Menlo Park, CA: AAAI Press/MIT Press, 291-316.

Franklin, S. and Graesser, A. (1996), "Is it an Agent or Just a Program?: A Taxonomy of Autonomous Agents", in *Proceedings of the Third International Workshop on Agent Theories, Architectures, and Languages*, New York: Springer-Verlag, 21-35.

Freeman, E. and Gelernter, D. (1996), "Lifestreams: a Storage Model for Personal Data", *ACM SIGMOD Bulletin*, **25**(1), 80-86.

References

Fritz, J. M. (1995), *An Investigation of the Effectiveness of Open Hypertext Techniques for Qualitative Decision Support,* D.Phil. Thesis, Department of Computer Science, University of York.

Gardner-Bonneau, D. (1999), *Human Factors and Voice Interactive Systems,* Norwell, MA: Kluwer Academic Publishers.

Geldof, S. and Velde, W. (1997), "An Architecture for Template Based (Hyper)text Generation", in *Proceedings of EWNLG'97, 6th European Workshop on Natural Language Generation,* Duisburg, Germany: Gerhard Mercator Universitaet, Inst. fuer Informatik, 28-37.

Gentner, D. and Nielsen, J. (1996), "The Anti-Mac Interface", *Communications of the ACM,* **39**(8), 70-82.

Gillie, T. and Broadbent, D. (1989), "What Makes Interruptions Disruptive? A Study of Length, Similarity and Complexity", *Psychological Research,* **50**(1), 243-250.

Gong, L. and Lai, J. (2001), "Shall We Mix Synthetic Speech and Human Speech? Impact on Users' Performance, Perception and Attitude", in *Proceeding of CHI 2001, Conference on Human Factors in Computing Systems,* Seattle, WA: 158-165.

Griss, M. L. and Pour, G. (2001), "Accelerating Development with Agent Components", *IEEE Computer,* **34**(5), 37-43.

Grosz, B., Scott, D., Kamp, H., Cohen, P., and Giachin, E. (1996), "Discourse and Dialogue", in R. Cole, J. Mariani, H. Uszkoreit, G. B. Varille, A. Zaenen, and A. Zampolli (Eds.), *Survey of the State of the Art in Human Language Technology,* Cambridge: Cambridge University Press, 227-254.

Hansen, P. M., Holtse, P., Nielsen, H., and Petersen, N. R. (1993), "Speech Synthesis - Teaching a Computer Spoken Language", *Teletknik,* (1-2), 52-65.

Heckerman, D. (2001), *A Tutorial on Learning Bayesian Networks,* (Rep. No. MSR-TR-95-06), Microsoft Research.

Hensley, P., Metral, M., Shardanand, U., Converse, D., and Myers, M. (1997), Proposal for an Open Profiling Standard, Technical Note, World Wide Web Consortium (W3C) [On-line], Available: http://www.w3.org/TR/NOTE-OPS-FrameWork.html

Horvitz, E., Jacobs, A., and Hovel, D. (1999), "Attention-Sensitive Alerting", in *Proceedings of UAI '99, Conference on Uncertainty and Artificial Intelligence,* Stockholm, Sweden: Morgan Kauffman, San Francisco, 305-313.

Houston, J. R. (1986), *Fundamentals of Learning and Memory,* 3rd ed., New York: Harcourt Brace Jovanovich, Inc.

References

Hovy, E. (1996), "Language Generation", in R. A. Cole, J. Mariani, H. Uszkoreit, A. Zaenen, and V. Zue (Eds.), *Survey of the State of the Art in Human Language Technology,* Cambridge University Press, 161-187.

Huhns, M. N. and Singh, M. P. (1998a), "Anthropoid Agents", *IEEE Internet Computing,* **2**(1), 94-95.

Huhns, M. N. and Singh, M. P. (1998b), "Cognitive Agents", *IEEE Internet Computing,* **2**(6), 87-89.

Huhns, M. N. and Singh, M. P. (1998c), "Personal Assistants", *IEEE Internet Computing,* **2**(5), 90-92.

Huhns, M. N. and Stephens, L. M. (1999), "Multiagent Systems and Societies of Agents", in G. Weiss (Ed.), *Multiagent Systems: A modern Approach to Distributed Artificial Intelligence,* Cambridge, MA: MIT Press, 79-120.

Internet Mail Consortium (1996), vCalendar - The Electronic Calendaring and Scheduling Exchange Format", Internet Mail Consortium [On-line], Available: http://www.imc.org/pdi/vcal-1.0.txt

Jameson, A. (2001), "Designing Systems that Adapt to Their Users", in *CHI 2001 Tutorial 6 Notes,* ACM SIGCHI.

Jenks, J. M. and Kelly, J. M. (1985), *Don't Do, Delegate!,* New York: Franklin Watts.

Jennings, N. R. (1999), "Agent-based Computing: Promise and Perils", in T. Dean (Ed.), *Proceedings of IJCAI 1999, Sixteenth International Joint Conference on Artificial Intelligence,* San Francisco: Morgan Kaufmann, 1429-1436.

Jennings, N. R. and Wooldridge, M. (1998), "Applications of Intelligent Agents", in N. R. Jennings and M. Wooldridge (Eds.), *Agent Technology: Foundations, Applications, and Markets,* Berlin: Springer-Verlag, 3-28.

Jennings, N. R. and Wooldridge, M. (1999), "Agent-Oriented Software Engineering", in F. Garijo & M. Bosman (Eds.), *Proceedings of MAAMAW-99, 9th European Workshop on Modelling Autonomous Agents in a Multi-Agent World: Multi-Agent System Engineering, Lecture Notes in Artificial Intelligence, Vol. 1647,* Heidelberg, Germany: Springer-Verlag, 1-24.

Jurafsky, D. and Martin, J. H. (2000), *Speech and Language Processing: An Introduction to Natural Language Processing, Computational Linguistics, and Speech Recognition,* New York: Prentice Hall.

Kautz, H. A., Selman, B., Coen, M., Ketchpel, S., and Ramming, C. (1998), "An Experiment in the Design of Software Agents", in M. N. Huhns and M. P. Singh (Eds.), *Readings in Agents,* San Francisco, CA: Morgan Kaufmann, 125-130.

Kirmeyer, S. L. (1988), "Coping With Competing Demands: Interruptions and the Type A Pattern", *Journal of Applied Psychology ,* **73**(4), 621-629.

References

Kozierok, R. and Maes, P. (1993), "A Learning Interface Agent for Scheduling Meetings", in W. D. Gray, W. E. Hefley, & D. Murray (Eds.), *Proceedings of the 1993 International Workshop on Intelligent User Interfaces,* New York: ACM Press, 81-88.

Kühme, T. (1993), "User-Centered Approach to Adaptive Interfaces", *Knowledge-Based Systems,* **6**(4), 239-248.

Lai, J., Cheng, K., Green, P., and Tsimhoni, O. (2001), "On the Road and on the Web? Comprehension of Synthetic and Human Speech While Driving", in *Proceeding of CHI 2001, Conference on Human Factors in Computing Systems,* Seattle, WA: 206-212.

Lamming, M., Brown, P., Carter, K., Eldridge, M., Flynn, M., Louie, G., Robinson, P., and Sellen, A. (1994), "The Design of a Human Memory Prosthesis", *The Computer Journal,* **37**(3), 153-163.

Lamming, M. and Flynn, N. (1994), "Forget-me-not: Intimate Computing in Support of Human Memory", in *Proceedings of Friend21: International Symposium on Next Generation Human Interfaces,* Meguro Gajoen, Japan: 125-128.

Langley, P., Thompson, C., Elio, R., and Haddadi, A. (1999), "An Adaptive Conversational Interface for Destination Advice", in *Proceedings of the Third International Workshop on Cooperative Information Agents,* Uppsala, Sweden: Springer-Verlag, 347-364.

Lansdale, M. and Edmonds, E. (1992), "Using memory for Events in the Design of Personal Filing Systems", *International Journal of Man-Machine Studies,* **36**(1), 97-126.

Larrey, P., Vigouroux, N., and Perennou, G. (1998), "Towards a Flexible and Contextually Appropriate Generation of Spoken Utterances", in *Proceedings of the Interactive Vocal Telephony Technology and Applications Workshop (ESCA/IEEE),* Turim, Italy: 124-129.

Larsen, S. F., Thompson, C. P., and Hansen, T. (1996), "Time in Autobiographical Memory", in D. C. Rubin (Ed.), *Remembering our Past: Studies in Autobiographical Memory,* Cambridge University Press, 129-156.

Laurel, B. (1997), "Interface Agents: Metaphors with Character", in J. M. Bradshaw (Ed.), *Software Agents,* Menlo Park, CA: AAAI Press/MIT Press, 67-77.

Lieberman, H. (1997), "Autonomous Interface Agents", in *Proceedings of CHI '97, Conference on Human Factors in Computing Systems,* Atlanta, GA: ACM Press, 67-74.

Litman, D. J. and Pan, S. (1999), "Empirically Evaluating an Adaptable Spoken Dialogue System", in *Proceedings of UM'99, 7th International Conference on User Modeling,* Banff, Canada: 55-64.

Logie, R. H. (1995), *Visuo-Spatial Working Memory*, Hove: Lawrence Erlbaum Associates.

Maes, P. (1991a), "The Agent Network Architecture", *SIGART Bulletin*, **2**(1), 115-120.

Maes, P. (1991b), "The Agent Network Architecture (ANA)", *SIGART Bulletin*, **2**(4), 115-120.

Maes, P. (1994), "Agents that Reduce Work and Information Overload", *Communications of the ACM*, **37** (7), 31-40.

Maes, P. (1997a), "Patti Maes on Software Agents: Humanizing the Global Computer", *IEEE Internet Computing*, **1**(4), 10-19.

Maes, P. (1997b), Toward a Truly Personal Computer, Microsoft Research Telepresence Group [On-line], Available: http://research.microsoft.com/acm97/pm/

Mallach, E. G. (1994), *Understanding Decision Support Systems and Expert Systems*, Boston, MA: Irwin Publishing.

Mander, R., Salomon, G., and Wong, Y. (1992), "A 'Pile' Metaphor for Supporting Casual Organisation of Information", in *Proceedings of CHI'92, Conference on Human Factors in Computing,* Monterey, CA: ACM Press, 627-634.

Massaro, D. W., Cohen, M. M., Daniel, S., and Cole, R. A. (1999), "Developing and Evaluating Conversational Agents", in P. A. Hancock (Ed.), *Human Performance and Ergonomics,* San Diego: Academic Press, 173-194.

Mathe, N. and Chen, J. R. (1998), "Organizing and Sharing Information on the World-Wide Web using a Multiagent System", in *Proceedings of ED-MEDIA'98, Conference on Educational Multimedia and Hypermedia,* Freiburg, Germany: Association for the Advancement of Computing in Education (AACE), 256-263.

McCrickard, D. S. (2000), *Maintaining Information Awareness in a Dynamic Environment: Assessing Animation as a Communication Mechanism,* PhD Thesis, College of Computing, Georgia Institute of Technology.

McTear, M. (1993), "User Modelling for Adaptive Computer Systems: a Survey of Recent Developments", *Artificial Intelligence Review*, **7** 157-184.

Microsoft (2001b), MSDN Library [On-line], Available: http://msdn.microsoft.com/library

Microsoft (2001a), Microsoft Agent Home [On-line], Available: http://www.microsoft.com/msagent

Millewski, A. E. and Lewis, S. H. (1997), "Delegating to Software Agents", *International Journal of Human-Computer Studies*, **46**(4), 485-500.

References

Mintzberg, H. (1973), *The Nature of Managerial Work*, New York: Harper and Row.

Mitchell, T., Caruana, R., Freitag, D., McDermott, J., and Zabowski, D. (1994), "Experience with a Learning Personal Assistant", *Communications of the ACM*, **37**(7), 81-91.

Mitchell, T. M. (1997), *Machine Learning*, Boston: McGraw-Hill.

Myers, I. B. (1974), *Manual for the Myers-Briggs Type Indicator*, Princeton, NJ: ETS.

Myers, I. B. (1993), *Introduction to Type: a Guide to Understanding your Results on the Myers-Briggs Type Indicator*, 5th ed., Oxford: Oxford Psychologists Press Ltd.

Mynatt, E. D., Back, M., Want, R., Baer, R., and Ellis, J. (1998), "Designing Audio Aura", in *Proceedings of CHI '98, International Conference on Human Factors in Computing Systems,* Los Angeles, CA: ACM Press, 566-573.

Nairne, J. S. (1996), "Short-Term / Working memory", in E. L. Bjork and R. A. Bjork (Eds.), *Memory,* 2nd. ed., London: Academic Press, 101-126.

Nass, C., Fogg, B. J., and Moon, Y. (1996), "Can Computers be Teammates?", *International Journal of Human-Computer Studies*, **45**(6), 669-678.

Nass, C. and Gong, L. (2000), "Speech Interfaces from an Evolutionary Perspective", *Communications of the ACM*, **43**(9), 36-43.

Nass, C. and Lee, K. M. (2001), "Does Computer-Synthesized Speech Manifest Personality? Experimental Tests of Recognition, Similarity-Attraction and Consistency-Attraction", *Journal of Experimental Psychology: Applied*, **7**(3), 171-181.

Nass, C. and Steuer, J. (1993), "Anthropomorphism, Agency and Ethopoeia: Computers as Social Actors", *Human Communication Research*, **19**(4), 504-527.

Nass, C., Steuer, J., and Tauber, E. (1994), "Computers Are Social Actors", in *Proceedings of CHI'94, International Conference on Human Factors in Computing Systems,* Boston, MA: ACM Press, 72-78.

Ndumu, D., Collis, J., and Nwana, H. (1998), "Towards Desktop Personal Travel Agents", *BT Technology Journal*, **16**(3), 69-78.

Negroponte, N. (1995), *Being Digital*, New York: Alfred A. Knopf.

Norman, D. A. (1993), *Things That Make Us Smart: Defending Human Attributes in the Age of the Machine*, New York: Addison-Wesley Publishing Company.

Norman, D. A. (1994), "How Might People Interact With Agents", *Communications of the ACM*, **37**(7), 68-71.

Nwana, H. S. (1996), "Software Agents: An Overview", *Knowledge Engineering Review*, **11**(3), 205-244.

O'Conaill, B. and Frohlich, D. (1995), "Timespace in the Workplace: Dealing With Interruptions", in *Proceedings of CHI'95, International Conference on Human Factors in Computing Systems,* Denver, Colorado: ACM Press, 262-263.

Olsen, D. R. (1999), "Interacting in Chaos", *Interactions*, **6**(5), 42-54.

Osgood, C. E., Suci, G. J., and Tannenbaum, P. (1967), *The Measurement of Meaning*, Publisher Urbana, University of Illinois Press.

Oviatt, S. (1996), "User-Centered Modeling for Spoken Language and Multimodal Interfaces", *IEEE Multimedia*, **3**(4), 26-35.

Oviatt, S. and Adams, B. (2000), "Designing and Evaluating Conversational Interfaces with Animated Characters", in J. Cassel (Ed.), *Embodied Conversational Agents,* Cambridge, MA: MIT Press, 319-345.

Papp, A. L. and Blattner, M. M. (1996), "Dynamic presentation of Asynchronous Auditory Output", in *Proceedings of Multimedia 96,* Boston, MA: ACM Press, 109-116.

Pascoe, J. (1998), "Adding Generic Contextual Capabilities to Wearable Computers", in *Proceedings of the Second International Symposium on Wearable Computers,* Pittsburgh, PA: IEEE Computer Society Press, 92-99.

Pashler, H. and Carrier, M. (1996), "Structures, Processes, and the Flow of Information", in E. L. Bjork and R. A. Bjork (Eds.), *Memory,* 2nd. ed., Academic Press, 3-29.

Pazzani, M. J. and Billsus, D. (1997), "Learning and Revising User Profiles: The Identification of Interesting Web Sites", *Machine Learning*, **27**(3), 313-331.

Preece, J., Rogers, Y., Sharp, H., Benyon, D., Holland, S., and Carey, T. (1994), *Human-Computer Interaction*, New York: Addison-Wesley.

Raman, T. V. (1997), *Auditory User Interfaces: Toward the Speaking Computer*, Norwell, MA: Kluwer Academic Publishers.

References

Raman, T. V. (1998), "Conversational Gestures for Direct Manipulation on the Audio Desktop", in *Proceedings of the Third International ACM Conference on Assistive Technologies*, 51-58.

Rao, A. S. and Georgeff, M. P. (1991), "Modelling Rational Agents Within a BDI-Architecture", in R. Fikes & E. Sandewall (Eds.), *Proceedings of KR&R 9, Knowledge Representation and Reasoning*, San Mateo, CA: Morgan Kaufmann Publishers, 173-181.

Raskin, J. (2000), *The Humane Interface: New Directions for Designing Interactive Systems*, New York: Addison-Wesley.

Reeves, B. and Nass, C. (1996), *The Media Equation: How People treat Computers, Television and New Media Like Real People and Places*, Stanford: CLSI Publications.

Reiter, E. and Dale, R. (1995), "Building Applied Natural Language Generation Systems", *Natural Language Engineering*, (3), 57-87.

Reiter, E., Robertson, R., and Osman, L. (1999), "Types of Knowledge Required to Personalise Smoking Cessation Letters", in W. Horn, Y. Shahar, G. Lindberg, S. Andreassen, and J. Wyatt (Eds.), *Lecture Notes in Computer Science, 1620*, Berlin: Springer-Verlag, 389-399.

Rhodes, B. (1997), "The Wearable Remembrance Agent: a System for Augmented Memory", in *Proceedings of ISWC'97, First International Symposium on Wearable Computers*, Cambridge, MA: 123-128.

Rhodes, B. and Starner, T. (1996), "Remembrance Agent", in *Proceedings of PAAM'96, First International Conference on The Practical Applications of Intelligent Agents and Multi-agent Technology*, London, UK: 487-495.

Rich, C. and Sidner, C. L. (1998), "COLLAGEN: When Agents Collaborate with People", in M. N. Huhns and M. P. Singh (Eds.), *Readings in Agents*, San Francisco, CA: Morgan Kaufmann, 117-124.

Robson, C. (1993), *Real World Research: a Resource for Social Scientists and Practitioner-Researchers*, London: Blackwell.

Roediger, H. L. and Guynn, M. J. (1996), "Retrieval Processes", in E. L. Bjork and R. A. Bjork (Eds.), *Memory*, 2nd ed., London: Academic Press, 197-236.

Russel, S. and Norvig, P. (1995), *Artificial Intelligence: A Modern Approach*, Upper Saddle River, NJ: Prentice-Hall, Inc.

Sagisaka, Y., d'Alessandro, C., Liénard, J., Sproat, R., McKeown, K., and Moore, J. D. (1996), "Spoken Output Technologies", in R. Cole, J. Mariani, H. Uszkoreit, G. B. Varille, A. Zaenen, and A. Zampolli (Eds.), *Survey of the State of the Art in Human Language Technology,* Cambridge: Cambridge University Press, 161-188.

Sanders, G. A. and Scholtz, J. (2000), "Measurement and Evaluation of Embodied Conversational Agents", in J. Cassel (Ed.), *Embodied Conversational Agents,* Cambridge, MA: MIT Press, 346-373.

Saunders, M., Lewis, P., and Thornhill, A. (2000), *Research Methods for Business Students*, New York: Pearson Education Limited.

Sawhney, N. and Schmandt, C. (2000), "Nomadic Radio: Speech and Audio Interaction for Contextual Messaging in Nomadic Environments", *ACM transactions on Computer-Human Interaction*, **7**(3), 353-383.

Schilit, B. and Theimer, M. (1994), "Disseminating Active Map Information to Mobile Hosts", *IEEE Network*, **8**(5), 22-32.

Schmandt, C. (1994), *Voice Communication with Computers*, New York: Van Nostrand Rheinhold.

Searle, J. (1969), *Speech Acts*, Cambridge: Cambridge University Press.

Searle, J. (1975), "Indirect Speech Acts", in P. Cole and J. Morgan (Eds.), *Syntax and Semantics 3: Speech Acts,* New York: Academic Press, 59-82.

Searle, J. (1979), "The Classification of Illocutionary Acts", *Language in Society*, (5), 1-24.

Shneiderman, B. (1992), *Designing the User Interface: Strategies for Effective Human-Computer Interaction*, New York: Addison-Wesley.

Shneiderman, B. (1993), *Sparks of Innovation in Human-Computer Interaction*, Norwood, NJ: Ablex Publishing Corporation.

Shneiderman, B. (1997), "Direct Manipulation Versus Agents: Paths to Predictable, Controllable and Comprehensible Interfaces", in J. M. Bradshaw (Ed.), *Software Agents,* Menlo Park, CA: AAAI Press/MIT Press, 97-106.

Shneiderman, B. and Maes, P. (1997), "Direct Manipulation vs. Interface Agents", *Interactions*, **4**(6), 42-61.

Shoam, Y. (1997), "An Overview of Agent-Oriented Programming", in J. M. Bradshaw (Ed.), *Software Agents,* Menlo Park, CA: AAAI Press/MIT Press, 271-290.

References

Shoam, Y. (1999), "What We Talk About When We Talk About Software Agents", *IEEE Intelligent Systems*, **14**(2), 28-31.

Silverman, B. G. (1997), "Computer Reminders and Alerts", *IEEE Computer*, **30**(1), 42-49.

Soltysiak, S. J. and Crabtree, I. B. (1998), "Knowing Me, Knowing You: Practical Issues in the Personalisation of Agent Technology", in *Proceedings of PAAM 98, Third International Conference on the Practical Application of Intelligent Agents and Multi-Agent Technology*, London, UK: Practical Application Co. Ltd, 467-484.

Speier, C., Valacich, J. S., and Vessey, I. (1997), "The Effects of Task Interruption and Information Presentation on Individual Decision Making", in *Proceedings of International Conference on Information Systems*, Atlanta, Georgia: 78-90.

Stevens, W. R. (1995), *TCP/IP Illustrated, Volume 1: The Protocols*, Reading, MA: Addison-Wesley.

Stewart, R. (1967), *Managers and Their Jobs*, London: MacMillan.

Sycara, K., Decker, K., Pannu, A., Williamson, M., and Zeng, D. (1996), "Distributed Intelligent Agents", *IEEE Expert: Intelligent Systems and Their Applications*, **11**(6), 36-45.

Tieger, P. and Tieger, B. B. (1995), *Do What You Are: Discover the Perfect Career for you through the Secrets of Personality Type*, Boston, MA: Little Brown.

Tulving, E. (1983), *Elements of Episodic Memory*, New York: Oxford University Press.

Van Mulken, S., André, E., and Müller, J. (1998), "The Persona Effect: How Substantial Is It?", in *Proceedings of HCI'98*, Sheffield, UK: 53-66.

Walker, M. A., Cahn, J. E., and Whittaker, S. J. (1997a), "Improvising Linguistic Style: Social and Affective Bases for Agent Personality", in *Proceedings of Agents'97, 1st International Conference on Autonomous Agents*, Marina Del Rey, CA: ACM Press, 96-105.

Walker, M. A., Fromer, J., Fabbrizio, G., Mestel, C., and Hindle, D. (1998), "What Can I Say?: Evaluating a Spoken Language Interface to Email", in *Proceedings of CHI'98, International Conference on Human Factors in Computing Systems*, Los Angeles, CA: ACM Press, 582-589.

Walker, M. A., Litman, D., Kamn, C., and Abella, A. (1997b), "PARADISE: A General Framework for Evaluating Spoken Dialogue Agents", in *Proceedings of the 35th Annual Meeting of the Association of Computational Linguistics, ACL/EACL 97*, Madrid, Spain: 271-280.

Wickens, C. D. (1992), *Engineering Psychology and Human Performance*, 2nd ed., New York: Harper Collins Publishers.

Williamson, A. G. (1998), "Moneypenny: Lessons from the Messy Desk", *Interacting with Computers*, **9** (3), 241-267.

Witten, I. H. (1982), *Principles of Computer Speech*, London: Academic Press Inc.

Wooldridge, M. (1999), "Intelligent Agents", in G. Weiss (Ed.), *Multiagent Systems: A Modern Approach to Distributed Artificial Intelligence,* Cambridge, MA: MIT Press, 27-77.

Wooldridge, M. and Jennings, N. R. (1995), "Intelligent Agents: Theory and Practice", *The Knowledge Engineering Review*, **10**(2), 115-152.

Zue, V. (1997), "Conversational Interfaces: Advances and Challenges", in *Proceedings of EUROSPEECH'97,* Rhodes, Greece: 9-14.

www.ingramcontent.com/pod-product-compliance
Lightning Source LLC
LaVergne TN
LVHW042331060326
832902LV00006B/110